EFFECTIVE TEACHING

EFFECTIVE TEACHING

PREPARATION
AND IMPLEMENTATION

By

LANCE E. BEDWELL, Ed.D.

GILBERT H. HUNT, Ph.D.

TIMOTHY J. TOUZEL, Ed.D.

DENNIS G. WISEMAN, Ph.D.

Coastal Carolina College of The University of South Carolina
Conway, South Carolina

CHARLES C THOMAS • PUBLISHER
Springfield • Illinois • U.S.A.

Published and Distributed Throughout the World by

CHARLES C THOMAS • PUBLISHER

2600 South First Street

Springfield, Illinois 62717

ISBN 0-398-05004-X

Library of Congress Catalog Card Number: 84-143

With THOMAS BOOKS *careful attention is given to all details of manufacturing and
design. It is the Publisher's desire to present books that are satisfactory as to their physical
qualities and artistic possibilities and appropriate for their particular use.* THOMAS
BOOKS *will be true to those laws of quality that assure a good name and good will.*

Printed in the United States of America
SC–R-3

Library of Congress Cataloging in Publication Data
Main entry under title:

Effective teaching.

   Bibliography: p.
   Includes index.
   1. Teaching.   2. Teachers—Psychology.   3. Teacher-
student relationships.   4. Behavior modification.
5. Students—Rating of.   I. Bedwell, Lance E.
LB1025.2.E417   1984   371.1'02   84-143
ISBN 0-398-05004-X

This book is dedicated to
OUR STUDENTS—
past, present, and future.

PREFACE

In analyzing the components of effective instruction, the popular refrain—"good teachers are not born, they are made"—is often heard. The truth in this rather simple statement echoes in schoolrooms across the country. Wanting to be a successful teacher is not enough, nor is love for children. The fact is, instruction is a complex process involving a multitude of interrelated skills as well as these important desires and feelings. For some, the development of effective teaching behaviors does not come easily. For others, the development does not come at all. Truly, everyone is not destined to be a teacher. Desire is a significant teacher characteristic as is a respect for learning and a concern for those who are about to learn. While these attributes are important characteristics of effective teachers, their impact is significantly diminished if the teacher does not have the requisite skill and knowledge in the art and process of instruction. Valuable assistance in developing these characteristics is presented in the six chapters that make up this text.

Important mental orientations which must be made toward planning for effective instruction are discussed in Chapter One, "THE TEACHER AS A PLANNER OF INSTRUCTION." The teacher's leadership style is carefully analyzed. Also, a planning format for subject matter presentation is systematically addressed and the actual implementation of formally planned lessons is considered in detail.

Chapter Two, "THE TEACHER AS A COMMUNICATOR OF INFORMATION," describes the teacher as an individual with an important message to be communicated. Through both verbal and non-verbal means, the effective teacher communicates stimulating ideas. Because the teacher is viewed as a communicator, the instructional message, that which the teacher communicates, is analyzed. A concept-based approach to instructional communication is proposed and described; above all else, effective teachers must send messages which are both meaningful and useful to learners. The acquisition of concepts and other significant learnings, leading to the development of sound generalizations, is dependent upon effective classroom communication.

Numerous generic characteristics of successful teachers are presented in Chapter Three, "THE TEACHER AS AN EFFECTIVE PERFORMER." It is recognized that these important teacher behaviors cut across grade level and content lines. Behaviors such as teaching based upon identified objectives, involving students in learning activities, and effective questioning are placed, along with several other important behaviors, in this category.

In Chapter Four, "THE TEACHER AS AN INSTRUCTIONAL STRATEGIST," both group and individual instructional strategies are identified. Characteristics and examples of each are enumerated along with a detailed analysis of considerations for their implementation.

Chapter Five, "THE TEACHER AS A MANAGER OF STUDENT BEHAVIOR," acquaints the reader with valuable information related to the teacher as the manager of the teaching-learning environment. In identifying effective managerial skills, this portion of the text describes varied management techniques and philosophies relevant to the development of leadership skills necessary to control student behavior in order that quality instruction can take place. Preventive measures to make problems less likely are stressed, along with techniques used to cope with problems when they do occur.

A significantly important characteristic of effective teachers is that they are fully aware of their responsibilities with respect to the evaluation of classroom performance. Chapter Six, "THE TEACHER AS AN EVALUATOR OF PERFORMANCE," describes those skills necessary for the teacher to fulfill this role. Test construction, various evaluative procedures, and the overall nature of evaluation are discussed. Building on the previously outlined areas of planning and implementing instruction, quality assessment is seen both as the logical conclusion to the lesson which has been taught and the guide to the direction of the teacher's future instructional efforts.

Like teaching itself, learning to become an effective teacher must be approached on an individual basis. Successful preparation, through study and practice, along with an instructional philosophy which focuses on both student needs and content responsibilities makes the possibility of becoming an effective teacher a reachable goal. The skills and guidance provided by *EFFECTIVE TEACHING: PREPARATION AND IMPLEMENTATION* give necessary direction and helpful insight into making success in teaching a reality.

USING THIS TEXTBOOK

The text has been structured in a format which provides opportunities for both practice and feedback. Each chapter is divided into sections beginning with a RATIONALE for the material being presented and ending with a FORMATIVE EVALUATION. The rationale, of course, emphasizes the importance of the material in the section. The purpose of the formative evaluation is to enable you to judge the extent to which you are understanding the material. FEEDBACK BOXES containing answers for each formative evaluation are provided in the APPENDIX. It is suggested that you discuss your formative evaluation results with a study partner and/or your instructor. If you encounter difficulties on any of the formative evaluations, you should return to the appropriate section for further study. MASTERY TESTS are not included; these are left to the discretion of your instructor.

LANCE E. BEDWELL
GILBERT H. HUNT
TIMOTHY J. TOUZEL
DENNIS G. WISEMAN

CONTENTS

EFFECTIVE TEACHING

CHAPTER ONE

THE TEACHER AS A
PLANNER OF INSTRUCTION

At the heart of any successful teaching episode is quality planning. There are many points to consider when preparing for high calibre instruction. For example, questions concerning *OBJECTIVES, STRATEGIES, RESOURCES,* and *EVALUATIVE CRITERIA* must be addressed. Beyond these issues, the teacher and the role this individual assumes in the classroom are of utmost concern in the teaching process. Teacher behaviors as they impact on student behaviors often prove to be the ultimate measure of success or failure in the lesson which has been carefully planned. The development of prerequisite skills in planning for and delivering instruction does not come naturally; it requires determined and knowledgeable preparation on the part of the teacher.

In order to assist you in the development of successful planning skills, this chapter presents sections dealing with many aspects of planning (e.g. planning for active student involvement and individual student differences). After studying this chapter, you should be able to complete the following performances.

1. Describe three leadership styles commonly associated with teachers.
2. Define centered-instruction.
3. List advantages of an authoritative, student-centered style of teaching.
4. Compare and contrast major characteristics of high and low ability learners.
5. Outline several suggestions for accommodating differences in learning styles, rates, and abilities.
6. Write performance objectives in each of the three domains of learning.

7. Classify cognitive performances according to Bloom's taxonomy.
8. Develop both short and long range plans for instruction using a three stage planning process.
9. Plan daily lessons according to a suggested format.

SECTION 1. PLANNING FOR ACTIVE
STUDENT INVOLVEMENT IN LEARNING

Any teacher entering the classroom for the first time will be confronted with basic decisions to make concerning just what type of teaching-leadership role is most preferred. Which teaching style is best? What teaching role should be assumed? In the end, of course, these decisions will be made on an individual basis. What suits one teacher may not suit another. Nevertheless, there is information available which relates in a pertinent fashion to these questions and which you should consider in the determination of your classroom teaching behavior. These data also lend assistance in dealing with the overall issue of student involvement in the learning process. As this is the case, consideration of the various styles of leadership that you may utilize is given in this discussion.

1.1. Leadership Styles

There is little doubt that the teacher's image as the instructional leader influences what types of success may be expected as a result of the teacher's instructional efforts. Different images project different messages to students, which in turn help to determine outcomes following the teaching process. A teacher's image is often referred to as *TEACHING STYLE.* Since the teacher is the leader of the learning group, one may conclude that a teaching style can, in reality, also represent a type of leadership style. Because of the impact that a teacher's leadership style has on student accomplishments, a knowledge of style as it relates to outcomes is essential.

A popular breakdown of leadership styles is a three category system, which includes the AUTHORITARIAN, LAISSEZ–FAIRE, and AUTHORITATIVE leadership approaches. In order to reach a logical and grounded conclusion concerning (1) one's most preferred style, (2) the question of student involvement in learning, and (3) student response to the various leadership approaches, it is helpful to investigate what the different styles mean in relation to student development, both personal and intellectual.

The authoritarian style of leadership is noted for its firmness of control. Authoritarian teachers demonstrate leadership by doing all of the planning and issuing all class directives; they might well be considered as analogous, in the dominative sense, to the captain of the ship. In the authoritarian classroom, the teacher acts as the primary active point of instruction and sees students as passive receivers of information. Consider the following example:

> Mrs. Peabody, a second grade teacher, always follows a definite routine for beginning class. At the moment the bell rings, she takes a position behind the teacher's desk and stares at the students until they become quiet and seemingly ready for instruction. She, typically, writes an outline of the day's activities on the chalkboard. Naturally, she sometimes makes errors in her haste to copy the material that she has selected. But, the students will never indicate that they have noticed because Mrs. Peabody has taught them well that she is the teacher and they are the students; her job is to know the subject and theirs is to learn it as she prescribes. She then proceeds to read from her notes and perhaps write on the chalkboard or transparencies while the students are expected to listen and learn. Following the lesson, the students are usually given worksheets to complete prior to the end of the class session while she stands, always at the front of the room, making certain that they keep busy. Her students are often bored because of the rigid nature of her class routine and the fact that they do not have an opportunity to participate very much in the typical lesson. However, students in her class do their work when she is present.

Mrs. Peabody is a good example of a distinction between efficient and effective. She is efficient in maintaining class order and in presenting the material she selects, but she is not effective in developing important, positive attitudes toward learning and a sense of autonomy in her students. Difficulties with Mrs. Peabody's type of leadership have been recognized for quite some time. For example, an early study by White and Lippitt (1960) concerning this style of instruction found that students in similar authoritarian groups tended to be apathetic, dependent, and unable to show serious initiative for self-directed work. When the teacher left the room, very little was accomplished. Students being instructed under this leadership style tended, on occasion, to display hostile behaviors toward fellow class members. However, while aggressive behaviors were evidenced in this manner toward classmates, little open resentment was shown toward the authoritarian leader. More recent studies of group leadership have produced similar results (Good and Brophy, 1980).

The laissez-faire teacher is found at the opposite end of the continuum from the authoritarian. Teachers operating with this style of instruction are really not committed to getting involved. Students are frequently left on their own to make their own decisions. The laissez-faire teacher tends to avoid giving directions, planning lessons, and, for all practical purposes, does not lead at all. Consider the case of Mr. Pinkerton:

> Working in a middle school, Mr. Pinkerton teaches sixth and seventh grade Language Arts. Mr. Pinkerton, unlike Mrs. Peabody, is often not even in the room when it is time to begin class. On arrival, he usually spends considerable time chatting with the two or three students near the front of the room while other students talk among themselves. When his class finally does begin, he usually has to ask the students to identify which page of the textbook the class is to study next. His opening remark is often the question: "What do we do today, group?" Mr. Pinkerton follows the text almost exclusively because he feels that since someone smarter than he went to much trouble to write it, he does not need to plan his lessons but, instead, merely follow the book. His class typically ends in the middle of a topic and, as they are leaving, the students yell questions concerning the nature of the next assignment. He often replies with, "Oh, just keep reading ahead."

Students under Mr. Pinkerton's laissez-faire leadership style seem to get along better than those enduring Mrs. Peabody's authoritarian style. Left on their own, Mr. Pinkerton's students will even complete some instructional tasks. As far as personal development, however, they tend to be insecure, continually seeking assistance from Mr. Pinkerton or some other leader figure.

In authoritative leadership situations, the teacher becomes a group leader rather than the "ship's captain" as was noted in the authoritarian style of teaching. The primary purpose of teaching as seen by those teachers employing this style of leadership is to "guide" their students in the pursuit of investigations in their own specified content areas. While the teacher is still the expert in relation to knowledge of the subject matter in question, student ideas, recommendations, and input play a major role as well. The classroom is arranged so that students may become active participants rather than passive recipients in the learning process; the students, as well as the teacher, play a major role in the learning process. For an example of how this may be done, consider Mrs. Porter's class:

> Mrs. Porter's kindergarten class routines vary considerably from day to day. Her entire approach is characterized by flexibility and concern for helping the students learn. She strongly believes that her job is to teach students—not subject matter content. On almost all lesson topics, students have a choice of ways in which they may actively participate because Mrs. Porter uses a variety of activities and strategies to accomplish the objectives. Her students even have some input into the selection of topics to be considered through the use of individual projects. Students in her class experience instruction in a variety of organizational patterns, individual, small group, and large group work, and feel free to communicate within and among groups as necessary. Unlike Mrs. Peabody, Mrs. Porter does not fear loss of classroom control during the group work because she realizes that there are several kinds of classroom noise (e.g. productive noise and disruptive noise). Through her enthusiasm and genuine interest in their progress, she has taught the students well that

learning can be interesting and even fun. Mrs. Porter's students feel free to discuss issues and ask questions. If she cannot answer a question fully, she directs the students to other sources of information available within the classroom and outside of the school setting. She does not consider herself the only source of knowledge.

Notice that the authoritative style is not a democracy (e.g. all decisions are not made by majority vote). However, students working with Mrs. Porter are more actively engaged in their own learning and experience feelings of personal control rather than teacher domination. Of the three styles outlined, the authoritative seems to be preferable; this preference is not without considerable research support (Bayles, 1960; Tjosvold, 1977; and Tjosvold and Santamaria, 1977). Moreover, Mahoney (1974) not only found greater academic success to be evident but reported that students tend to enjoy their learning more when they are able to make significant choices in their daily schedule of activities. Interestingly enough, these findings are repeated even when the responsibilities identified by the students are identical to those previously identified by the teacher.

The general conclusion is simple yet powerful. When students are given the opportunity to be a part of their own learning in an active decision-making sense, they are going to learn more and enjoy school more than when they are not able to become an important part of this process.

1.2. Centered Instruction

Although much is known supporting the authoritative, student-centered classroom in theory, its application has not been widely adopted. Very few people would argue against the importance of the teacher being able to deliver a motivating, well-organized lecture or conducting demonstrations and student recitations. These are, of course, prime strategies utilized in the teacher-centered approach. But, as an overall teacher behavioral style, the student-centered design for instruction must be considered more preferred in the majority of teaching situations. In teacher-centered instruction, because of the focus of the approach, the teacher is the star of the classroom; the student is passive. If possible, why not have thirty stars instead of one? This seems to make more sense. As opposed to the teacher-centered style, the student-centered approach is directed toward the student during the instructional process, not the teacher. Students are active as opposed to passive. Such strategies as the language experience approach to reading, group discussion, oral reporting, role playing, debating, brainstorming, and inquiry are relevant approaches to center the focus of instruction on the student and, therefore, move toward authoritative leadership in a student-centered classroom.

How you involve the learner as an active participant naturally requires a rather extensive knowledge of the total learning group. Fortunately, we have instruments to help us gain this information. The obtaining of some form of systematic feedback from students often provides us with a sound basis for student-centered strategies. One instrument available for such an investigation is the Learning Environment Inventory (LEI). Anderson and Walberg (1974) have noted that, while the LEI serves to identify student opinion, scores are also correlated with student achievement as well. The LEI poses classroom characteristics or situation statements to which students are asked to respond. A few items from the LEI are presented as follows:

1. Class decisions tend to be made by all the students.
2. Members of the class don't care what the class does.
3. The class is disorganized.
4. The class has difficulty keeping up with its assigned work (Good, Biddle, and Brophy, 1975).

A second valuable resource is the School Sentiment Index (SSI). Like the Learning Environment Inventory, this instrument is also designed to systematically obtain information detailing student perceptions concerning the learning setting. Sample items from the SSI are listed below.

1. My teacher would let the class plan an event alone.
2. My teacher doesn't explain things very well.
3. I would rather do almost anything else than study.

4. I don't do very much reading on my own (Good, Biddle, and Brophy, 1975).

Data from instruments such as these can be helpful in providing information to the teacher concerning student satisfaction with, or perception of, the learning environment. Naturally, if dissatisfaction is identified, students should be helped to feel some degree of ownership in the learning process so that, in turn, they will feel more satisfied with it.

Formative Evaluation: Section 1*

1. Name and describe three leadership styles commonly associated with teachers.
2. List three advantages of the authoritative style of leadership.
3. Define CENTERED INSTRUCTION.
4. Why might one use the LEI or the SSI?

SECTION 2. PLANNING FOR INDIVIDUAL DIFFERENCES

Effective teachers think of their classes as being made up of individuals, not large group units. Therefore, you must view the classroom as a group of separate learners; at the very least, a class must be seen as a conglomerate of several small groups or a combination of small groups and distinct, individual learners. A common misconception held by many teachers is that all of their students are equally able to gain information from classroom instruction. However, in a typical elementary or secondary classroom, a teacher, when making a presentation designed to be suitable for a large group, will most assuredly present material too difficult for some students while not challenging others.

This is not a great revelation to educators; it has been known for many years that some students have great difficulty in school, while others have to put forth little effort to do well. However, some educators have often been guilty of assuming that a teacher's

---

*See the Appendix for suggested answers to these questions.

obligation is fulfilled when correct information is presented in a sequential manner and when questions that the students might pose are answered. Regardless of the fact that this assumption has persisted for decades, it is obviously flawed. Not only do students vary in their ability to learn, students often vary in their rate of learning even when they are of similar ability. In other words, the excuse given by some educators that their classes are homogenously grouped and do not need further grouping is invalid. Of course, when students vary in ability to learn, the variance in rates in learning and the speed at which new material is mastered is likely to be even greater. Superimposed over the diversity created by differences in ability and rate of learning is the fact that many students do not learn equally well from all types of learning experiences; they differ in what has been termed *LEARNING STYLE*.

Essentially, one of the most difficult tasks that you as the teacher must accomplish is to adjust your instruction to the learning abilities, learning rates, and learning styles of all students. At the very least, this adjustment will be difficult and will occupy much of your planning time. In fact, you will find that the best planning efforts will sometimes fall short of helping all of the students with their learning needs. No matter how complex the learning needs of a class may be, you will need to begin planning for these needs by thinking of ways to best group the students for the most appropriate instruction. Grouping students to enhance learning is a skill effective teachers at all grade levels must possess. A skillful teacher knows how to arrange groups on a flexible basis in order that individuals within the class will learn as much as they can at an optimum rate.

Most educators agree that learners of different learning abilities cannot be taught with the same instructional strategies because they learn in different ways and at different speeds. Simply put, teachers cannot teach high ability students using the same strategies they use to teach low ability students if they wish to be effective with all learners. Different strategies must be used to accommodate the styles, rates, and abilities of all learners in any classroom.

2.1. Working with the High Ability Student

Before you read the following portion of this section, carefully study Figure 1-1 which provides an outline of some of the more definitive characteristics of high ability students.

HIGH ABILITY STUDENTS:

- are able to complete their work faster than many of their classmates;
- have an extensive background of competencies;
- are ready to tie new information to their relatively large accumulation of experiences;
- have a history of academic success;
- are confident;
- are eager to become involved in new learning experiences;
- work well on their own;
- often are class leaders;
- are frequently outgoing.

Figure 1-1. Characteristics of high ability students.

In order to challenge the more advanced and faster working student, you must design strategies to allow these students to complete the required assignments in a more realistic time frame; at the same time, you can provide such students with opportunities to explore an enriched curriculum. For example, an elementary teacher may choose to use a learning center designed for advanced students, while a secondary teacher may provide the necessary materials and resources for students to pursue an individual project. In each case, the students who finish the required assignment would have an opportunity to pursue those learnings in which they have a special interest and which serve as enrichment. Work on enrichment activities such as these could typically take place while other students are completing the required assignments. High ability students, when working through a given curriculum area, should be encouraged to work independently at an individualized rate of speed. In other words, they should work in a curriculum that is individualized and self-paced. Essentially, an individualized, self-paced curriculum is one in which students are accorded an opportunity to individually experience instruction geared to their ability level and to complete such instruction at their own rate. Working with high ability students in this way will:

1. Allow the students to extend themselves by completing more work in a shorter time span and going into greater depth on given topics
2. Diminish the amount of wasted instructional time during the school year
3. Allow the teacher to spend more directed instructional time with low ability students
4. Make it possible for advanced students to progress through the curriculum fast enough to allow them extra time which can be used for other activities such as tutoring classmates of lesser ability

A fact of instructional reality is that teachers often spend too much time giving direct instruction to the students who need it the least while the less motivated, lower ability students suffer from the absence of needed direct teacher guidance. Although the use of an individualized strategy is strongly advised for high ability pupils, it is important to realize that such an independent approach to learning may be very ill-advised for low ability students. Only highly skilled students with a background of successful learning experiences are likely to have the competencies and motivation needed to work effectively on their own.

2.2. Working with the Low Ability Student

Take a moment to examine Figure 1-2 in order to gain an understanding of the more salient characteristics of low ability students. Low ability learners need to move through the curriculum at a pace that is commensurate with their personal needs while receiving a great deal of close attention from the teacher. These students are rarely able to benefit from large group or independent instruction; however, such students usually make progress in a dyadic situation with the teacher or a tutor. Immediate reinforcement and feedback are of the essence. Essentially, the teacher should look for those things that the low ability learner is doing well and reward (reinforce) the student through the use of teacher praise. Thus, the teacher must find curriculum materials that are of interest to each slow learner which are written on a level that is simple enough to guarantee success. When instructing a low ability student, you must remember that it is much worse to place the learner in material which is too difficult than to place such a student in material which is too easy. The low ability student is one who most assuredly has had a history of failure and frustration. If such students are to realize success, it is imperative that they be given an opportunity to view themselves as capable individuals making progress in a non-threatening environment.

LOW ABILITY STUDENTS:
  • require more time to learn a concept or skill;
  • have a minimal level of readiness for new instruction;
  • have generally had few past experiences with which to link new information;
  • have a history of failure;
  • are unsure of themselves;
  • are hesitant to become involved in new learning situations;
  • tend not to work well in groups;
  • may be difficult to motivate;
  • are often more successful with concrete as opposed to abstract work;
  • frequently require visual, active presentations;
  • tend not to work well independent of close supervision.

Figure 1-2. Characteristics of low ability students.

The most realistic, non-threatening environment for low ability students is a situation where they are working closely with a supportive teacher in a curriculum area where they do not have to worry about adjusting their rate or style of learning to other students in the class. The importance of reinforcing the low ability student in a highly supportive environment cannot be overstated

(Purkey, 1976; VanHouten, 1980). The teacher simply must not approach the low ability student with a corrective attitude. Rather, the teacher must concentrate on what the learners do correctly, not on their errors. If low ability students are constantly being corrected and reminded of their inabilities, they are likely to become anxious and withdraw from the instructional situation.

The low ability student, by definition, is a student who does not have the skills and knowledge that are required to function in the typical curriculum for average learners at their grade or level. The teacher needs to accept the student's inabilities and avoid judging by standards suitable for the average student. It is an unrealistic goal to expect such students to come up to the norm in the span of one school year; a more appropriate goal would be to expect them to make steady, although perhaps slow, progress from the point at which they are presently functioning. The teacher should be concerned much more with what these students learn than what they do not already know. One might think of low ability learners as if they were glasses that needed filling; in the past much water has been spilled instead of going into the glass, now is the time to reinforce what goes into the glass, not to worry about what has spilled outside.

2.3. Adjusting Instruction to Learning Styles

In addition to the fact that students learn at different rates and have different levels of learning ability, students do not all achieve at their optimal level through the same instructional methods. It is apparent that while some students can achieve well through some methods, others find it difficult to learn when certain other methods of instruction are used. Dunn and Dunn (1979) have suggested that there are eighteen different elements that make up all of the possible learning styles; these elements can be categorized into one of the following headings: (1) environmental elements, (2) emotional elements, (3) sociological elements, and (4) physical elements. Barbe and Milone (1981) further suggested the need to investigate areas of sense perception in conjunction with learning styles in order to create the optimal learning environment (See Fig. 1-3). Obviously, if there are this many elements that can affect the learning styles of students, a teacher has a great many stimuli to be aware of in trying to develop the best of all possible learning environments for each student.

Environmental Elements

The first set of learning style stimuli discussed is that set dealing with the classroom environment. Some students seem to learn well only in a quiet setting; noise disrupts their learning processes. Other students, however, are very able to learn in a busy, active environment which might seem noisy to some. The amount of light also has an effect on the learning capabilities of some students. It has been noted that while light variations do not affect as many learners as sound variations, some students should not sit near windows or bright lights if they are to do their best work. Room temperature has also been found to have an effect on learning. Although it is a rare classroom where the temperature can be controlled by the learners, some students need to be warm when they learn and others simply cannot function unless they feel the temperature is cool. Consequently, the classroom should be arranged so that there are variations in room temperature. At the very least, the teacher needs to be aware of how close or how far away from heaters and air conditioners that certain students sit. A final consideration about the environment is the degree of casualness or formality in the teaching-learning atmosphere. Some students cannot learn in a restrictive environment that requires them to sit quietly without moving. One can only speculate about how many children have become behavior problems because they simply could not adjust to the rigid, restrictive environment of the classical teaching-learning setting. Of course, there are many other students who cannot learn unless they are in an environment that provides a quiet, peaceful setting.

Emotional Elements

Motivation is an important element in determining how well a student will learn a given body of information; however, great variance exists among students in terms of how much motivation they exhibit for different learning activities. Some students show little interest or at the most a very short attention span when

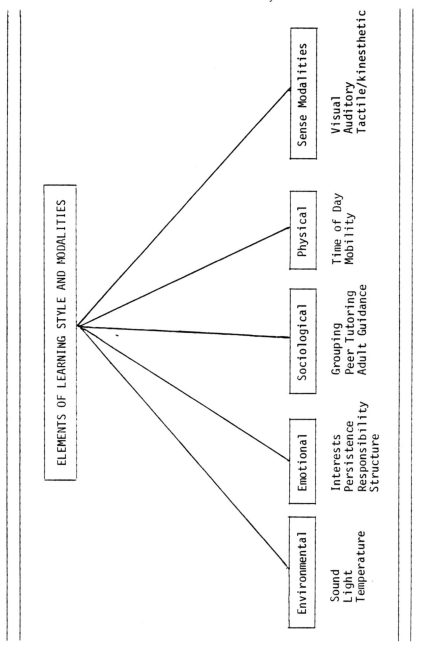

Figure 1-3. Basic elements of learning style and modalities affecting the learning environment.

many activities are undertaken. Obviously, these students need special instructional strategies to help them learn. Such learners need to be encouraged to make free choices in order to vary the way they work in the learning environment. Teachers must allow students to work in groups and practice self-evaluation. Persistence is also a very important aspect of a learner's style. Some students can only stay on task for about twenty minutes, while others can work an hour or more at the same assignment. Because of this variance in student persistence, it is suggested that students who seem to have short attention spans be given assignments that have a specific time limit that is realistic for the person involved. It is important that this time limit be set so that the student can legitimately be required to come to closure. Another important emotional element is that of responsibility. Many students seem unable to work on any task unless they are closely supervised; these students find it quite difficult to work independently in a self-paced situation. Such learners need less demanding work until they build their confidence. Highly related to the other elements of the emotional stimuli is what has come to be referred to as *structure*. Students often have a need for frequent supervision in order to get a task completed. Students who have special learning styles based on their emotional needs are the ones who probably need the closest attention from the teacher. Students who do not have these same needs are more likely to be able to work independently.

Sociological Elements

A third set of elements has been clustered together which designate the sociological elements of learning style. Students often vary greatly in terms of the type of learning group they desire; this variety ranges from learning alone to learning in large groups. Teachers need to encourage students to choose the type of group setting in which they work best, remembering that some may enjoy peer tutoring while others will desire a higher level of adult guidance.

Physical Elements

Another set of learning style stimuli is referred to as physical elements. For example, some students evidently learn best when they are eating or drinking; no doubt, few teachers would be able to accommodate such a learner to meet this type of learning need. As difficult as some teachers may find it to adjust to a learner's need for the intake of food or drink, it does seem reasonable to suggest that the students' schedules could sometimes be adjusted to the fact that they may learn better during certain times of the day. Accordingly, if a student learns best during the latter part of the morning, this is the time to provide the most demanding tasks. Finally, a number of students need to be mobile before they can satisfy their learning needs completely. Such students tend to function best in an informal learning environment because of their need to move, stretch, and even walk around before they can adjust well to the teaching-learning environment.

It is somewhat unrealistic to suggest that a teacher can develop a completely different learning environment for each and every student in the classroom. However, it is reasonable to suggest that a teacher be conscious of the fact that some of the students' learning may be affected by group size, room temperature, time of day, and room design.

How many students are greatly affected in the public school by the fact that their learning style needs often go unsatisfied is difficult to determine. As Fischer and Fischer (1979) point out, many students are eclectic learners and can adjust their learning to any instructional style. These students often do very well in school, and there is a tendency for teachers to give them high evaluations. Since it is the best of students who adjust to any teaching style, teachers often conclude that all students should be able to make these adjustments. Dunn, Dunn, and Price (1981) suggest that all students simply cannot adjust their learning to all teaching styles. The fact is, many learners are unable to meet their full learning potential because they cannot learn in the manner that the teacher has planned for the total class. This type of student seems to suffer greatly when the teacher feels that all learners should be taught in the same way in large groups.

Sense Modalities

High ability students, by definition, adapt well to the instructional styles of their teachers; therefore, it is the style of the low ability learner that is in need of more careful analysis. Barbe and Milone (1981), among other researchers, suggest that the greatest analysis should be done in the area of sense perception. These channels of perception are usually referred to as sense modalities. Some students can learn best visually, while others learn best through the senses of hearing and touch. The important aspect of matching instructional styles with learning styles is the fact that many students are unable to learn well through certain sense modalities or in certain learning environments. It is, therefore, important that they not be required to attempt learning in situations that could only lead to anxiety and failure. Teachers need to vary styles of instruction with students who are having difficulty until a best style is determined. When the best style is finally determined, there is little need for variation. The goal of the teacher is not to vary styles for each student but to find the optimal instructional style for each student and then use it. The result will be a variety of styles within the same classroom, not within the instructional program of a given learner.

Formative Evaluation: Section 2*

1. Compare and contrast the major characteristics of high and low ability learners.
2. List several suggestions for dealing with students of differing abilities in your class.
3. What are some of the ways in which the teacher can accommodate differences in learning rates?
4. What is meant by learning style? How might you accommodate differences in learning style within the same classroom?

---

*See the Appendix for suggested answers to these questions.

SECTION 3. PLANNING INSTRUCTIONAL OBJECTIVES

Instructional planning involves deciding *WHAT* you are going to teach, *HOW* you are going to teach, and *HOW WELL* you expect your students to know the material when you have finished. If the teacher does not have these planning points well in mind, inconsistent instruction and classroom confusion may well be expected. Not only may the students become confused, but the teacher may also lose direction. Good planning, of course, will not insure good teaching, but it is a very important prerequisite if one desires quality classroom interaction. As a matter of fact, it is the first step to good classroom management that we discuss later in Chapter Five.

An obvious purpose of teaching is to facilitate learning on behalf of the students in the classroom. But, how is one to know if learning has been facilitated? If the teacher is not certain of what it is that is being facilitated, it will be impossible to determine when it has been accomplished. It is for this reason that a formal planning aid such as learner objectives becomes necessary. Through the use of well-planned objectives tailored to the learner or learning group, the teacher has a much clearer indication of how learning may be enhanced.

There are many types and styles of learner objectives that a teacher could adopt and use. The three-part objective described by Mager (1962) will be used here as a recommended model. Mager stated that objectives should consist of (1) a performance statement identifying the terminal behavior of the student, (2) a conditions of performance statement, and (3) a criterion statement to indicate quality of performance expected by the teacher. This type of objective provides answers to the following questions:

> Where am I going?
> How shall I get there?
> How will I know when I have arrived?
> (Mager, 1968, p. vii)

The answers to these questions are, of course, fundamental to the process of good planning.

3.1. Performance Statements and Domains of Learning

Performance statements are, as the name implies, statements describing the behavior that the learner will be able to perform following instruction in order to demonstrate that learning has taken place. These statements typically consist of a verb followed by the object of that verb. All learning (i.e. changes in behavior or performance) may be classified into three basic categories or domains: cognitive, affective, and psychomotor (Bloom, 1956; Krathwohl, 1964; Harrow, 1972). See Figure 1-4 for the major categories of each domain. Thinking of learning as involving one of three discrete categories or domains has proven very useful in planning and assembling instruction. *COGNITIVE* behaviors or performances are intellectual. They involve such mental skills as knowing, understanding, and thinking. Behaviors in this domain may be thought of as those usually emphasized in formal education. Any curriculum contains a certain, rather large, body of information that educators feel is important for the students to learn. Along with this body of information, teachers strive through their instruction to develop rational thinking abilities in their students. Learning in the *AFFECTIVE* domain consists of attitudes, interests, and appreciations. Behaviors or performances in this domain are products of feelings, emotions, and values. The emphasis in formal education involves attempting to generate learner enthusiasm for the subject matter the teacher is presenting, but, in addition, the development of a positive response to learning is also a primary goal of a formal education, regardless of the subject matter. The *PSYCHOMOTOR* domain involves motor or neuro-muscular skills such as handwriting, typing, assembling or using apparatus, and performing athletic/movement skills. With the exception of quality physical education and early childhood programs, the psychomotor domain receives less emphasis than the other domains in the formal education environment; teachers, in actuality, spend little time developing performances in this domain. See Figure 1-5 for a brief summary of the three domains and examples of performance statements in each. You should remember that performance statements identify behaviors that the learner will be able to exhibit in order to demonstrate that learning has followed

DOMAIN	CATEGORIES		DESCRIPTION
COGNITIVE:	1. Knowledge	-	*involves recall of information*
	2. Comprehension	-	*refers to understanding something*
	3. Application	-	*the use of abstractions in particular situations*
	4. Analysis	-	*the dissection of a communication into components revealing the relationship between the parts of the whole*
	5. Synthesis	-	*the putting together of ideas or things in a unique creation*
	6. Evaluation	-	*the judgement about a person, place, or thing*
AFFECTIVE:	1. Receiving (Attending)	-	*an awareness of the existence of certain ideas so as to become willing to receive or listen to them*
	2. Responding	-	*a response which goes beyond attending; it implies some commitment to be involved*
	3. Valuing	-	*a profession that something has worth*
	4. Organization	-	*the elementary internalization of values into a system*
	5. Generalization	-	*the more refined internalization of values which are consistent and interrelated with other values*
PSYCHOMOTOR:	1. Reflex Movements	-	*involuntary movements; precursor to voluntary, fundamental movements*
	2. Basic-Fundamental Movements	-	*simple, learned movements, (e.g., crawling, walking, grabbing) which are inherent and form the basis for complex movements*
	3. Perceptual Abilities	-	*all perceptual modalities that are carried to the brain for interpretation*
	4. Physical Abilities	-	*general body vigor such as endurance and flexibility demonstrated by efficiency in performing complex movement tasks*
	6. Non-Discursive Communications	-	*behaviors related to expressive or interpretive movement which communicates a message to the viewer*

Figure 1-4. Major categories of the taxonomies in the cognitive, affective, and psychomotor domains.

instruction. Moreover, you should also be aware that considerable overlap exists among the domains.

It must be noted that within each domain, performance statements may reflect varying degrees of learning. For example, the performance statement *CONDUCT AN OUT OF SCHOOL PROJECT* indicates a more positive attitude toward the subject than the statement *ACTIVELY PARTICIPATE IN CLASS DISCUSSIONS.* Similarily, *RECITE THE FIRST MULTIPLICATION TABLE* indicates less intellectual activity than *WRITE A PARAGRAPH ABOUT YOUR PET.* Thus, it is very useful in planning, particularly in the cognitive domain, to differentiate between levels of difficulty in learning. Of course, it is also very useful to differentiate between levels of the psychomotor and affective domains. However, due to the content emphasis of public school curricula, we will stress the levels of the cognitive domain. Knowledge gained studying the cognitive domain should be readily transferable to your work in the other two domains should you wish to develop your planning around the specific levels of each domain. Obviously, you should develop plans in each domain regardless of whether or not you divide the domains into discrete categories.

3.2. Cognitive Levels

Although educators have agreed that there are many levels of thinking or cognition, no attempt at delineating the levels of thinking gained general acceptance until a committee of the American Psychological Association addressed itself to the problem (Bloom, 1956). This committee, under the direction of Benjamin Bloom, developed a taxonomy or classification system for educational objectives in the cognitive domain. The resultant taxonomy was composed of the following six major levels: *KNOWLEDGE, COMPREHENSION, APPLICATION, ANALYSIS, SYNTHESIS,* and *EVALUATION.* While the individual categories have been further divided into subclasses, only the six major classifications need be emphasized for planning purposes.

The major classification levels listed in the cognitive domain constitute a hierarchy; that is, they are ranked, with knowledge

DOMAIN	SAMPLE PERFORMANCE STATEMENTS
Cognitive: Intellectual Activities	• define energy in your own words • identify the rhyming words • formulate a generalization to explain recent weather trends • write a paragraph about your summer vacation • discriminate between a triangle and a square • solve problems using the given formula
Affective: Attitudes, Interests, Appreciations	• volunteer to care for the aquarium after school • take care of the school garden • conduct an after school research project • rewrite a book report voluntarily • bring current news stories to class • voluntarily pick up trash in the lunchroom
Psychomotor: Motor Skills	• roll a kickball • color a picture • assemble a model airplane • copy a graph from the chalkboard • measure the classroom • focus a telescope on a given point

Figure 1-5. Sample performance statements for the three domains of learning.

being the lowest and evaluation being the highest. In other words, to function effectively at the more complex levels (application, analysis, synthesis, and evaluation), the learner must first master the lower and simpler mental processes (knowledge and comprehension). For example, if a student solves a problem at the analysis level, it is assumed that the learner has the ability to deal with this same subject matter at the preceding levels.

For consistency in classifying performances, you should categorize behaviors in the highest (most complex) category that is appropriate. If a student is required to use knowledge, comprehension and application, the performance statement should be classified under the application category.

KNOWLEDGE, the lowest level of the cognitive domain, includes situations and conditions in which the student is expected to remember, memorize, or recall information previously learned. Knowledge level functions are those which develop almost directly from one's experiences, particularly those experiences at the concrete level. Remembering is the key intellectual process involved. The student is expected to store certain facts derived from experience and then, at some later time, be able to recall this information with minimum assistance. Knowledge level performances typically refer to the recall of facts, concepts, or principles. Examples of knowledge level performance statements are:

- Name three types of sentences
- Match the meaning of selected road signs with the correct picture
- Recall the date of Darwin's voyage

COMPREHENSION, the level that is perhaps most often emphasized in schools today, requires the ability to know the meaning of material or ideas and make some use of the information. Comprehension builds on knowledge in that the learner has achieved a higher level of understanding of the information which has been memorized and recalled. Performance statements, in this category, indicate that the learner understands a particular fact, concept, or idea. Examples of comprehension level performance statements include:

- Explain the kind of information found on a particular chart
- In your own words, define subtraction
- Paraphrase written statements, retaining the original meaning

APPLICATION is essentially the act of applying some understanding to a new or unique situation without being told to do so. Bloom describes the distinction between the levels of comprehension and application thus: "A demonstration of 'Comprehension' shows that the student *can* use the abstraction when its use is specified. A demonstration of 'Application' shows that he *will* use it correctly, given an appropriate situation in which no mode of solution is specified" (Bloom, 1956, p. 120). It is useful to think of the student understanding a principle or rule at the comprehension level and then using that principle or rule in a practical situation at the application level. Application, then, requires the learner to remember, comprehend, and also to apply the proper generalization at the right time and place. Obviously, there is a great deal of difference in knowing how to multiply and knowing when to multiply. Application requires students to go beyond correctly demonstrating a skill; they must be able to apply the proper abstraction without being told or shown. Examples of application level performance statements are:

- Calculate how much paint will be needed to paint our classroom
- Select and use the appropriate verb wherever it has been left out of a list of sentences
- Demonstrate what our class should do if we were to see a tornado coming

At the *ANALYSIS* level, students should be able to break an idea into its constituent elements or internal organizational principles and perceive relationships among those elements or principles within one "whole" or among several "wholes." Analysis, in its fundamental form, is seeing similarities among and differences between things. Although higher on the taxonomic scale, analysis may be easier to understand than some of the previous levels because analysis basically involves breaking down material into its component parts and finding relationships among them. Performance at this level requires the student to 'get into' something to see clearly what is there. Examples of analysis level performance statements are:

- Identify, in a written passage, which statements are statements of fact and which are hypotheses
- Identify the bias of a writer in an article
- Distinguish between opinion and fact in a story

While analysis involves reducing wholes to identify their component parts, *SYNTHESIS* is the ability to put known parts together to make a unique entity or whole which is new to the learner. Using a musical analogy, when composers attempt to develop a new composition, they may well begin with basic chords and, using music theory principles, develop these logically into a melody. It should be remembered that students must have mastered material in the area at the preceding levels before they can be successful at the synthesis level. Even then, developing something that is unique is often not an easy task. Performance statements dealing with synthesis require students to create something that is distinctly their own idea. The product to be created may be a communication (e.g. poem, essay, editorial), a plan of operation (e.g. diagram, outline, model), or a set of abstract relations (e.g. unique interpretation). The distinctive quality of synthesis is the freedom it allows students in deciding what is to be produced. A performance statement dealing with synthesis, in other words, never has only one correct response. Examples of synthesis level performance statements are:

- Make up a story about the forest
- Write a poem about winter
- Design a model bridge

EVALUATION, the highest level of the cognitive domain, includes making judgments about the worth of material for a given purpose according to specific criteria. Performances at this level also involve a justification of the judgment which is made by reference to facts, examples, or specific criteria of another sort. Evaluation means, then, considerably more than simply saying that one thing is better than another. The judgment must have some basis, or criterion, for being made in the first place. Care must be taken in writing evaluation level performance statements so as to exclude those dealing primarily with values, opinions, or feelings which more properly are part of the affective domain. Evaluation requires the identification of standards and ascertaining the degree to which whatever is being evaluated meets the standards. Whenever students are required to assess, appraise, or judge some event, message, object, or situation on the basis of distinct criteria, the intellectual skill of evaluation is being developed. Examples of evaluation level performance statements are:

- Rate information in the *Weekly Reader* on the basis of accuracy, completeness, and relevance of the included data

- Compare the worth of the scientific contributions of Einstein and Newton
- Appraise the quality of a given paint according to durability and retention of gloss

Any cognitive performance statement can be categorized into one of these six levels. Because certain mental processes tend to overlap into several categories, the exact classification of a performance statement is sometimes difficult. This does not necessarily decrease the instructional quality of that performance statement, because a wide range of intellectual activities for students is provided as a result of this type of planning.

Each of the different intellectual skills can be adapted to any subject area and grade level. Slow students and bright students alike should be able to perform at each level of thinking with some measure of sophistication. Of course, students of marginal mental capacity may experience more difficulty in analyzing, synthesizing, and evaluating. Often, slower learners can engage in these higher mental processes if the subject matter is familiar to them, because lower ability students do not function well at higher levels when using abstract ideas.

In practice, the cognitive domain might be appropriately used in the development of curricula which address both lower as well as higher level thinking skills. Through the categorization of performance statements as they relate to the cognitive domain, you can readily see what mental challenges the learner will experience.

Figure 1-6 presents a brief summary of the typical behaviors and the definitions of the six levels of the Taxonomy of the Cognitive Domain; becoming familiar with this taxonomy is an important step in using this very valuable aid in planning and sequencing instruction.

Through the use of this category system, the most basic part of a quality objective—the performance statement—is more clearly defined. With the learners' expected performance better delineated, the teacher has a more lucid indication of the answer to the earlier question: "Where am I going?"

	Typical Action Verbs*	Definition
Evaluation	Appraise, compare, criticize, judge, justify, select	To evaluate is to make a judgement based on specific criteria: more than choice is involved. One must also provide a rationale for whatever evaluation is made.
Synthesis	Compare, design, devise, formulate, hypothesize, plan	Synthesis involves organizing elements into a new structure, putting parts into a whole, creating new forms or ideas, or developing plans.
Analysis	Detect, infer, relate, distinguish, differentiate	Analysis is the breakdown of something to reveal its parts or structure and make clear what they are and how they relate to one another.
Application	Calculate, solve, determine, compute	This level involves the use of facts, ideas, principles, or formulas in *new* situations. The appropriate fact, idea, or formula must first be selected and then used in the given situation.
Comprehension	Convert, estimate, explain, paraphrase, summarize	This level emphasizes gaining the meaning or intent of something. The learner must do more than recall memorized knowledge.
Knowledge	Define, identify, list, name, state	Knowledge involves remembering or recalling specific facts, definitions, terms, names, or formulas.

Figure 1-6. A summary of the taxonomy of objectives for the cognitive domain (*taken from Gronlund, 1970).

3.3. Criterion Statement

As explained in Part 3.2, performance statements help to clarify educational objectives by using behavioral terms which are explicitly stated. A second important component of an instructional objective, the criterion statement, serves to further clarify expected student performance by defining how well the student is expected to complete the specified performance.

While it is very important to know *WHAT* the learners are expected to be able to do, it is also important to know *HOW WELL* they are expected to perform. This latter point becomes crucial for three reasons: (1) it serves to clarify the initial performance statement of what is expected of the learners, (2) it becomes a valuable aid in helping identify individual students who may need remedial instruction, and (3) it provides information for the teacher to use in revising instruction.

The criterion statement is an expression of the level of learner proficiency expected as a result of mastering the stated objectives. The teacher may express this in a variety of fashions. For example, if the performance statement involves solving addition problems with two digit numbers, the criterion statement may be stated in terms of the number correct out of the total number possible, such as nine out of ten. A criterion could also be stated in terms of a percentage of correct responses, for example, 90 percent; of course, the teacher may expect 100 percent proficiency. In fact, if the criterion statement is absent from an objective, 100 percent proficiency by the learner should be expected. The criterion along with the conditions statement adds greater specificity and a higher dimension of quality to a performance statement. However, the performance statement remains the heart of any quality instructional objective.

3.4. Conditions Statement

The conditions statement essentially describes what the students will be given at the time they are to demonstrate accomplishment of the learning involved in the performance statement. It may be useful to think of a conditions statement as a description of the setting in which the learners will function before or during their evaluative performance. For example, the learner may be provided with pictures to match with names for performance statements such as: *MATCH THE NAME OF AN ANIMAL WITH ITS HABITAT.* On the other hand, the student will often simply use paper and pencil to demonstrate the performance as in: *WRITE A BRIEF SUMMARY OF A STORY.* In this instance, the conditions statement may be implied; it is not necessary to state *GIVEN PAPER AND PENCIL.* Previous instruction may at times also be referred to in the conditions statement. The conditions statement, *GIVEN CLASS DISCUSSION AND A FILMSTRIP,* describes information that the learner will need to complete a performance statement such as: *GIVE EXAMPLES OF THE USE OF THE QUESTION MARK.*

3.5. Assembling Objectives

After one has written precise performance statements and developed possible criterion and condition statements, all that remains to arrive at a well-stated objective is to combine the three components. The following should be considered as a complete objective:

- After studying a unit on plants and observing plant growth, name four life requirements of plants.

The performance statement is *NAME FOUR LIFE REQUIRE-MENTS OF PLANTS.* The expression, *AFTER STUDYING A UNIT ON PLANTS AND OBSERVING PLANT GROWTH,* is a statement of the necessary conditions for mastery of the performance. The criterion statement is an implied 100 percent. Another example is as follows:

- Given a variety of straight line segments, measure the length of each line segment to the nearest centimeter.

In this example, the performance statement is *MEASURE THE LENGTH OF EACH LINE SEGMENT.* The expression, *GIVEN A VARIETY OF STRAIGHT LINE SEGMENTS,* describes the conditions inherent in the testing of the students' ability to perform the measurement. The criterion statement is embodied in the phrase *TO THE NEAREST CENTIMETER.* This indicates the level at which the student must perform; it is an example of the use of a qualitative, as opposed to a quantitative, criterion. Consider the following objective:

- Given the names of twenty common animals, identify the habitat of at least eighteen.

This objective represents the use of a quantitative criterion, i.e. eighteen of twenty must be correct. The conditions statement indicates that the learner will receive a list of animal names and be expected to write an answer beside each name.

Formative Evaluation: Section 3*

1. Identify the performance statements, criterion statements, and conditions statements in each of the following objectives:
   a. Given regulation track shoes and the use of an outdoor cinder track, run one mile in seven minutes or less.
   b. Given a current map of Africa, list all of the countries that lie in the Sahara Desert area.
   c. Write, without the use of aids, the definition of all spelling words in unit one.
2. Choose a topic and write three cognitive objectives.
3. Choose as you did in number two and write three psycho-motor objectives.
4. Write three affective domain objectives.
5. Classify your objectives for question two according to cognitive level.
6. Arrange the objectives in question four in an order from low affective response to high affective response.
7. Arrange the objectives in question three in order of skill difficulty.

SECTION 4. PLANNING EFFECTIVE INSTRUCTION

Kaye Wittwer, an English teacher from Montana, described a vivid picture of the unprepared teacher: "Teachers without plans too often waste major portions of class time in irrelevant activity or discussion. Flexibility may come to mean sloppiness, and spontaneity can turn out to be the coach discussing his newest football play with his math class" (Wittwer, 1971, p. 55).

Wittwer's comment indicates a belief in the importance of plan-

---

*See the Appendix for suggested answers to these questions.

ning for professionals in the field of education. This emphasis on planning, however, is not just voiced by professional educators but by professionals in all fields. Whether a lawyer preparing a court brief, a nurse assessing the psychological needs of patients, or an architect evaluating the impact of certain aesthetic barriers on handicapped individuals, all professionals must invest tremendous effort and thought before their actions are effectively implemented in their respective fields. When you enter the classroom as an effective teacher, you must enter it as an effective planner as well.

In describing the qualities of good teachers, Rosenshine (1971), Rosenshine and Furst (1971), and Good and Brophy (1980) have identified planning as one characteristic that is of great import. Organization in teaching is often described by students as a prime trait of their favorite teachers, whereas poor teachers are usually described as unorganized or not well planned. However, the most unfavorable aspect of unorganized teaching, in the public's opinion, is that it leads to lower student achievement than the instruction of a well-structured, organized teacher. Figure 1-7 provides an overview of a planning process that is intended to give you the background necessary to become an effective planner who will be able to avoid the inherent problems of unorganized instruction. It should be helpful to study Figure 1-7 before continuing your work in this section.

4.1. Pre-Instructional Development Stage

The major responsibility of the teacher during the pre-instructional development stage is to identify the direction that learning should take. In other words, the teacher will need to identify both the subject matter goals and the readiness levels of the students. Readiness levels will be determined following an analysis of important cognitive, affective, and psychomotor factors related to each learner.

Teachers who begin teaching a class without a clear conception of the overall goals of instruction are, in all likelihood, wasting time. If the student is to enter the school system in kindergarten and optimally progress through the next twelve years, it is neces-

STAGES	CONSIDERATIONS		
	Content Characteristics	Student Characteristics	Community Characteristics
PRE-INSTRUCTIONAL DEVELOPMENT STAGE	1. Goals and Objectives 2. Subject Matter 3. Activities	1. Cognitive entry behaviors 2. Affective entry behaviors 3. Psychomotor entry behaviors	1. Socio-economic levels 2. Occupational offerings 3. Rural/Urban milieu 4. Special community needs
INSTRUCTIONAL PLANNING AND IMPLEMENTATION STAGE	GOALS OBJECTIVES PROCEDURES/MATERIALS EVALUATION		
POST-INSTRUCTIONAL STAGE	Evaluation of Pre-Instructional Development Stage and Instructional Planning and Implementation Stage		

Figure 1-7. A process for planning effective instruction (adapted from Orlich, 1980).

sary for all of the teaching staff to coordinate their efforts toward the achievement of certain goals and objectives. The Phi Delta Kappa goals as identified by Spears (1973) are an excellent source (see Fig. 1-8); from these, numerous objectives can be devised. While objectives are considered as more immediate outcomes, goals, on the other hand, identify intended learnings that are broad and long-range in nature. A knowledge of important goals will help develop the necessary background for planning, but, because of the broad, unspecified nature of goals, teachers will often need further direction. It is for this reason, in part, that teacher's guides and packaged curricula are developed by and for teachers.

If a teacher is well versed in subject matter, these necessary content characteristics will form a foundation for proper planning. Perhaps classroom examples will clarify some of these preinstructional planning ideas.

> Mrs. Brown, a fourth grade teacher, begins each year without regard for students' experiences and achievement. Classroom instruction is rigidly scheduled with little flexibility shown. She seldom makes adjustments in her teaching; whole group instruction is utilized with absolutely no individualization.

> In the sixth grade, Mr. Jones, however, never sets up a group without carefully examining students' past achievement, skill attainment, and reading ability. He also gives students an interest survey and carefully examines their social characteristics. Adjustments are made as needed based on feedback from student performance and teacher observation.

Mrs. Brown and Mr. Jones are two generalized types of teachers. One believes that children are like robots that are programmed to fit a mold. The other believes that children are so variable that each child must be carefully assessed and placed in appropriate groupings based on past achievement and other data. Such an awareness of cognitive, affective, and psychomotor entry behaviors will allow teachers to vary planning according to the needs of the students. Teachers who are unable to decide on a correct diagnosis, or to alter their decisions when necessary, often find students frustrated, misbehaving, and achieving less than their

THE GOALS OF EDUCATION

1. Learn how to be a good citizen

2. Learn how to respect and get along with people who think, dress, and act differently

3. Learn about and try to understand the changes that take place in the world

4. Develop skills in reading, writing, speaking and listening

5. Understand skills and practice democratic ideas and ideals

6. Learn how to examine and use information

7. Understand and practice the skills of family living

8. Learn to respect and get along with people with whom we work and live

9. Develop skills to enter a specific field of work

10. Learn how to be a good manager of money, property, and resources

11. Develop a desire for learning now and in the future

12. Learn how to use leisure time

13. Practice and understand the ideas of health and safety

14. Appreciate culture and beauty in the world

15. Gain information needed to make job selections

16. Develop pride in work and a feeling of self-worth

17. Develop good character and self-respect

18. Gain a general education

Figure 1-8. Suggested goals for education (from Spears, 1973).

potential. It has been reported by Bloom (1976) and Harvey and Horton (1977) that when teachers plan for alterations in their teaching, student achievement can rise significantly. Mrs. Brown would be well advised to instigate more diversity in her planning endeavors.

4.2. Instructional Planning and Implementation Stage

It is during this stage of planning that actual lessons are structured for later implementation. If teachers are burdened with an unworkable planning format or one that is not flexible, the production of quality instructional plans will be greatly hampered. Many teachers across the country are required by boards of education and/or building principals to prepare lesson plans on a weekly basis. This is due to the extreme importance of quality planning. With these points in mind, we would like to suggest the instructional planning format outlined in Figure 1-9.

Teacher _____

Lesson Title _____

Unit _____

GOAL(S):

OBJECTIVE(S):

PROCEDURES AND MATERIALS:

EVALUATION:

Figure 1-9. A lesson planning format.

The lesson planning format outlined in Figure 1-9 contains five major components. We will examine each component separately.

Unit

Notice that at the top of the suggested planning format, you are asked to provide the name of the unit in addition to the title of the lesson and your name. A unit refers to a segment of work and may be defined in many different ways. For example, to some teachers it consists of one to two weeks of instruction; to others, it may constitute six weeks of instruction. Regardless of its length, however, a unit is essentially a series of experiences or body of information related to a general topic; to be complete, a unit must include required materials such as tests and audiovisual aids.

Typically, unit planning has been thought of as a method of structuring the curriculum in order to organize several kinds of activities, or even subject areas, so that they focus upon one general topic. This type of planning can be utilized to assure that the learning rates, abilities, and styles of the students, as well as their experiential backgrounds, are taken into consideration during ongoing daily lessons. For example:

Mr. Rose is a third grade teacher who utilizes unit planning. He is currently teaching a unit on fractions. He plans to have five groups working on a variety of projects which will culminate in five separate activities to be shared by the entire class. Mr. Rose began his planning by generating five major goals; in this particular case, there is one goal statement for each group. After the goals were generated, Mr. Rose created several specific instructional objectives based on each goal. In this unit, one goal deals with problem solving. A specific objective was written as follows: Given ten problems from *Riddles for the Superintelligent*, the student will explain in writing the steps needed to solve six problems. Each group was given five to ten such specific objectives. Mr. Rose then met with each group to suggest ways to accomplish the objectives. He is always ready to take student suggestions and often modifies certain objectives to coincide with learner interests. During their group meetings, Mr. Rose makes certain that all students understand exactly how committee and individual work is to be evaluated. In Mr. Rose's class, several activities go on at once. The students are involved in some talk because Mr. Rose understands the importance of sharing ideas in a socially stimulating environment. However, he never allows students to disturb the other learners. Mr. Rose has definite plans for the culmination of the unit after three weeks; such culminating activities will include role

playing, the exhibition of art work, the reading of individual poems and essays, and the exhibiting of projects.

You should think of most daily lesson plans as small parts of a larger, more encompassing plan called a *UNIT.* It is not suggested that all instruction must be planned within a unit format. Too many important and interesting lessons will be found to stand alone in any instructional program (Shepherd and Ragan, 1982). Nonetheless, several advantages of a unit planning system may be identified (See Fig. 1-10).

As noted in Figure 1-10, by developing units and associated goals one may also complete quality long range planning. The long range planning process must include, (1) identification of goals, (2) selection of unit topics for the goals, (3) specification of the approximate time requirement for each topic, and (4) determination of an appropriate sequence for the units. Once these four steps are completed, you have essentially outlined your long range plans. It now remains for you to prepare individual units as needed. Keep in mind that a unit should include at least (1) goals and objectives, (2) experiences and/or subject matter, (3) evaluation information, and (4) required materials.

Advantages of the Unit Format in Planning

---

1. It unifies several subject matter fields around a general topic.

2. The unit lends itself to students learning HOW to learn on their own.

3. The students' rates, abilities, and styles of learning can be taken into account.

4. The experiential background of the students and the resources of the community can easily shape planning.

5. Unit planning helps the teacher to get away from an over-reliance upon a single textbook.

6. A format is provided to allow the teacher to be flexible and creative.

7. Unit utilization aids in the development of quality long-range plans.

Figure 1-10. Advantages of unit planning.

Goals and Objectives

The goals referred to here are those from the unit which are appropriate for the particular lesson you are planning. They should appear on the lesson plan to aid you in keeping in mind the expected broad outcomes. As with all planning, they serve to remind you where you are going. Objectives should also be clearly specified as outlined in Section 3. Each objective must be stated in performance terms with the appropriate conditions and criteria specified.

Procedures and Materials

The materials specified under this heading refer to those instructional materials which would be required to complete the lesson. In some lessons, this may simply be the chalk and chalkboard; in others, more extensive materials may be required. For example, you may wish to show films, complete a laboratory exercise, or work with instructional aids such as globes, cuisenaire rods, or attribute blocks. Such activities require considerably more materials. It is convenient to first plan the procedures portion, then go back over what you have written and underline the necessary materials. This will serve to remind you to collect necessary materials prior to beginning the lesson.

In order to develop the procedures portion of the typical lesson plan, the ROPES format—a process for planning lesson procedures which addresses previously stated objectives—may be helpful. The ROPES process (Berenson, Berenson, and Carkhuff, 1978) has been found to be extremely beneficial to use and applicable to a variety of teaching situations. As ROPES is a process for planning procedures only, you will find it necessary to have already determined your goals and objectives for the lesson. The ROPES components are: R (review), O (overview), P (presentation), E (exercise), and S (summary).

As a systematic planning format, the ROPES approach has been extensively field tested with extremely positive evaluations. The advantage of this system is the flexibility with which it can be used. The sequence of procedures recommended can be adapted to most lessons whether they emphasize skills, principles, concepts, or associations. Further credibility is given the system due to its relevance to all grade levels and for all subject matter. We will consider each of the ROPES components separately in the following discussion.

R-Review: There are many ways in which teachers can begin their class presentations. Depending upon the purpose of the instruction that is to follow, Gage and Berliner (1975) mention that the teacher might begin the lesson by focusing on (1) a motivational attention-getting beginning, (2) a simple interaction that establishes rapport between teacher and students, or (3) a way of relating past experiences to the class presentation. The function of the review is to build upon the readiness level determined by the cognitive, affective, and psychomotor entry behaviors of students. For example, if the topic to be studied were reducing fractions, a necessary step before teaching fractions may be to review the skills of division. By specifying and summarizing the attributes and processes of division, the teacher is more assured that the student has the major prerequisite knowledge that is necessary to learn the new objective of the lesson. The review should be a short part of the overall lesson, lasting from perhaps one to five minutes.

O-Overview: The overview, given to students near the beginning of the lesson, should introduce the content to be taught. An outline of the topics to be discussed and information as to how they are related to real world applications is also appropriate. Simply giving directions regarding how to do an activity is an insufficient orientation. Elaboration, description, and insight are the focal points in developing the successful overview. The overview portion of the lesson is very brief, being typically less than five minutes in duration. At the beginning of a lesson on physical geography, for example, the teacher could write on the board: *LANDFORMS ARE LAND SURFACES THAT HAVE CHARACTERISTIC SHAPES AND COMPOSITIONS;* drawings of plateaus, hills, and mountains may be included with this beginning. This preparatory structure would facilitate learning about landforms in the lesson to follow. Ausubel (1968) has found that students are more able to associate past learnings with present learnings when given some preparatory understanding of what they are about to study. In fact, Mayer (1979) states that when given such an overview, student learning of future material is also enhanced.

P-Presentation: The major portion of each lesson will be some type of presentation structured by the teacher. Where the review and overview are typically composed of only one activity, the presentation should be composed of several activities. These will primarily be a combination of showing, telling or doing activities. In reference to the previous example with landforms, the teacher could include a variety of these activities that influence students to (1) observe the drawing on the chalkboard, (2) listen to the teacher explain the different kinds of landforms, (3) compare their map with the standard on the board, (4) get feedback from the teacher about their answers, (5) see additional examples of landforms in pictures and/or slides, and (6) respond to questions about landforms and participate in other showing, telling, and doing activities. An important key in using such showing, telling, and doing methods is to vary their implementation for the purpose of maintaining the students' interests and in improving retention (Cooper, 1977; Gage and Berliner, 1975). The change of pace from one perceptual sense to another, from one task to another, and from previously learned material to novel material enhances learning. Teachers who vary their activities have faster paced lessons that are usually characterized as motivating and interesting. The presentation is generally the major portion of a lesson, typically taking as much as three quarters of the class time and usually no less than one quarter.

E-Exercise: When a basketball player practices the correct form in shooting free throws, when a fourth grade student practices the multiplication tables, when a student in English practices sentence combining, all are getting exercise. They are, in effect, applying what they have learned by shooting, reciting, and writing. This is exercise in the sense of practicing, but it also has the added benefit of providing feedback for the teacher and the student. Without watching the ball go into the hoop, without checking the multiplication tables, without examining the different sentences formed, the student or teacher would have no real knowledge, no feedback, of how well the material is being mastered. Knowledge of feedback is effective because it enhances the students' likelihood of being more responsive and productive. Therefore, if the exercise that the teacher requires the students to do is to be optimally beneficial, the teacher must be sure to provide ample amounts of feedback. The practice or exercise that students are asked to complete is often written but can include oral drill, recitation or physical manipulation, and demonstration. It should be a type of performance that has been taught in the presentation but could also include some material from content previously mastered. The purpose of the exercise component is to allow students the opportunity to actively apply what they have learned. The length of this component in ROPES is variable. In a second grade spelling lesson or a high school history lesson, the exercise portion of instruction could be as short as five minutes. However, when conducting a values clarification or a science laboratory activity, this process could include one-half of the lesson and perhaps even more.

S-Summary: The conclusion of a lesson is often neglected because teachers tend to concentrate their attention on the body of the presentation, not because the ending of a lesson is considered unimportant. Since the presentation component may be lengthy, usually between one-quarter and three-quarters of a class session, the use of a summary at the end of a lesson helps insure that the main points of the lesson are reinforced. Summaries can be structured by the teacher in many ways. Some teachers prefer to have students answer questions as a summary activity at the end of the lesson. These answers can be accepted orally, in writing by individuals, or by the whole class. Such variation will improve the classroom climate by keeping the lesson routine novel, not monotonous. Other variations are also possible; for example, many teachers choose to present a summary either orally or on the chalkboard. Also, the use of test-like questions is an excellent way to conclude the class; these have been shown by McKenzie (1979, 1980) to be important behavioral tools in raising achievement. In addition, elaborate summaries may involve the use of prepared posters or transparencies to save time in the presentation. Such an approach provides students with materials to examine or copy after the lesson. It is important to note that summaries may also have diagnostic benefits that help teachers in the planning of future lessons. Following ROPES will allow the teacher to develop activities that are consistent with the psychology of learning.

Evaluation

The final portion of any good lesson plan deals with evaluation. Evaluation is an integral, ongoing part of the teacher's responsibility. It is a tool in providing the teacher with feedback information for meeting future student needs. Consequently, teachers must prepare evaluation instruments to comprehensively assess student learning efforts and achievement. Evaluation usually occurs daily but can occur weekly, monthly, or, in the case of standardized tests, yearly. Generally speaking, the more frequently students are evaluated and receive feedback, the better their achievement.

Daily evaluation, as a desired goal, can be achieved in many ways. Evaluation might simply consist of the teacher asking questions orally during the lesson with subsequent feedback to students about the accuracy of their answers; also, a written response should often be required. In fact, short quizzes could be given daily. Recitation, drill, and question-answering serve to provide students with feedback about their degree of proficiency. Such approaches as these communicate to students and teachers whether the correct material is being learned and whether they result in increased achievement (Bloom, 1980).

In planning lessons, it is advisable to not only (1) have one or more definite objectives identified, (2) plan appropriate, stimulating instruction, (3) prepare a culminating evaluation exercise but, also, (4) develop test-like situations that function as learning aides during instruction which can later be used in preparing for student evaluation. These four steps in planning for instruction are beneficial teacher routines and are sound preparation for effective instruction.

Because of frequent and multiple forms of evaluation, and variation in student ability, experience, and achievement, teachers are faced with many difficulties in planning and evaluating; for example, students complete assignments at different speeds and with different levels of understanding. Properly grouping or working with learners on an individual basis will help meet many student needs. But, without an orderly management of assignments, any teacher can become burdened with a mass of paperwork or even confused as to which assignments are due at a particular time and what those students who have completed assignments early should do next. We will address these concerns in Chapter Six.

Figure 1-11 is an example of a completed lesson plan for a fourth grade language arts class. You should study the plan and compare it to the criteria identified in the lesson plan checklist (See Fig. 1-12). We believe that all checklist items for this lesson plan could be checked "yes." For example, differences in rates of learning and ability levels were accommodated by providing practice worksheets on differing levels and an enrichment learning center for those who finish early. Differences in learning style were also accommodated primarily by the variation in showing, telling, and doing activities. Study Figures 1-11 and 1-12 and see if you agree.

4.3. Post-Instructional Stage

Successful teaching, like any other complex activity, is impossible without a recognition of the importance of changes and improvements. The final stage of the instructional process, the post-instructional stage, is a quality check; it is a means to insure that when improvements are necessary, there is a process through which they may be accomplished. This stage can also be seen as a

Teacher *Joan Smith*

Lesson Title *Compound Subjects*

Unit *Sentence Structure*

GOAL(S): *To develop competent language skills*

OBJECTIVE(S): *Given five sets of two simple subject sentences, combine each set into a single sentence.*

PROCEDURES AND MATERIALS:

Review simple subjects and provide a short overview
Show set of three cartoons. Ask students to make-up simple subject sentences appropriate for first two cartoons. Write sentences on the chalkboard. Have students state how these sentences can be combined to make one sentence for the third cartoon.
Introduce and define compound subjects.
Discuss in a question and answer session the process of combining subjects
Discuss attributes:
The subjects are always joined by the conjunction "and"
The sentences must have the same predicate
Provide two non-examples
Show the class four sentences on a poster. Ask which sets of two sentences can be combined and why.
Recap what has been studied so far and repeat definition
Orally provide pairs of simple subject sentences and ask individual students to make a compound subject sentence.
Discuss nonattributes of compound subject sentences
It does not matter what type of noun or pronoun is used.
It does not matter what verb is used.
Summarize and repeat definition
Provide each sub-group with practice sentences on worksheets (two different levels of difficulty). Those who finish early are to work at the enrichment learning center

EVALUATION: *Distribute the five sets of simple subject sentences and ask the students to write one sentence combining each set.*

Check and return papers tommorrow

Figure 1-11. A sample lesson for fourth grade language arts.

LESSON PLAN CHECKLIST

	YES	NO
GOAL(S)		
Is each goal statement a long-range aim or purpose in my area of study?	___	___
OBJECTIVE(S):		
Does the objective include conditions, performance and criteria for evaluation?	___	___
Is it consistent with the stated goal?	___	___
PROCEDURES AND MATERIALS:		
Did I address the ROPES components? Review (optional)	___	___
Overview	___	___
Presentation	___	___
Exercise	___	___
Summary	___	___
Did I identify (underline) the necessary materials?	___	___
Have I provided motivation for learning?	___	___
Did I provide for differences in: rate of learning	___	___
learning styles	___	___
ability levels	___	___
EVALUATION:		
Have I provided for student demonstration of learning that is consistent with the stated objective?	___	___
Have I provided for the communication of feedback information to the student?	___	___

Figure 1-12. Lesson plan checklist.

means to develop certain instructional or management routines that result in increased stability of classroom activities and reduction in time lost to interruptions. Such routines, when established, provide the teacher with fewer decisions to make on a daily basis and streamline both planning and instruction (Yinger, 1979). The post-instructional stage is designed to determine if teaching encounters have been successful and, if not, to provide information to make alterations so that the results of future activities will be effective teaching and learning.

Analyzing the Pre-Instructional Development Stage

When students are not making satisfactory progress, the teacher must determine the cause for the learning difficulties. The first place to look for these causes is the pre-instructional development stage (see Fig. 1-13).

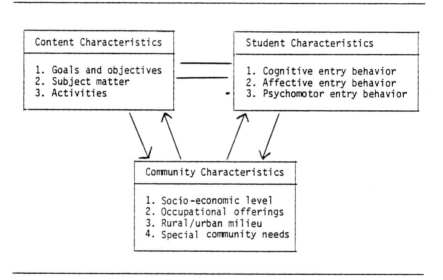

Figure 1-13. The pre-instructional development stage.

One of the important components of the pre-instructional development stage involves the content characteristics of planning. When analyzing content, there are three questions that teachers should ask. The first question is, "Do I really know what my students are expected to do?" When unsure of how to answer this question, the teacher should develop or select more appropriate goals and objectives. The problem might be that the objectives of the teacher and the school district are not congruent. This is often a frequent occurrence and can be corrected easily if the teacher has mistakenly addressed the wrong or inappropriate objectives; the teacher might simply use the district's goals during the next school year. Secondly, the teacher should ask, "Is the poor achievement due to my lack of subject matter knowledge?" In a situation such as this, the teacher may need to give further study in the particular area under consideration. There are professional associations in all areas that provide excellent conferences, books, ancillary materials, and professional interaction that aid in the development of subject matter competence. Participation in these will furnish numerous experiences for improving subject area knowledge. Another difficulty within content characteristics is the actual methods utilized during instruction. Ineffective methods cause less-than-anticipated achievement. Because of this, a final question to analyze content characteristics is, "Are my instructional methods producing desired results?" Difficulties with inappropriate methods can, at times, be corrected through discussion with peers and supervisors. Many times, however, inappropriate activities will be resolved best by proposing alternative methods and attempting to match these to student characteristics. This has been identified as the second set of variables in the pre-instructional stage: student characteristics.

Student characteristic variables, according to Bloom (1976, 1980), are among the most crucial in determining student achievement. Entry behaviors, which are the cognitive, psychomotor, and affective learnings that students possess when they begin a learning task, are possibly the most important characteristics to examine when analyzing student success. Accordingly, if students possess the necessary entry behaviors (i.e. readiness for learning), almost all students can attain mastery of the given material. Students whose achievement is below expectancy could be given a diagnostic test, either commercial or teacher-prepared, to determine if they have the prerequisites needed to master the new material. If students do not have the needed competencies, they should be developed through careful planning and implementation of remedial instruction. While perhaps difficult for the teacher to respond to quickly and easily, entry behaviors obviously have a great impact on school achievement. Finally, affective entry behaviors, by their very nature, must be approached longitudinally since affect is developed globally, over time. The teacher, in this situation, is advised to examine the whole classroom climate, i.e. (1) the leadership style of the teacher, (2) the application of learning styles to actual classroom practice, (3) the communication between teacher and student (see Chap. 2), and (4) the management techniques that develop rapport between teacher and student (see Chap. 5).

Components in the pre-instructional development stage also include a collection of community-related matters that may significantly alter the teacher's curriculum. Today, due to society's mobility, teachers may grow up in one state, be educated in another, and finally teach in yet a third. Indeed, it is likely that many teachers will have students of different races, cultures, and perhaps even language backgrounds. Such diversity means that a teacher could receive an excellent education, be prepared to teach a complete curriculum, but could still have students miss the goal of high achievement because their instruction lacked relevance. Awareness of community characteristics will help address this problem of relevance. Many teachers have taught in classrooms where extreme social, cultural, and economic differences exist among the students. Teachers who often lack an awareness of such differences find it difficult to relate to such conditions. In fact, teacher-student communication is frequently hampered by the overt differences existing in their common background of experiences. In a like manner, the occupational orientation and the size (rural vs. urban) of the community should have an impact on the instructional strategies of the teacher. For example, a teacher living in Detroit, Michigan might often use, as explanations during instruction, the *AUTOMOBILE INDUSTRY* when introducing the topic of multiplication (10 cars produced per hour, how many produced in 8 hours?), the *DETROIT LIONS FOOTBALL TEAM* when showing proper capitalization (Detroit Lions; lions at the zoo), the *MASS TRANSIT SYSTEM* when discussing community helpers (the bus driver), and other such terms characteristic of Detroit and of the northern, urban area around Detroit. A teacher in rural South Carolina, conversely, should often use examples such as *TOBACCO FARMING* when discussing percentage (Mr. Bagwell buys his tobacco on speculation for $1.70 per pound and sells it for $1.80 to a tobacco company. What was his percentage of profit?), the *AGRICULTURE INDUSTRY* when assigning paragraph writing (Topic: "The importance of the agricultural industry to the state's economy"), the *SMALL TOWN* when discussing population patterns in social studies (What is the difference between a town and a city?), and other terms associated with the South and rural areas. Teachers could incorporate numerous examples in their instructional plans in areas where there are unique community needs. For example, in the Mount Saint Helens area of Washington, teachers might want to use examples of volcanoes during instruction. Indeed, this topic is so unique and significant to the region that the study of volcanoes should receive not just special instructional treatment but should receive a greater curricular focus. It is noted that community characteristics are often overlooked in teaching, but they should very clearly influence the daily instructional endeavors of teachers and possibly the ongoing curriculum.

Analyzing the Instructional Planning and Implementation Stage

Even though much of the teacher's evaluation of success must rightly be focused on what happens before instructional encounters are implemented, a great deal of evaluation energy should be focused on the planning and implementation stage. Once the teacher has given sufficient time to reflect on goals, objectives, student entry behaviors, and community characteristics, lesson plans developed can then be judged on their own merits. In particular, the adequacy of the instructional procedures should be analyzed. For example, proper review and overview could have been omitted as is frequently the case. The teacher must make sure that these procedures are inserted in future plans so that improved performance will result. It must be noted that the materials and resources used in the classroom should also be evaluated for effectiveness in instruction. This can be done by analyzing use, content (of items such as filmstrips), and presentation as they correlate with stated goals and objectives. Finally, the evaluation of student assessment procedures should not be overlooked. It is, unfortunately, all too often assumed that standardized tests, because they are produced by a textbook or test company, are valid for all situations. This is patently not the case. Each test, or other evaluation instrument, whether commercially or self-prepared, must be carefully matched to the instructional objectives that the teacher is attempting to reach. When the assessment is not coordinated with the instruction that precedes it, all parties involved become frustrated—the students because they were not adequately prepared and the teacher because the results were less than anticipated. In addition to the lack of coordination between objectives and student assessment, another reason that evaluation may produce poor results is that the students may have not had ample opportunities during instruction to become familiar with procedures which approximate the teacher's final evaluation. Teachers help insure success on tests when they:

1. Clearly inform the students of the instructional objectives
2. Teach toward these objectives
3. Give students opportunities to demonstrate mastery of these same objectives
4. Guide students to apply what has been learned to new situations

The planning concerns analyzed in the post-instructional stage can have a great impact on the quality of instruction that a student receives. Teachers following this suggested planning approach will insure a well-planned, professionally conceived instructional program.

Formative Evaluation: Section 4*

1. Name and briefly describe three major stages in the planning process.
2. Assume you are responsible for an early childhood, elementary, or secondary class made up of predominately high ability students who read, on the average, one grade above grade level. Select two goals from the list in Figure

---

*See the Appendix for suggested answers to these questions.

1-8 and identify a series of three unit titles in a subject matter area of your own choosing for each.

3. Choose one of the units identified in question two and briefly outline the necessary components you would have in it.

4. Using the format described in this section, choose a lesson topic for one of your hypothetical units and write a lesson plan using the guidelines presented in this section. Remember, all lessons do not involve just the cognitive domain.

5. Describe the purpose of and the procedures involved in the Post-instructional Stage.

REFERENCES

Anderson, G., and Walberg, H. Learning Environments. In H. J. Walberg (Ed.): *Evaluating educational performance: A sourcebook of methods instruments, and examples.* Berkeley, CA: McCuthan, 1974.

Ausubel, D. *Educational psychology: A cognitive view.* New York: Holt, Rinehart and Winston, 1968.

Barbe, W. B., and Milone, M. What we know about modality strengths. *Educational Leadership,* 1981, 38(5), 378–380.

Bayles, E. *Democratic educational theory.* New York: Harper and Row, 1960.

Berenson, D., Berenson, S., and Carkhuff, R. *The skills of teaching: Lesson planning skills.* New York: Human Resources Press, 1978.

Bloom, B., Englehart, M., Furst, E., Hill, W., and Krathwohl, D. *Taxonomy of educational objectives. Handbook I: Cognitive domain.* New York: David McKay, 1956.

Bloom, B. *Human characteristics and school learning.* New York: McGraw-Hill, 1976.

Bloom, B. The new direction in educational research: Alterable variables. *Phi Delta Kappan,* 1980, 61(5), 382–385.

Cooper, J. (Ed.). *Classroom teaching skills: A handbook.* Lexington, MA: D.C. Heath, 1977.

Dunn, R., and Dunn, K. Learning styles/teaching styles: Should they . . . can they . . . be matched? *Educational Leadership,* 1979, 36(5), 238–244.

Dunn, R., Dunn, K., and Price, G. Learning style: Research vs. opinion. *Phi Delta Kappan,* 1981, 62(9), 645–646.

Fischer, B., and Fischer, L. Styles in teaching and learning. *Educational Leadership,* 1979, 36(5), 245–254.

Gage, N., and Berliner, D. *Educational Psychology.* Chicago: Rand McNally, 1975.

Good, T., Biddle, B., and Brophy, J. *Teachers make a difference.* New York: Holt, Rinehart, and Winston, 1975.

Good, T., and Brophy, J. *Educational psychology* (2nd ed.). New York: Holt, Rinehart, and Winston, 1980.

Gronlund, N. *Stating behavioral objectives for classroom instruction.* New York: Macmillan, 1970.

Harrow, A. *A taxonomy of the psychomotor domain: A guide for developing behavioral objectives.* New York: David McKay, 1972.

Harvey, K., and Horton, L. Bloom's human characteristics and school learning. *Phi Delta Kappan,* 1977, 59(3), 189–193.

Krathwohl, D., Bloom, B., and Masia, B. *Taxonomy of educational objectives. The classification of educational goals. Handbook II: Affective domain.* New York: David McKay, 1964.

McKenzie, G. Effects of questions and test-like events on achievement and on-task behaviors in a classroom concept learning presentation. *Journal of Educational Research,* 1979, 72(6), 348–351.

McKenzie, G. Improving instruction through instructional design. *Educational Leadership,* 1980, 37(9), 664–667.

Mager, R. *Preparing instructional objectives.* Palo Alto, CA: Fearson Publishers, 1962.

Mager, R. *Developing attitude toward learning.* Palo Alto, CA: Fearson Publishers, 1968.

Mahoney, M. *Cognition and behavior modification.* Cambridge: Ballinger Publishers, 1974.

Mayer, R. Can advance organizers influence meaningful learning? *Review of Educational Research.* 1979, 49(2), 371–383.

Orlich, D. *Teaching strategies: A guide to better instruction.* Lexington, MA: D. C. Heath, 1980.

Purkey, W. *Self-concept and school achievement.* Englewood Cliffs, NJ: Prentice-Hall, 1976.

Rosenshine, B. Teaching behaviors and student achievement. London: International Association for the Evaluation of Educational Achievement, 1971, 99–100.

Rosenshine, B., and Furst, N. Research in teacher performance criteria. In B. O. Smith (Ed.), *Research in teacher education: A symposium.* Englewood Cliffs, NJ: Prentice-Hall, 1971.

Shephard, G., and Ragan, W. *Modern elementary curriculum.* New York: Holt, Rinehart, and Winston, 1982.

Spears, H. Kappans ponder the goals of education. *Phi Delta Kappan,* 1973, 55(1), 29–32.

Tjosvold, D. Alternative organizations for schools and classrooms. In D. Bartel and D. Saxe (Eds.), *Social psychology of education: Research and theory.* New York: Hemisphere Press, 1977.

Tjosvold, D., and Santamaria, P. The effects of cooperation and teacher support on student attitudes toward classroom decision-making. Paper presented at American Educational Research Annual Meeting. New York, 1977.

Van Houten, R. *Learning through feedback: A systematic approach for improving academic performances.* New York: Human Sciences Press, 1980.

White, R., and Lippitt, R. *Autocracy and democracy: An experimental inquiry.* New York: Harper and Row, 1960.

Wittwer, K. Quoted in *Today's Education,* 1971, 60(9), 55–56.

Yinger, R. Routines in teacher planning. *Theory Into Practice.* 1979, 18(3), 163–169.

CHAPTER TWO

THE TEACHER AS A COMMUNICATOR OF INFORMATION

Communication takes place throughout the educational environment even before the teacher enters the classroom. Consider the following examples of some of the teacher communications which take place just within the classroom, and you will see that teaching is communication and communication is, in many ways, teaching. The classroom teacher:

- Listens to students respond
- Talks about assignments
- Explains a new concept
- Listens to announcements from the principal
- Writes information on the chalkboard
- Reads instructions for an activity
- Corrects students' homework
- Talks with teacher aides
- Reviews student papers
- Asks questions about student understanding
- Presents overviews of main ideas
- Announces forthcoming activities

Of course, the above list is certainly not exhaustive of all of the teacher communications in any given classroom. For example, you may have noted that it only deals with examples of what has been termed *verbal communication*. The classroom teacher indeed communicates in these and in many other ways. For example, the verbal and nonverbal communication skills of individual teachers can also do a great deal to help school/community relations. Teachers who are quite proficient in communication skills are better able to present the school's goals and objectives to parents and community groups. Individual teachers may wish to further school and community relations by instituting a short weekly column in the local newspaper dealing with school news and views or by speaking to local citizens groups. Such teacher activities can have a tremendous payoff for the schools as well as the teachers themselves.

Because teachers are expected to communicate often and well, we have provided information in this chapter on several aspects of the communication role of teaching. Following the section concerning types of communication, the various types of knowledge to be communicated are elaborated. The chapter concludes with a special example of communicating information. Since concepts comprise such a significant part of the curriculum, this type of information is given special attention. In this final section, you will learn specific characteristics of planning concept lessons and be able to further apply the planning skills derived from your study of Chapter One. Specifically, in this chapter, you will learn to complete the following performances:

1. Define the communication process in terms of three basic parts.
2. Distinguish between verbal and nonverbal language.
3. Describe suggestions for improving verbal language communication in the classroom.
4. Describe effects of six types of nonverbal language symbols.
5. Differentiate among facts, generalizations, values, and concepts.
6. Explain what is meant by the term *concept.*
7. Describe the relationship between concept attainment and skills instruction.
8. Describe the process that occurs when a concept is learned.
9. Plan a concept lesson utilizing a three-step systematic approach.

SECTION 1. TEACHING AS COMMUNICATION

Since the classroom teacher must become somewhat expert in the area of communication in order to be effective, it is very important to be aware of the many facets of communication likely to be utilized in the classroom. With this in mind, we present here a basic definition of communication and provide examples of its many aspects.

1.1. A Definition of Communication

Communication is a process, not a set of isolated events. Since it is a process, it involves the existence of key elements necessary to make it effective. In the classical model of the communication process (See Fig. 2-1), three key elements are identified: source, message, and destination. As you may note from Figure 2-1, communication must have a beginning point, a message to be sent, and an ending or receiving point. The message, or idea, is sent to its destination by the source. The signal by which the message is sent is referred to as language.

In essence, an idea or message exists with the source or message-sender who develops symbols or language so that a receiver or message-recipient may understand the communication. In teaching, the teacher, possibly with input from students, identifies what is to be communicated and develops procedures so that students will understand what is being transmitted. Communication, then, may be thought of as a transaction in which changes or exchanges occur (Sereno and Bodaken, 1975). Once the transaction has successfully taken place, a meaning has been communicated from the teacher to the student. The learner has changed because something is now known that was not known earlier. The teacher has also changed, as this individual now looks upon the student with new information, therefore, in a new light. It is clear that the meaning attached to each message is one of the most central features of communication; it is this meaning which must be communicated.

In its most basic form, then, communication involves a sender, a receiver, a meaningful message, and a language with which to send the message. The language possibilities which exist in this process are included in two broad categories: verbal and nonverbal (See Fig. 2-2). Whether the teacher uses primarily verbal or nonverbal language messages, the language which is chosen involves the use of some type of language symbols to make up the

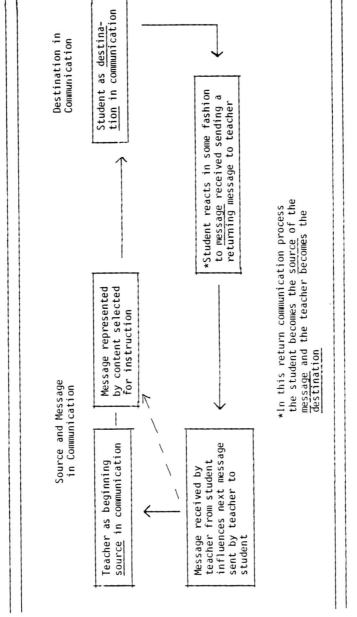

Figure 2-1. Source, message, destination model of communication as applied to a teaching situation (influenced by Shramm, 1945).

basis of the actual transmission. In communication, that which someone attaches meaning to is referred to as a symbol.

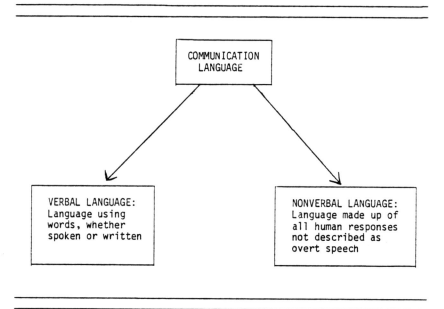

Figure 2-2. Communication as verbal and nonverbal language.

1.2. Verbal Communication

Words, whether they are spoken or written, are verbal symbols. These symbols relate to ideas about things. Linguists have identified four basic verbal language vocabularies: reading, listening, writing, and speaking. Communication problems, which may arise using any of the four vocabularies, develop primarily because senders and receivers do not share the same meaning for the words used or because they put the words together in different patterns when speaking. Such communication breakdowns can occur quickly when word symbols are abstract as opposed to concrete. For example, words such as *FAIR, JUST, HELPFUL,* and *LOVE* are generally more easily misinterpreted because of their abstractness than such words as *CHAIR, HOUSE, CAR,* and *COW* which are less abstract. Abstract concepts are also much more difficult to understand when common background experiences are absent (Berger, 1970). Because of this, it is imperative that teachers (especially those in multicultural settings) further their understanding of the students in their class through the use of such techniques as the inventories described in Chapter One.

Various thoughts occur at different levels of sophistication and abstraction. The clearest communication occurs when language, thus thoughts, is made as concrete as possible. It is a major part of the teacher's responsibility to make sure students still understand messages that are communicated in abstract language. This can only be accomplished if the teacher provides experiences for the student with the language being used in order to develop familiarity and, ultimately, some level of concreteness as the abstract symbols become more clearly understood. Although the communication of abstract messages is sometimes difficult for the student to receive, they are a necessary part of that which must be learned in school. It is often the understanding of these abstractions that provides the greatest utility for the student.

More than any other aspect of communication, the skill of listening is the least studied and the most taken for granted. No matter how much teachers would like for listening skills to develop spontaneously, skills in listening may not develop naturally even though the spoken language surrounds the learner daily. Competency in the listening process requires awareness, concentration, and practice. You should realize, with regard to listening skill development, that the ability to be an effective listener is not necessarily dependent on one's intelligence or reading skill. In fact, many linguists have suggested that one's ability to read as well as one's measured intelligence are dependent, at least in part, on an individual's ability to listen.

Various techniques may be utilized to enhance listening and other forms of verbal communication in your classroom. Carefully consider the following guidelines.

1. Reading communication should be integrated into all subject matter areas in an interdisciplinary approach on a

school-wide basis. To relegate such communication development to the reading or language arts specialist at the elementary level, or the remedial or English teacher at the secondary level, is to attack only a small part of the problem. Whether the question is textbook reading communication, chalkboard reading communication, or merely teacher notes as a form of reading communication, the point remains the same. There exists a sender, a message, and an intended receiver. Unless the learner has mastered the reading process, the appropriate message may not be received.

2. Students should be encouraged to feel that they have something important to say. They, like teachers themselves, need encouragement, praise, and a forum to express their ideas. Written messages such as "interesting ideas" serve as positive reinforcers. Such reinforcers are important even if the student's work is not of the highest calibre. To assist the student in maintaining a positive approach to the task, the teacher ought to develop a constructive blend of reinforcement with necessary criticism.

3. For students to understand what you say, they must obviously have a solid understanding of the verbal symbols you use. There is, naturally, a direct relationship between words and thoughts. When the teacher uses certain words, the student has certain thoughts. In successful communication, the intent is to develop better control over what thoughts the student has when certain words are uttered. Be alert for word misunderstandings. Ask frequent questions designed to determine student comprehension of your verbal presentation.

4. Be a good listener yourself. Pay close attention to student responses in all language vocabularies: reading, listening, speaking, and writing. The role of the teacher as a model of effective communication can have a significant impact on students in learning to communicate.

5. Provide opportunities for students to practice their verbal communication skills in all four language vocabularies. For example: Read aloud occasionally to help them de-

velop listening skills and provide extensive opportunities for them to write in order to improve their writing skills.

6. Design your classroom physical environment to encourage and enhance the enjoyment of communication. For example, take care in making seating and grouping arrangements to insure that everyone can see, hear, and participate.

1.3. Nonverbal Communication

Imagine the teacher as a picture sending out messages or symbols, without actually using verbal communication. Even though this may sound odd, as you have often heard, a picture is worth a thousand words. Nonverbal language communication involves transactions through nonverbal symbols rather than verbalizations (Crable, 1979). Given the rather recent popularity of this medium of communication as an area for empirical investigation in classroom communication, there is still a great deal yet to be understood. A helpful working definition for nonverbal communication from a teaching standpoint has been provided by Knapp (1972). Nonverbal communication may be considered as all of those human responses which are not identified as overtly spoken or written words.

It is unusual for verbal or nonverbal symbols to occur in isolation from one another; they generally occur together. Knapp has estimated that in simultaneous verbal and nonverbal communication, approximately 65 percent of the meaning of the communication is created by nonverbal messages. Research also seems to indicate that when verbal and nonverbal messages conflict, the nonverbal symbols are the ones to be believed (Galloway, 1982). In studying this area, it is important to remember that nonverbal symbols do not really mean anything by themselves; their meanings are given by the receiver. For example, a yawn may mean boredom to one or fatigue to another. A teacher's wink may be a positive reinforcement or simply an indication that something has irritated the eye. Someone's hand waving could mean goodbye or help. Interpretation depends, to a great extent, on the context of the message and the background of the receiver.

Of particular interest to the classroom teacher are the following types of nonverbal symbols (See Fig. 2-3): (1) kinesics, (2) proxemics, (3) haptics, (4) oculesics, (5) vocalics, and (6) environmental factors (McCroskey, 1972).

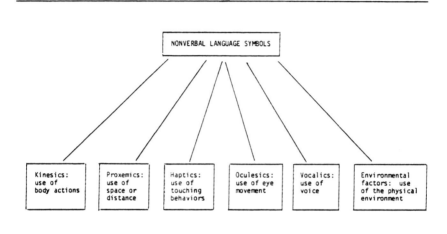

Figure 2-3. Nonverbal language symbols relevant to classroom communication.

KINESICS refers to communication through body actions. Included in this area are head movements, postures, body movements, and facial expressions. In reference to teaching behaviors, posture which includes leaning toward someone is generally seen as expressing warmth or positive feelings; leaning away expresses more negative or cold feelings (Mehrabian, 1969). Similar conclusions are drawn concerning head movements. Head nodding is seen as acceptance, while shaking the head suggests less acceptance. Ekman (1965) notes that such interpretations are far from absolute and only point to general impressions or feelings. Thus, kinesic messages are presently only open to some general conclusive interpretations, many quite well-known: the "V" to communicate victory, the hand motion across the throat to communicate death, fingernail biting to cue emotions, the smile to communicate warmth, and the frown to communicate dissatisfaction. It is again, however, the context of the kinesic message that often provides for the most accurate interpretation.

The use of space or distance for communication is referred to as *PROXEMICS*. People tend to define their own territory, and then protect it. Some teachers are notorious for defining their territory as that space around their desk or in front of the room. These kinds of proxemic messages notify the students that there is an area best suited for them and one best suited for the teacher. In this context, students should not go into the teacher's space unless invited. Such a territorial arrangement for a classroom learning environment generally proves to be quite counterproductive. Individuals become protective and defensive. This type of proxemic setting often results in a breakdown of positive communication. Too, when seatwork is assigned, a greater percentage of students complete their work when the teacher circulates about the room during the work time. This type of nonverbal communication lets the students know that the teacher is interested in their performance. Although somewhat of a simple criterion for success, the academic payoff is clear. When students attend to the task at hand, their achievement improves.

Nonverbal language communication through touching behaviors is known as *HAPTICS*. Touching is a common method of communicating among early childhood and elementary school teachers and their students. Unfortunately, when interacting with adolescents, touching is often reserved for the display of extreme emotions. Many educators point to the warmth shown by a hand on the shoulder but, in the same instant, point out how this may be misinterpreted by secondary students. While touching is a basic means of nonverbal communication, difficult interpretation makes its use awkward in some teaching situations. Teachers are advised not to be "afraid" to touch but to be alert to the various interpretations that touching may invoke. Indeed, there are people who are touchers and those who are non-touchers. A non-touching adolescent may label a touching teacher as overly forward or aggressive. Younger students, however, may perceive the non-touching teacher as unfriendly or cold-natured.

The study of how the eyes and eye movements can communicate is termed *OCULESICS.* The eyes most assuredly do influence communication. Argyle and Dean (1965) have identified four major factors that determine how much eye contact will exist in a communication transaction. First is the role of the communicator. In a communication transaction, the person receiving the message usually demonstrates more eye contact than the person who is initiating the message to be sent. Second is the nature of the topic to be communicated; eye contact is easier with impersonal topics. If the topic is personal, eye contact generally decreases. Gender is the third factor; women tend to engage more in eye contact than men. It is not known if this finding transfers to female as opposed to male students. The fourth factor is relationship. If the persons communicating are friends, greater eye contact will be established. In the role of classroom leader, the teacher can improve communication channels by establishing good eye contact with the students. When the students are speaking, eye contact from the teacher should be evident. This tells the students that the teacher is interested. No eye contact communicates disinterest. Eye messages can serve the teacher in many ways. Perhaps the two most significant ways are to promote positive relationships in the classroom and to communicate some form of teacher dissatisfaction to the students in order to then influence behavior change.

The study of how the voice can communicate various types of messages is termed *VOCALICS.* While judgments about people are continually made based on vocal quality, research shows that these judgments are accurate only about 50 percent of the time (Knapp, 1972). Nevertheless, as decisions about individuals are made, whether right or wrong, they are all too often assumed accurate and acted on accordingly. Thus, it is crucial that the teacher have a good working knowledge of just what can be done and communicated with the voice. Students prefer listening to voices that change in inflection; they do not prefer a voice with a lack of pitch variety as seen in a monotonic presentation. On the other hand, voices which have patterns of a singsong nature are as annoying as a monotone. Changes in pitch, volume, and the rate of speech create interesting communication transactions with more favorable student reactions (Crable, 1979). Many teachers, the novice as well as the experienced, include in their verbal repertoire the distracting overuse of repeated words or phrases. Vocalizations such as *UM, ER, OK,* and *AH* are often used to fill a pause in the speech pattern, however, they generally communicate the feeling that the teacher is nervous or excited (Goldman-Eisler, 1961). The pattern of "filling" speech pauses in this manner also sometimes communicates that the individual is attempting to keep control of the conversation or situation (Maclay and Osgood, 1959). The pause is definitely a communicator in a nonverbal sense. When pauses are few and not obvious, the teacher is seen as being extroverted and outgoing, perhaps even confident. The intended use of the pause in teaching, sometimes called "wait time" when following a question, can also be used to the teacher's advantage in provoking student thought and investigation (Rowe, 1972). It is the overuse or unplanned use of the pause that is of concern here. In its flagrant usage, this speech pattern displays a lack of confidence and evidences an insecurity on the part of the teacher. Effective teachers will occasionally tape record their classroom interaction in order to analyze their abilities in vocalics.

ENVIRONMENTAL FACTORS in nonverbal communication refers to the setting which has been established in the teacher's classroom. The importance of the appearance of the room cannot be overemphasized. Cold, stale, nondecorated rooms, in general, push learners away. Bright, colorful, decorated surroundings tend to draw them in. It is important for the teacher to remember that the display of student work can be a very significant part of an inviting atmosphere. Students whose work or contributions have a place in the environment become a greater part of the classroom themselves. Constructive use of bulletin board and wall space, desk arrangement, and even personal touches such as plants say a great deal about the teacher's concern for the learning environment and, most definitely, testify to the professional energy level produced. Thus, one's work place reflects both one's personality and professional efforts. The need to create a comfortable place in which to work is no different for teachers than other workers. The warm, inviting environment is preferred over the cold.

Consider the following summary points related to nonverbal communication.

1. *KINESIC* messages can be easily misinterpreted. Head and body movements should be utilized based on student comprehension of meaning.
2. Based on the concept of *PROXEMICS,* teachers should move around the room (from center to center, table to table, or desk to desk) as often as possible. Teachers should remain alert to the impact of proxemics related to classroom management principles.
3. Teachers need to be cautious to the varied interpretations given to touching behaviors. Through *HAPTICS* teachers can, however, display extreme warmth and caring to students.
4. Look at your students while you are speaking to them. Communication through the eyes, *OCULESICS,* quickly displays interest, concern, and value.
5. Develop an exciting voice. Be lively, sincere, and motivating through *VOCALICS.*
6. Create a warm, bright, "bringing in" classroom. Keep students comfortable in a learning-designed setting. Remember the significance of *ENVIRONMENTAL FACTORS.*

Formative Evaluation: Section One*

1. Define the communication process, including reference to three key factors.
2. Distinguish between verbal and nonverbal language.
3. List the four verbal communication languages.
4. Describe three suggestions for improving verbal language communication in the classroom.
5. Name six types of nonverbal language symbols and describe an effect of each.

SECTION 2. TYPES OF LEARNING: COMMUNICATING KNOWLEDGE

Look at the pages of any early childhood, elementary, or secondary textbook and you will note at least four kinds of information being communicated:

---

*See the Appendix for suggested answers to these questions.

1. Generalizations
2. Value statements
3. Factual statements
4. Concepts

GENERALIZATIONS explain a total situation or summarize a large body of data. *VALUE STATEMENTS* function either as justification for a course of action or as a basis of rating objects, events, persons, or situations. *A FACTUAL STATEMENT* is merely something verifiable or thought to be verifiable. Value and factual statements have little value to the thinking process, except when they are given some kind of order in the construction of concepts or generalizations. *CONCEPTS* define some feature of a situation. Concepts are felt to be the actual basis of all thinking and knowing. Teachers sometimes say that thinking is impossible without the proper concepts (Hunt and Metcalf, 1968). Because of the significance of concepts in the understanding of thinking processes and to the logic of teaching and learning, they will be discussed at some length in this section.

2.1. Facts, Generalizations, and Values

The easiest mistake a person can make with concepts is to confuse them with facts. In one study, an attempt was made to rate, according to their relative importance, 938 "concepts" in United States history (Hunt and Metcalf, 1968). Nearly every alleged concept on the list was actually a factual statement such as *CHRISTOPHER COLUMBUS, ATTEMPTING TO REACH ASIA BY SAILING WEST ACROSS THE ATLANTIC, DISCOVERED AMERICA IN 1492.* This statement is definitely not a concept; it is a fact. A convenient way to describe a fact is to consider it as a well-grounded, clearly established unit of information. It is a fact, for example, that George Washington was the first president of the United States. There is an important difference between teaching facts and teaching concepts. The teacher uses facts while teaching or communicating concepts, but it is possible to communicate many facts without teaching a single concept. As we noted in

Chapter One, factual knowledge represents the lowest level of the cognitive domain.

Another confusion arises when concepts are defined as generalizations. The basic difference to be pointed out is that concepts are definitions and axioms. Generalizations, in comparison, possess a synthetic content. Their truth or believability rests upon their proof through the investigation of evidence. Such expressions as *PEOPLE MIGRATE WHEN THEY ARE HUNGRY,* or *GENERALS ARE BABES IN POLITICS,* are often erroneously labeled as concepts. Actually, they are generalizations. Generalizations are perceived as law-like statements which express a relationship among concepts. Part of the special nature of generalizations is their predictive power. According to Martorella (1977), generalizations have the following qualities.

1. They are true or have been verified by the best tests of evidence available (i.e. facts).
2. They predict things in the sense of allowing one to make "if . . . then" statements.
3. They apply to all relevant cases without exceptions.
4. They express significant relationships among concepts.

The generalization, *PEOPLE WHO HAVE COMMON INTERESTS ARE ATTRACTED TO ONE ANOTHER,* is a law-like statement expressing a relationship between the concepts *PEOPLE, COMMON INTERESTS,* and *ATTRACTION.* A major goal of teaching is the development in the student of the ability to create sound generalizations. The teaching of both facts and concepts must not be an end in itself. In considering the acquisition of information for its future use, the generalization statement has greater applicability.

It could be argued that most decisions, whether claimed to be intellectual or not, are motivated by one's values. An individual's values serve as reasons for completing actions and as the basis for rating the worth of something. Such statements as *THE ROSE IS A BEAUTIFUL FLOWER, DOCTOR SEUSS IS THE BEST AUTHOR OF CHILDREN'S BOOKS,* and *COMMUNIST SYMPATHIZERS CANNOT BE TRUSTED* all reflect rating decisions which, in a given situation, could be the reason for an action taken or a position held. As compared to other areas of knowledge such as facts, generalizations, and concepts, values are much more tentative. They are grounded in belief systems, sometimes based on small and, at other times, large amounts of knowledge. Considering their relationship to classroom instruction, values or value statements are frequently felt to hold greater controversy because the universal acceptance of a value is something which cannot be, and perhaps should not be, expected. It is recommended that values be explored as a formal part of instruction because they serve to provide clarity in the understanding of concepts and generalizations. Taught as ends in themselves, values lead to a slanted, narrowed, and less-than-open investigation of knowledge and its usage.

Analyze the following examples of factual statements, value statements, and generalizations:

Factual Statements
1. There are 12 inches in a foot.
2. Red is a primary color.
3. George Washington was the first president.
4. A circle has 360 degrees.
5. Each state is allowed two senators in Congress.

Value Statements
1. Harvard has the best library in the country.
2. Bill Cosby is the funniest comedian.
3. Jefferson Square is the dirtiest section of town.
4. F. Lee Bailey is the most talented trial lawyer in the country.
5. The movie *SUPERMAN II* is well worth seeing.

Generalizations
1. Changes in climate affect the way one lives.
2. Friends generally help one another.
3. New challenges are sometimes confusing.
4. Clubs are made up of common interest areas that tie people together.
5. Domestic animals often have difficulty when returned to the wild.

It may appear to be somewhat off target to spend so much valuable time dealing with conceptual development and other logical aspects of the teaching process. The logical tools of language and thought, however, are the real basis of communication in the learning process. Concepts are often referred to as "the building blocks of knowledge." However, it would be erroneous to assume that all that is to be taught in schools could neatly be classified as facts, concepts, generalizations, and values. Many subject matter areas have a skill orientation as well. The understanding of and instruction in skill areas, however, is enhanced by an accompanying understanding of related concepts associated with the skill performance. One of the major reasons for learning concepts is to use them in solving problems. In some subject matter areas, the activity of using problem-solving skills is a natural extension of concept development wherein a most important process takes place within the learner (Gagné, 1977). In essence, problem-solving skills, through concept development, cause the student to become engaged in rather high level cognitive skill performances. Skills in the areas of algebra, reading, map and graph interpretation, for example, involve the development of an approach to seeking solutions dependent on an understanding of related concepts. While the argument is made that activities of this type are skill oriented (and indeed they are), their successful attainment is based on a sound understanding of relevant and related concepts.

2.2. Concepts

The distinction made here in reference to the study of the concept is that a concept "defines." The verbal expression of a concept is thought of as its definition or the concept rule. Some concepts, however, are almost never communicated verbally. Bruner (1956) offers a helpful interpretation of the term concept when he defines a concept as a category. He would have one think of a concept as a basket into which one may place those objects that belong together because of their attributes (i.e. characteristics). These categories typically include a range of discriminately different items which are treated as if they are the same. For example, many discriminately different wars are placed together to form a category called *CIVIL WAR*. This is done in accordance with certain relevant criteria. Bruner calls these relevant criteria the *DEFINING ATTRIBUTES OF THE CATEGORY;* they are the various characteristics of the concept. A particular war can be classified as *CIVIL WAR* only by first defining *CIVIL WAR* according to its attributes and then showing that the war in question has those unique characteristics. Merrill and Tennyson (1977) describe a concept as being a set of specific objects, symbols, or events which are grouped together on the basis of shared characteristics and are referred to by the same name. Thus, students have learned a concept at that point in time when they can name the concept and identify its class membership.

Basically, a concept is a mental image accounting for your level of familiarity with, or understanding of, objects, events, or the relationships among objects and/or events. Following the mental image idea, you could think of the phrase *IN YOUR MIND'S EYE* when considering what is pictured when a concept is brought to mind. Concepts might well be thought of as "hooks" upon which to hang new experiences. When you are confronted with a novel situation for which there are no "hooks," you must either force the information on an incompatable hook or create a new one. Concepts serve to organize knowledge and keep it from becoming unwieldy and dysfunctional. If students do not have the appropriate mental hooks, the concept cannot be appropriately communicated.

The strength of a concept depends upon the number of established relationships between it and other concepts. Of great importance is the fact that your concepts are really your own, a somewhat private, mental image generated by thinking about personal experiences. In the communication process, you can only utilize available language to attempt to make interpretations of a concept understandable to others. Whether a person exposed to these communication techniques is able to produce an appropriate concept or image is dependent upon many factors. Clearly, the potential for error is tremendous. Obviously, the communication of verbal language may be the weakest technique a teacher can use to communicate concepts to students. Most individuals benefit from visual presentations of concepts. Wherever possible, the use of pictures, actual objects representing concepts under study, or hands-on experiences is highly recommended.

2.3. Types of Concepts

Concepts have been placed in varied categories typically based upon their comprehension difficulty. As a classroom teacher approaches the decision of which concepts to teach, the complexity of the concepts selected will have bearing on how easily students will be able to form the desired mental image.

A popular distinction made in the classification of concepts is the degree to which they are perceived as concrete or abstract. Concrete concepts are those which may be perceived directly through one of the five senses: taste, smell, sound, touch, and sight. The abstract concept is one, on the other hand, which cannot be perceived through the senses. Concrete concepts are much easier for the teacher to communicate than those which are abstract. It is far easier to communicate an image of *HOUSE,* something which can be touched and seen, than it is to provide such an image of *BEAUTY* which is a very abstract concept.

Conjunctive, Disjunctive, and Relational Concepts

Bruner (1956) has suggested that, classified according to their nature, there are three kinds of concepts: the conjunctive, the disjunctive, and the relational. Various teaching strategies are affected by the kind of concept being taught.

A *CONJUNCTIVE CONCEPT* is defined by the simultaneous presence of several critical attributes which are required for the existence of the concept. Most of the research on the teaching of concepts has dealt with concepts of this type. A good example of a conjunctive concept is *SOCIAL CLASS* when it is defined according to several attributes: a person's occupation, source of income, neighborhood, and type of housing. Note that a conjunctive concept connects its attributes with the coordinating conjunction *AND.* The conjunctive concept is typically learned by looking for elements that are common to several examples.

A *DISJUNCTIVE CONCEPT* is defined by various sets of alternate attributes. A disjunctive concept separates these attributes with the coordinating conjunction *OR*. An example of a disjunctive concept is *CITIZEN*. A citizen may be defined as a person who was born in this country, one whose parents were born in this country, or an individual who has passed certain examinations. Another example of a disjunctive concept would be a *STRIKE* in baseball. A strike is a pitch within a certain zone, a pitch that the batter misses, or a pitch that the batter hits outside the foul lines when the count is less than two strikes. Any of these alternate definitions is acceptable.

The concept *TRIANGLE*, which is conjunctive, can be taught by confronting the student with an array of triangles, each one very different from the others, and asking the learner to determine what all of the triangles have in common. It would be a mistake to try to teach a disjunctive concept in this manner. Imagine an American baseball coach trying to teach an Australian aborigine an understanding of the antics on a baseball field. The coach might start with an attempt to teach the concept *STRIKE*. After each strike, the coach could say to the aborigine, *THAT WAS A STRIKE*. If the aborigine then tried to invent a concept of strike based upon an attribute or set of attributes common to all strikes, the aborigine would fail and likely feel that baseball was too complicated a game to understand. This kind of frustration will be created in a student when a teacher attempts to teach disjunctive concepts as if they were conjunctive. The teacher would be better advised to begin by providing the student with a basic knowledge level definition of the concept. This definition would include all of the different instances of the concept which are possible. From this knowledge base, the teacher can then proceed to examples of each instance to reinforce the learned definition.

The *RELATIONAL CONCEPT* is that kind of concept which shows a connection among attributes. A numerical law of physics is one example of a relational concept; density is defined as mass per unit volume. If we know the values for two of the attributes, the other may then be computed. Another example of a relational concept is *AREA OF A RECTANGLE*, defined as a relationship between *LENGTH OF RECTANGLE* and *WIDTH OF RECTANGLE.*

For an understanding of this concept, the learner must have a knowledge of what is meant by the related concepts of *LENGTH* and *WIDTH.* If either of these concepts has been misinterpreted, the relational concept of *AREA OF A RECTANGLE* will not be clearly communicated. As might be imagined, the relational concept represents a rather complex aspect of knowledge.

It is easy to confuse the relational concept with a generalization. The earlier generalization statement that there is a testable relationship between people, common interest, and attraction is not a relational concept but a generalization. An example of a relational concept would be *COMMON INTERESTS* defined as a relationship between people and that which attracts people to each other. The difference between a relational concept and a generalization is best seen in the way that each is developed and supported by fact. A relational concept structures the facts, while a generalization is based upon the facts.

Formative Evaluation: Section Two*

1. Differentiate among facts, generalizations, values, and concepts and provide at least two examples of each.
2. Explain what is meant by the term concept.
3. Distinguish between conjunctive, disjunctive, and relational concepts.
4. Describe the relationship between concept attainment and skills instruction.

SECTION 3. COMMUNICATING THE CONCEPT

Now that you know a great deal about communication and understand the vocabulary of verbal and nonverbal language (e.g. symbols, senders, and receivers), this information clearly must transfer to the teaching act itself. It has been established that teachers are communicators and that their entire professional

---

*See the Appendix for suggested answers to these questions.

effectiveness rests on how well and what they communicate. Since so much of the teacher's efforts at communication involve the teaching of concepts, we have given special consideration to the teaching of concepts in this section. You will learn a systematic procedure for planning and implementing lessons designed to teach specific concepts and apply what you have learned about communicating concepts to the actual development of lesson plans. Later in this text, additional strategies for the application of these skills will be provided.

3.1. A Perception of Concept Acquisition

Before you can teach concepts, you need to have some under-standing of how concepts are learned. We feel that concepts are largely derived through inductive reasoning. Induction is the process where the student collects an assortment of separate pieces of information and puts them together in a manner which makes them meaningful. The learner creates a mental image which synthe-sizes these pieces of information. The mental image is what is termed the learner's concept of whatever is being investigated. Any new information perceived by the person holding the concept can force a revision or expansion of this concept to make it even more meaningful (Wiseman, 1975). This revision or expansion is arrived at through a combination of inductive and deductive processes.

What actually occurs in most school or formal learning settings related to concept learning is a process which combines, in some way, both deductive and inductive features of thinking (Carroll, 1970). The teacher, by providing descriptions and definitions of the concept in question, employs deductive aspects of thinking. The component parts of a selected definition identify the critical attributes or critical aspects (i.e. characteristics) of the concept necessary for its understanding and existence. In contrast, by citing numerous positive and negative instances of the concept, the teacher employs inductive aspects of thinking. Learning is apparently facilitated more by the use of positive rather than negative instances, although both are necessary to develop the concept for instruction. The student is frequently provided, by the teacher, with a verbal presentation of the concept. This typically involves the stating of a concept rule or definition—a deductive process. The learner is then assisted in attaining the concept by learning to make correct identifications of positive and negative instances—an inductive process. Perhaps the ultimate value of formal inductive procedures in concept learning is to provide learners with the opportunity to test their understanding of the concept, its definition, and description.

3.2. A Systematic Approach to Concept Instruction

Assume that you plan to teach a middle school social studies unit on the topic of *WAR*. You have already decided that one of your broad goals will be: *DEVELOP AN UNDERSTANDING OF THE DIFFERENT TYPES OF WARS AND THEIR EFFECTS.* Furthermore, you have tentatively planned to teach a lesson on *CIVIL WAR* which has the following objectives:

1. After studying several examples, define "civil war" using at least two characteristics of the concept.
2. Given a short history of the Vietnam war; explain in writing why you think this war was or was not a civil war; two reasons must be provided.

How should you proceed in order to teach the concept *CIVIL WAR?* As with any type of classroom teaching, the communication of a concept should be approached formally and systematically. Due to the importance of proper concept attainment, confusion should not arise out of awkward or inappropriate instructional procedures being selected. Procedures for instruction should be chosen with both the difficulty of the concept and intellectual sophistication of the students in mind. Thus, we suggest that you, during the instructional planning and development stage, proceed as outlined in Figure 2-4. Using the concept *CIVIL WAR*, we will elaborate on each portion of the proposed systematic approach in this figure. Before reading further, however, a knowledge of the following important concept-related terminology should prove to be helpful in this area of study.

1. CONCEPT RULE: The basic, verbalized, definition of the concept.
2. CRITICAL ATTRIBUTE: An essential defining characteristic of the concept.
3. NONCRITICAL ATTRIBUTE: Defining characteristic often associated with the concept but not really necessary to make a complete definition.
4. EXAMPLE: Positive instance of the concept.
5. NONEXAMPLE: Negative or not an actual instance of the concept.
6. CUES: Suggestions, directed thoughts, or "hints" for the student to think about as the concept is being communicated.

INSTRUCTIONAL PLANNING AND

DEVELOPMENT STAGE

---

1.   ANALYZE THE CONCEPT

2.   PLAN THE LESSON PROCEDURES AND MATERIALS PORTION TO INCLUDE:

Set Induction

Presentation of Examples and Nonexamples

Use of Cues, Questions, and Further Directions

Assessment of Minimal Level Concept Mastery

3.   PLAN THE EVALUATION PORTION OF THE LESSON TO INCLUDE:

Assessment of Advanced Levels of Concept Mastery

Figure 2-4. A systematic approach to concept instruction (adapted from Martorella, 1977).

Analyzing the Concept

When preparing for concept instruction, the teacher should carry out a number of significantly important tasks. As a beginning point, you as the teacher must determine (1) whether or not the concept is significant enough to actually be formally taught, (2) if the concept is best learned through formal means, and (3) if there is sufficient agreement on the critical attributes of the concept to make its communication clear. In this initial phase of concept teaching, you must analyze the appropriateness of the concept and its level of complexity for the student group in question. Besides assessing the appropriateness or relevance of the concept for formal instruction, analyze the concept to help organize the basic elements of the lesson. In this activity, the following questions might be asked:

- What is the concept rule or definition to be communicated?
- What are the important critical and non-critical attributes of the concept?
- What examples and nonexamples of the concept will be included to enhance communication?
- What are some basic questions or cues which may be used in the lesson to facilitate concept understanding?

Figure 2-5 presents the results of an analysis of the concept *CIVIL WAR.*

Planning the Procedures/Materials Portion

As with any lesson introduction, the introduction to a concept lesson should be eye-catching and interesting. The introduction should present the concept to be studied, could include the rule or definition, and must serve to set the stage for the formal lesson which is to follow. The beginning of the instructional sequence might include a short story or a description of a concept-related experience. It could contain a series of questions to stimulate thinking on the part of the learner directed toward an investigation of the concept. This part of the lesson is sometimes referred to as the lesson's *SET INDUCTION.* That is, it is a period of the instructional sequence wherein a special "set" is established on which the forthcoming lesson will build. The set induction deter-

Concept: CIVIL WAR

Concept Rule or Definition: *A civil war is a war between different sections or factions of the same country*

Critical Attributes: 1. *Occurs within a country*
2. *Participants are citizens of the same country*
3. *Begins with an uprising against some form of government*

Non-Critical Attributes:

1. *Length*
2. *Nation involved*
3. *Point in history*
4. *Cost*
5. *Historical significance*
6. *Numbers involved*

Examples: 1. *U.S. Civil War*
2. *French Revolution*
3. *Bolshevik Revolution*
4. *War of the Roses*

Non-Examples: 1. *World War I*
2. *World War II*
3. *Spanish-American War*
4. *War of 1812*

Questions and Cues: -*What might cause one group of citizens to conflict with another?*
-*Was the Korean conflict a civil war?*
-*What does the word "civil" mean?*
-*How can civil wars be resolved?*
-*Think about inter-country and intra-country conflict.*
-*Describe how citizens might feel fighting one another.*

Figure 2-5. Analysis of the concept: civil war.

mines the tone for the lesson and pulls together a common learner outlook for the concept under investigation. For the concept *CIVIL WAR*, the introductory questions below are a good example of a set induction that could be used:

- Did any of your ancestors fight in a civil war?
- Which war?
- Why do you think they fought in this war?

One common element in concept instruction lessons is the presence of examples and nonexamples of the concept. Such examples and non-examples have been referred to as positive and negative instances of the concept. Experiences in the lesson which portray the concept are called positive instances; those which do not are called negative instances. It is recommended that, where possible, all examples and non-examples, positive or negative instances, be presented simultaneously. In this manner, where such experiences are presented in close succession, the learner can compare all of the cases quickly. If the concept is understood, the learner should be able to point to examples in new and novel situations. The student should also be able to discriminate instances which do not represent the concept.

Returning to our *CIVIL WAR* concept, you would, therefore, present the examples and non-examples listed in Figure 2-5 in close succession and in as short a time period as possible. As these instances are presented, the learner will develop the ability to discriminate between that which is defined as *CIVIL WAR* and that which is not.

Throughout the concept lesson, the teacher should draw close attention to the finer differences among the examples used. This is to say, an understanding of gross as opposed to specific differences is not sufficient for sound conceptualization. In making reference to such differences, the teacher should have the learner focus on both the attributes and nonattributes of the concept. The teacher should also ask questions to determine the degree to which the learner is advancing and at the same time encourage the learner to ask questions. Verbal cues should be given as suggestions to note differences among examples and non-examples which vividly or explicitly delineate the concept. Too, direction from the teacher might be included to help the learner to actively investigate and take note of critical and non-critical attributes as well as various instances of the concept portrayed in the presentation. Refer to Figure 2-5 for attributes, nonattributes, sample cues, and questions for the concept *CIVIL WAR*. Making use of these, as outlined above, in teaching the concept *CIVIL WAR* will serve to develop an in-depth acquaintance with the concept among your students.

Prior to the close of any concept teaching episode, it is important that the teacher conduct some type of formative student assessment. This ongoing assessment will help the teacher to determine whether or not the level of concept understanding acquired by the learners meets the standards established prior to instruction. Evaluation at this juncture might be either formal or informal. Its importance, however, is crucial for the identification of future instructional directions. If the learners do not hold a satisfactory image of the concept at this point, it would be an error on the teacher's part to proceed further to more complex concepts. Perhaps further examples, non-examples, questions, and cues are needed to assist the learner in acquiring the appropriate understanding of the concept. This type of assessment represents an important form of feedback for both the teacher and the learners. Such information enables learners to better comprehend their own level of understanding and provides the teacher with valuable data to assist in the determination of future instruction.

Planning the Evaluation Portion

At the end of the lesson, the teacher must refer back to originally identified objectives for the lesson in determining evaluative procedures. One of the main reasons in beginning instruction with clearly stated objectives is to give the teacher guidance in providing sound, objective-referenced assessments. In assessing for in-depth levels of concept formation, the teacher might seek answers to the following questions; these dimensions of assessment recognize an increasingly complex understanding of concept acquisition:

- Can the learner identify both critical and non-critical attributes of the concept?
- Can the learner separate positive instances of the concept from negative instances?

- Can the learner relate the newly acquired concept to other concepts?
- Can the learner use the concept in a novel way?

If the answers to these questions are in the affirmative, the teacher may appropriately conclude that the concept has been communicated well. Identifying examples, non-examples, critical and non-critical attributes, the concept rule, relating the concept to other concepts, and actually using the concept in a novel way clearly point to a high level of learning.

Final evaluation for the concept lesson on *CIVIL WAR* could be completed by preparing formal test questions based on the lesson objectives. These could be included on a weekly quiz or as part of a larger unit examination. Possible test questions for this lesson are included on the completed lesson plan (See Fig. 2-6). If the students are able to answer these questions, they will have progressed to the point of being ready to learn to use the concept *CIVIL WAR* in a novel fashion. Before going on to the formative evaluation for this section, carefully study the completed lesson plan (See Fig. 2-6) and satisfy yourself that all aspects of quality lesson planning have been considered.

Formative Evaluation: Section Three[*]

1. Describe the process that is thought to occur when one learns a new concept.
2. Describe a three-step systematic approach to planning concept lessons.
3. Select a concept and analyze it for instruction according to procedures outlined in Part 3.2.
4. Plan a lesson utilizing the remaining steps in the three-step approach for the concept you analyzed in question three.

---

[*]See the Appendix for suggested answers to these questions.

Teacher _____*John Smith*_____

Lesson Title _____*Civil War*_____

Unit _____*Wars and Their Effects*_____

GOAL(S): *Develop an understanding of the different types of wars and their effects.*

OBJECTIVE(S): *After studying examples, define 'civil war' using at least two characteristics.*

Given a short history of the Vietnam war, explain in writing why you think this war was or was not a civil war; two reasons must be provided.

PROCEDURES AND MATERIALS:
Set induction questions
Review Vietnam war and provide a short overview
Introduce and define civil war
Discuss in a question and answer session the general characteristics of war. List on chalkboard
Discuss critical attributes of civil war
    Occurs within a country
    Participants are citizens of same country
Provide two non-examples
Make use of cues and questions: Was the Korean Conflict a civil war?
                              What might cause a civil war?
Recap and repeat definition
Discuss non-critical attributes of civil war.
  Length, nation involved, point in history, cost, historical significance.
Summarize and repeat definition.
Use a simulation game as a summary. Distribute handout *explaining roles and scenario*
Use remaining time to help individual students with their unit projects

EVALUATION:
Questions for Exam
1. *Define CIVIL WAR using at least two characteristics.*
2. *Was the Vietnam War a CIVIL WAR? Why or why not? Provide two reasons.*

Figure 2-6. Completed plan for example concept lesson.

REFERENCES

Argyle, M., and Dean, J. Eye contact, distance, and affiliation. *Sociometry*, 28, 1965, 289–304.

Berger, Allen. "So you want to know." *Wilson Library Bulletin.* Vol. 45, No. 3 (November, 1970).

Bruner, J. S., Goodnow, J. J. and Austin, G. A. *A study of thinking.* New York: Wiley, 1956.

Carroll, J. B. The formation of concepts. In *Concepts in the social studies* by Barry K. Beyer and Anthony N. Penna (Eds.), Bulletin 45. Washington, D.C.: National Council for the Social Studies, 1970.

Crable, Richard E. What can you believe about rhetoric? In *Exploration in speech communication.* Edited by John J. MacKay. Columbus, OH: Charles E. Merrill Publishing Company, 1979.

Ekman, Paul. Differential communication of affect by head and body cues. *Journal of Personality and Social Psychology,* 1965, 2, 726–735.

Gagné, Robert M. *The conditions of learning,* 3rd ed. New York: Holt, Rinehart and Winston, 1977.

Galloway, C. Please listen to what I'm not saying. Presentation to Reflections: An Invitation To Successful Teaching, Coastal Carolina College of the University of South Carolina, Myrtle Beach, South Carolina, April, 1982.

Goldman-Eisler, Frieda. A comparative study of two hesitation phenomena. *Language and Speech,* 1961, 4, (January–March), 18–26.

Hunt, Maurice P., and Metcalf, Lawrence E. *Teaching high school social studies.* New York: Harper and Row Publishers, 1968.

Knapp, Mark L. The Field of Nonverbal Communication. *On Speech Communication.* Edited by Charles J. Stewart. New York: Holt, Rinehart and Winston, 1972.

Maclay, H., and Osgood, C. E. Hesitation phenomena in spontaneous English speech. *Word,* 1959, 15, 19.

Martorella, Peter H. "Teaching concepts." In Classroom teaching skills: A handbook. Edited by James A. Cooper. Lexington, MA: D. C. Heath and Company, 1977.

McCroskey, James C. *Introduction to rhetorical communication,* 2nd. ed., Ch. 6. Englewood Cliffs, NJ: Prentice-Hall, 1972.

Mehrabian, Sue. Significance of posture and position in the communication of attitude and status relationships. *Psychology Bulletin,* 1969, 71, 359–72.

Merrill, M. David, and Tennyson, Robert D. *Teaching concepts: An instructional Design Guide.* Englewood Cliffs, NJ: Educational Technology Publications, 1977.

Rowe, Mary Budd. "Wait-time and rewards as instructional variables: Their influence on language, logic, and fate control" (Paper presented at the National Association for Research in Science Teaching, Chicago, April, 1972.)

Schramm, Wilbur (Ed.) How communication works in *The process and effects of mass communication.* Urbana, IL: University of Illinois Press, 1945.

Sereno, Kenneth, and Bodakan, Edward. *Trans-per: Understanding human communication.* Boston, MA: Houghton Mifflin Company, 1975.

Wiseman, Dennis G. "The Logical Aspects of Classroom Instruction." In *The General Teaching Model* by Henry G. Walding, School of Teacher Education, Coastal Carolina College-USC (Copyright-Summer, 1975).

CHAPTER THREE

THE TEACHER AS AN EFFECTIVE PERFORMER

The purpose of this chapter is to explore those general teacher behaviors that are related to successful instruction. Determining those behaviors which lead to effective classroom instruction is difficult and has occupied a significant facet of educational research for some time. Thus, this chapter is focused on effective teacher performance in the complex instructional environment. We will examine many teacher behaviors in order to assist you in effectively addressing this intricate social system. Such a review of the instructional environment will help put the need for appropriate teacher skills and performances in the proper perspective. Specifically, after studying this chapter, you should be able to demonstrate the following performances:

1. Name and describe eight generic characteristics of effective instruction.
2. Provide examples of the implementation of eight generic characteristics of effective instruction.
3. Classify questions according to cognitive level.
4. Preplan lesson questions at various cognitive levels for given topics.
5. Describe fourteen suggestions for better classroom questioning practices.

SECTION 1: GENERIC CHARACTERISTICS
OF EFFECTIVE INSTRUCTION

It is possible, through some effort, to generate a list of characteristics common to effective instruction. While this list may never be exhaustive, many of the qualities that are frequently found in instruction by successful teachers can be enumerated. All of these generic characteristics of effective instruction are not necessarily found in every good lesson. Nevertheless, a master teacher would be expected, when necessary, to have the ability to develop lessons that have all of these qualities.

Since educators vary in their estimations of what constitutes effective instruction, the task becomes one of listing the qualities that most agree should be included, not necessarily listing all of the characteristics found in everyone's description of a model lesson. The following characteristics would likely be found on almost any insightful educator's listing. Lessons should:

1. Be *APPROPRIATE* to the *DEVELOPMENTAL LEVEL* of the students
2. *ADDRESS* the *STATED OBJECTIVES* in the lesson plan
3. Have a *MOTIVATIONAL ASPECT* which will stimulate the students' desire to attend to the lesson
4. Be organized around *A VARIETY OF GROUPING STRUC-TURES* within the classroom in order to accommodate the learners' styles, rates, and abilities
5. Have opportunities for all *LEARNERS* to *BECOME ACTIVELY INVOLVED* in the learning activities
6. Allow students to *FUNCTION* at least *AT THE APPLICA-TION LEVEL* of learning
7. Provide the teacher an opportunity to *DETERMINE IF* all *STUDENTS ARE LEARNING* from the instructional activities
8. Be designed so as to *ALLOW STUDENTS FEEDBACK* concerning their level of competency

1.1. Appropriate Developmental Level

The concept of "grade level" often causes confusion when elementary and secondary teachers prepare for classroom instruction. Too frequently, teachers assume that all students, at a given grade level, are developmentally equal. This antiquated concept of human growth and development is inconsistent with classroom reality. Learners at a given chronological age will usually vary substantially in their physical, emotional, social, and intellectual development. Individual learners, additionally, will likely vary significantly in aspects of their personal development. For example, students who are highly developed intellectually may be far behind their classmates (i.e. age-mates) in emotional development.

It is essential for the classroom teacher to understand the characteristics common to learners at a given grade level; on the other hand, the teacher must be cautious not to allow this information to be used to stereotype learners. Such information should be used as a beginning point for the analysis of individual student needs. The determination of a student's developmental level might typically begin with age-group characteristics. Even though there is great developmental variance within age groups, it must be noted that there also exists a similarity among learners of the same age. The interests, attitudes, habits, and skills of a seven-year-old are usually quite different from those of a fourteen-year-old. Therefore, teachers of these students will, no doubt, approach similar topics with very different strategies. Curriculum areas such as death education, sex education, and values clarification, to name obvious examples, are very sensitive to the maturational levels of learning individuals. The selection of strategies for areas such as these should be approached with care and caution. For example, one should not approach the topic of "human reproduction" with eight-year-olds in the same manner that one would approach the same topic with biologically mature adolescents.

As important as age is in helping a teacher to determine appropriate levels of subject matter interest and difficulty, psychologists, such as J. McVicker Hunt (1964), have also stressed the impact of environmental factors on the developmental process. No teacher can assume that all students in a given group are ready for the same instructional strategies simply because they are all of approximately the same age. Similarly, to declare that instruction should be appropriate to the developmental level of certain students is clearly not to suggest that teachers must always follow a given textbook or curriculum guide.

Piaget (1970) described in detail the factors that he recognized as determiners of cognitive development; a knowledge of these factors is helpful for a teacher to more completely understand the individual developmental differences of a group of learners.

1. Piaget agreed with the traditional maturationists that bio-logical maturation is a determiner of a learner's cognitive development. His stages of cognitive development (i.e. sensorimotor, preoperational, concrete operational, and formal operational) are loosely associated with identified age spans. That is, Piaget concluded that children of given age groups are very similar in respect to the way they function when performing certain cognitive tasks. It is important to keep in mind that Piaget discussed these stages as being several years in duration; he did not sug-gest that cognitive levels change on a yearly basis.

2. Piaget stressed the importance of life experiences in the development of cognitive abilities. Experiences that stu-dents have will aid them in cognitive development to the degree that these experiences are rich in variety and eas-ily understood. To the point that they have experiences explained in language that is easily understood, these experiences will be meaningful. It was also Piaget's posi-tion that intellectual development was directly related to the amount of oral conversation in which learners engage. Not only should students be encouraged to discuss activities, a teacher must also attempt to describe these activities in everyday language that stimulates thinking and furthers understanding.

3. Piaget stated that learners need to expand their concep-tual structures in order to develop cognitive ability. This expansion takes place when the learner has the opportu-nity to fit new examples of the characteristics of the con-cept into an existing pattern or when the learner can discover new characteristics of the concept which must, in some way, alter the existing pattern before they will neatly fit into the conceptual structure. (Refer to Chapter 2 for a detailed discussion of the nature of a concept.)

After you, as the teacher, begin to determine the developmental level of the learners, it will only then become possible to adjust the curriculum in such a way as to provide each student with greater opportunities for success. Unfortunately, even after exhaustive diagnosis and preparation, it may still be impossible for even the best diagnostician to accurately match all materials to the developmental level of a given learner thus guaranteeing continued success. However, the following basic guidelines have been identified to assist you in providing instruction appropriate to each learner's developmental level.

1. Concepts are developed more easily from the concrete to the abstract. As a result, some learners who have great difficulty learning an abstraction from a science textbook might readily understand the same material when presented in the form of a classroom demonstration.

2. When it is necessary to present certain material in a vicarious manner (e.g. through the use of books, tapes, or films), it often will be necessary to precede the presentation of materials with certain direct, more concrete experiences. This is to suggest that some learners may find a unit of instruction more meaningful if it is introduced with such activities as field trips, visits from community experts, or presentations of realia.

3. The ability of learners to use and understand language is central to developmental level. The length and complexity of sentences are often the factors that interfere with student understanding of the directions that they receive from their teachers. Furthermore, some learners function at a developmental level which necessitates their receiving verbal feedback while they are at work; receiving the teacher's simple explanation will help these learners form more complete concepts. It seems reasonable to suggest that many students, who have been previously thought of as deficient in mental abilities, are actually able to learn but unable to understand the language used in the public schools.

4. Another component of a learner's developmental maturity is the degree to which it is possible to attend to a learning task over time; this component is usually described as a learner's attention span. All learners do not have the ability to attend to a learning task for extended

periods of time. If a teacher fails to adjust instruction to the learner's ability to stay on task, a student with a short attention span is likely to have academic difficulty. If a learner is given too much work to complete relative to personal attention span, that student is apt to receive poor grades based on the fact that much of the work will be unattempted or completed with little concentration.

5. Lastly, because of learner differences in emotional development, teachers must pace learning experiences in such a way as to insure that all learners will experience some level of satisfaction in the classroom environment. If the teacher allows too many activities to occur simultaneously for an individual learner, the student may become overstimulated resulting in mental confusion and low performance. Another outcome could be that the student becomes emotionally unable to adjust to the environment. This lack of adjustment could cause aggressive behavior problems or withdrawal. The teacher must be aware that some learners can become overstimulated and receive inappropriate kinds of reinforcement from the same learning environment which is quite satisfying to other students.

1.2. Address Stated Objectives

A major emphasis of this text is the importance of using objectives as the foundation of instruction. Simply stated, instruction should be purposefully designed in order to help learners reach the stated objective(s). Teachers who develop lessons without being guided by specific learner outcomes are commonly guilty of "teaching books" instead of students. Too often, teachers require learners to work through a textbook page by page without ever considering the purpose of teaching in the selected content area or whether or not the students are really benefitting from the instruction. Such teachers are, in fact, focusing on the textbook, not interacting with the learners. Before any instruction takes place, the way or ways the lesson is going to benefit the students as they strive to learn should be ascertained. Objectives guide instruction and, at the same time, provide an organizational structure making meaningful student evaluation possible.

Objectives are not always stated in terms of the performance of the entire class. In an effort to individualize instruction, certain objectives may only be appropriate for a small percentage of the total student population. As a result, many lessons will be designed for small groups or possibly even one student. Regardless of the number of students involved, whole group or small group, all *PLANNED INSTRUCTION,* as developed in the systematic model discussed in Chapter One, should be aimed at helping learners reach some specific, stated objective.

During the planning of the lesson, more than one objective per instructional group may be listed. Nevertheless, it is not unusual for the teacher to discover that all objectives cannot be addressed in one lesson; this simply means that the remaining objectives may be addressed in a future instructional period. Because of the need to maintain an important flexibility determined often by individual learner needs and talents, a teacher should not force the addressing of all planned objectives in every lesson. To illustrate this point, consider these objectives related to the study of the concept *DEMOCRACY.*

The student will be able to:
1. From memory, define the terms republic, representation, democracy, government, constitution, and non-democratic state
2. Given two different countries, one representing a democratic and one representing a non-democratic state, compare and contrast the countries in a paragraph discussion pointing out no less than three differences
3. Given three separate descriptions of governmental systems, identify the type of governmental structure utilized by each using no less than two pieces of supporting evidence for each identification
4. Using any desired references, create a hypothetical country to include the following: population, geographic region, technological orientation, agricultural orientation, and governmental system using a democratic model

While all of these objectives may be quite relevant as desired outcomes related to the study of the concept *DEMOCRACY,* all, obviously, could not be appropriately addressed in only one or even two class sessions. In spite of this, all observed instruction should be targeted toward at least one of these stated objectives. If this is not the case, the teacher should adjust the instructional activity to make it relevant to the list of identified objectives. The points being made are these:

1. Instruction should not take place without a prior identification of stated objectives.
2. Instruction observed should be characterized by a link between the stated objectives and the instructional activity by the teacher.
3. Ultimately, evaluation which occurs following instruction should be based on objectives which were established and communicated to students before the start of the instructional sequence.

1.3. The Motivational Aspect

A well-planned lesson at any grade level will not be effective if students do not attend to the instruction provided by the teacher. Teachers often plan well and present the material to the learners in a well-organized format but have students who fail to respond positively because the lesson is not interesting to them. Most teachers feel that students must share some responsibility for their own learning; this is certainly a legitimate position. However, teachers do have the greater responsibility of making their lessons interesting to the degree that students feel excited about learning. In order to be effective, teachers must motivate their students by stimulating their interest. This is an essential of quality instruction.

To help insure this, quality instruction should, at least, include a presentation of the lesson's rationale; such a rationale will provide the teacher with an opportunity to stimulate the group's interest in the content area. A rationale will also serve as a means to stimulate student interest by helping the learners identify more closely with the learning activity. Far too often students are asked, or told, to proceed through learning activities without ever being informed of the importance of the area of study to either their daily lives or their future. A rationale statement, or the reason for spending time in the selected area of study, helps assist students in identifying the importance of the content. Obviously, those students who see the relevance of study in a particular area will approach their studies with greater energy and determination than those students who do not see this importance. Regardless of the grade level, this is a most important thought to consider.

Good and Brophy (1973) have stated that the modeling of enthusiasm is a skill necessary for all teachers regardless of the age of their students. Students tend to respond positively to an enthusiastic teacher and become interested in the same things that interest their instructor. Enthusiasm is conveyed through the display of a sincere interest in the subject matter and through both vigor and dynamic behavior. Truly effective teachers, through their enthusiasm, project the notion that they enjoy their work. Rosenshine (1970), as well as other researchers, has reported that enthusiastic teaching tends to promote greater academic gains for the students involved. This has obvious implications for the classroom. Teachers who desire to have high achieving students must make an effort to capture their interest even before instruction begins. Students are not likely to be motivated to learn in a dry, stale classroom with a teacher who seemingly would rather be doing something else.

Probably no other part of the lesson is as important as the introduction, because it is at this point that the teacher is most concerned with establishing high motivation. If students are not motivated to attend to the beginning of the lesson, it may be difficult for interest to be recaptured as the instructional sequence develops. Because of this, effective teachers often plan "attention grabbers" for the introduction of a lesson with the purpose of stimulating learner interest. See Figure 3-1 for examples of several attention grabbers. During the course of a lesson, student interest may wane. When this occurs, it will be necessary to implement new motivational strategies to insure student interest throughout the rest of the instructional episode. Teacher dynamics is the key factor in any motivational strategy; teachers can move, touch, show surprise, inflect their voices, and be dramatic. It has often been suggested that teachers need an actor's flare to be successful.

Good and Brophy (1973) stated it well when they noted that there needs to be a bit of Tom Sawyer in all teachers.

Ten Examples of Attention-Grabbers

-use carefully planned introductory questions

-provide a dramatic demonstration

-use role playing by the teacher

-show slides without accompanying narration and ask students to guess what the slides are about

-pose an unpopular argument or point of view

-ask a riddle to start discussion

-play a record or cassette tape and ask the class to analyze its content

-present a puzzling problem for solution

-use a puppet to introduce a new idea

-use an open-ended mystery story

Figure 3-1. Examples of attention-grabbers.

1.4. A Variety of Grouping Structures

Chapter One emphasized the importance of using a variety of grouping structures to accommodate the rates, styles, and abilities of individual learners. Effective teachers, whether in elementary or secondary school, regardless of the class setting or content studied, cannot afford the luxury of constantly teaching lessons to the entire class without ever subgrouping for instruction. As a teacher, you must develop the ability to teach whole groups, small groups, and individuals in a planned sequence and as the need arises. The position taken here is that effective teachers usually vary group size during a given instructional episode in order to address the learning needs of their students. It is often possible for the teacher to introduce a lesson to the entire group but, after this initial experience, find it necessary to address special learning needs with small group or one-to-one instruction.

To be sure, many teachers feel there are several positive aspects of whole group teaching.

1. A greater depth and breadth of content can be covered in a shorter period of time.
2. The teacher can be assured that all students have the opportunity to hear the same delivery, which will, perhaps, eliminate possible confusion in direction-giving and enhance consistency.
3. Whole group instruction gives many teachers the feeling of being in "control" of the instructional scene, thereby affording them the chance to deal with all student questions for the benefit of all students.
4. In a management sense, whole group instruction is seen by many teachers as reinforcing their position of authority which enables them to maintain "better" classroom control.

While it is not argued that the above list consists of unimportant instructional concerns, it must be noted that numerous positive characteristics are also associated with both the small group and one-to-one organizational formats.

1. Many students who feel uncomfortable in the large group setting will participate orally in small group discussions.
2. Personal interaction and socialization skills may be addressed in such settings where the large group makes in-depth attention to these skill development areas less likely.
3. Independent learning patterns are more easily fostered where students are either working on their own or in small groups.
4. The teacher is provided greater opportunities to work with students on an individual basis and to get to know them personally in situations where small group and one-to-one structures are employed.

It is difficult to imagine any class being so homogeneous that effective instruction can continually be delivered using a whole group format. It may be safe to assume that teachers are concentrating *MORE ON CONTENT* and *LESS ON STUDENTS* when small group and individual instruction are not practiced. Teachers report that it is much easier to plan for and to evaluate instruction when everything is done with the entire class. However, instructional decisions should be based upon that which is best for the learners, not that which is easiest for the teacher.

1.5. Active Involvement of Learners

Quality instruction allows students an opportunity to take an active part in learning. Effective instruction does not continually allow learners to sit passively while the teacher assumes the dominant, active role. Obviously, levels of student activity will vary across lessons, but, with few exceptions, every lesson should provide students the opportunity to do more than passively listen to instruction.

At the very least, students should be given the opportunity to engage in some speaking and/or writing activities during the course of every lesson. As minimal as this amount of activity may seem, providing learners an opportunity to speak or write will give them a time to express themselves publicly and to center their attention on the selected learning task. Allowing students to communicate during the learning experience will provide the teacher with valuable information about the level of the students' understanding. Of course, writing and speaking also provide learners opportunities to receive feedback concerning their level of competency.

Active involvement in classroom instruction frequently serves to address the affective portion of the classroom environment. Students who feel a part of the class, and, in actuality through instruction are a part of the class, in turn seek out higher levels of instructional involvement. Without question, instruction which involves learners as active participants in the learning enterprise provides for the most successful instructional climate.

1.6. Working at the Application Level

Most teachers are aware of the importance of encouraging students to become actively involved in the learning process. However, some of these same teachers do not routinely stress the importance of having high cognitive level student performance during instruction. Too frequently, students are simply required to answer questions which demand rote memory of lectures and discussions or, at most, a low level comprehension of textbook materials or teacher explanations. It is necessary that learners be given the opportunity to demonstrate, not only to the teacher but to themselves, an ability to put their learning to some practical use.

As discussed in Chapter One, there are six levels of cognitive performance that can take place in any learning environment. Students who are not challenged to extend their cognitive processes are actually being encouraged to spend most of their valuable learning time engaging in the rather low level mental activities of memorizing or restating the words of their teachers and textbooks. At the very least, learners should be encouraged to apply their newly acquired knowledge on a daily basis.

In order for you to insure that your students have the opportunity to function at least at the application level, a specific structured sequence of learning activities which allows for the application of knowledge must be planned. The most basic activities will enable the learner to develop the required foundation of knowledge upon which higher levels of cognition can be developed. After knowledge is developed and students are able to comprehend the basic concepts of the body of information under study, they are then able to apply their new information to "real life" situations. Opportunities should be developed for students to demonstrate their skills in unique situations. For example, after the study of internal rhyming techniques, students could be provided the opportunity to write poetry. If students use internal rhyming in their writing where such a technique is appropriate, but, without being told to do so, they will be applying their new knowledge and comprehension.

Competent, effective teachers will never be able to guarantee that all students will function at the application level in every area of study. Nevertheless, it may be assured that students can frequently have learning activities designed to allow them the opportunity to apply what they have learned. While perhaps not possible in all situations, application is clearly relevant in most.

1.7. Determination of Student Learning

One of the most serious mistakes a teacher can make is to assume that learning has taken place simply because instruction was conducted. Good teachers are routinely, actively involved in strategies designed to monitor and reinforce student progress. To be effective, you must have the ability to determine when learning is taking place. While this determination is not always easy to make, guidelines such as the following should be of some assistance in dealing with this important aspect of instruction.

1. Provide some type of evaluation at the end of each learning task in order to identify what students have learned and what they still need to learn before they can master the stated objectives. Bloom (1976) stated that this feedback-corrective procedure is one of the most powerful determiners of effective instruction.
2. Assess the nonverbal communication of students in order to determine anxiety, stress, confusion, and other factors.
3. Ask questions and examine students' work while they are involved in the learning task to determine if they are making progress.
4. Develop precise learning objectives as guides to instruction and evaluate the attainment of these objectives often and systematically. Much of this evaluation need not be complex because its purpose is diagnostic, not grading.
5. Move around the classroom examining student work in order to identify problems so that, in turn, proper feedback can be given as quickly as possible. When students seem confused or perplexed, ask questions of them in order to determine the source of the confusion and then help them to correct the problem.

1.8. Students Receive Feedback

Students, when involved in learning tasks, need to obtain information concerning how well they are performing. However, providing quality feedback is a very complex and difficult task to master. It may very well be that one of the most powerful determiners of effective teaching is the proper use of informational feedback. Biehler and Snowman (1982) have pointed out that feedback is most effective when learners are confident in their response, even if the response is incorrect. This is, before students can benefit from being told that they have made an incorrect response those students must have self-confidence in their abilities to perform the task. Feedback has little effect on learners if they have little or no self-confidence. This is true even if the correct response is being provided.

The list of considerations provided in Figure 3-2 is designed to help insure that you make proper use of feedback.

Formative Evaluation: Section 1[*]

1. List eight generic characteristics of effective instruction.
2. Choose two of the eight generic characteristics of effective instruction and provide a brief description.
3. Pick three of the eight characteristics named in question one; provide at least two examples of how each may be implemented.

SECTION 2: QUESTIONING: A BASIC TEACHING PERFORMANCE

It should be evident from the preceding discussion that a variety of teaching skills are needed to effectively carry out successful instruction. Some teaching behaviors are basic to virtually any lesson; one such behavior is teacher questioning.

A widely accepted goal of education is the development of higher thinking abilities in students. Since questions used by teachers have long played an important role in guiding the per-

---

[*]See the Appendix for suggested answers to these questions.

FEEDBACK CONSIDERATIONS

---

1. Feedback should not be used to promote a lack of confidence in learners (i.e. to promote a negative self-concept). If students are told of their mistakes too often, they are likely to form a negative self-image which will then result in poor performance in the classroom.

2. Feedback should be immediate and positive in order to build slow learners' self-confidence in the learning task.

3. Accelerated learners seem to benefit from being told when they have made mistakes. Actually, telling students of high self-confidence that they have correct answers has been found to have minimal positive effect on their performance because it simply confirms what was already known (Biehler and Snowman, 1982).

4. Immediate feedback functions best when a student is working with factual information or learning a specific task such as the operation of a piece of equipment.

5. When accelerated learners are involved with complex, higher level thinking, it is often more productive to delay feedback. Such learners are likely to think about the task at a later time and then give themselves internal feedback concerning the correctness of their responses. This is essentially true after formal thought processes have been developed.

Figure 3-2. Considerations involving the proper use of feedback.

formance of students, it follows that the use of questions is one of the basic means available to the teacher for stimulating student thinking. The use of questions has been called "by far the most influential single teaching act" (Taba, Levine, and Elzey, 1964). Depending upon the skill of the instructor, teacher questioning can shape the learning environment by setting the students' expectation levels and by guiding their study toward deeper levels of understanding.

2.1. Questioning Practices

Teachers, at all levels, ask a tremendous number of questions each day. Research indicates, however, that the emphasis of most of these questions is on the lower levels of cognition. Hoetker and

Ahlbrand (1969), in a review of studies spanning a half century, conclude that the dominant mode of thinking as exemplified by teacher questions is the memorization and recall of facts. The following classroom scene reflects a typical questioning practice. Consider the questioning approach used by Mr. Smith in his fourth grade classroom.

Mr. Smith:	Today, class, we are going to continue our study of dental health. I hope that you read the chapter for today. Johnny, did you?
Johnny:	Sort of—I got as far as I could.
Mr. Smith:	Well, that's not good enough! You must study better than that. Maybe Colleen has done her work. Colleen, what can happen if people don't brush their teeth?
Colleen:	They get cavities.
Mr. Smith:	Right! Now who can tell me how to avoid cavities? Robert?
Robert:	Brush your teeth after every meal.
Mr. Smith:	And what else did the book say to do? George?
George:	Floss your teeth.
Mr. Smith:	What did the text say about the food you eat? Harry?
Harry:	Don't eat sweets.
Mr. Smith:	Why, Harry?
Harry:	They cause cavities.
Mr. Smith:	Anything else?
Harry:	I think that's all.

Now analyze the following class discussion of Mrs. Jones' first grade class.

Mrs. Jones:	Class, today let's explore what we know about the people in our community. What kinds of people who work in our community help to make it a good place to live: Mary, can you name one?
Mary:	The policeman, I think.
Mrs. Jones:	That's great. Joe, what are some of the things that policemen do to help our community?
Joe:	Well, they help stop robbers; they help you if you

	get lost, and they help people if something bad happens to them.
Mrs. Jones:	Perfect. Who else in our community helps us? Billy?
Billy:	The postman.
Mrs. Jones:	What does the postman do to help us?
Billy:	The postman makes sure that we get our mail. The postman also helps us get our mail taken to other people.
Mrs. Jones:	Those are good answers. Debbie, what do you think things would be like if there were no policemen or postmen?
Debbie:	I don't think it would be very good. There probably would be a lot of people who would hurt other people.
Mrs. Jones:	That's too bad isn't it? You may be right. But what about the postman? Chuck?
Chuck:	Well, for one thing, we wouldn't ever get any letters or packages. There would be no way to send things.
Mrs. Jones:	Good ideas! Barbara, this might be kind of a hard question, but, who do you think helps our community the most? The policeman or the postman?
Barbara:	I think the policeman.
Mrs. Jones:	Why?

You may have noticed that Mr. Smith jumps from subtopic to subtopic requesting factual information without ever going into depth on any one aspect of the major topic. Some students are not enjoying the discussion either (e.g. Harry); their answers are correspondingly narrow and brief. Mr. Smith would be well advised to structure his questions in such a fashion that students are challenged to think about relevant points and build on them.

Mrs. Jones, on the other hand, is more systematic in her style of questioning. Mrs. Jones asks students for factual information and for descriptions (explanations). Mrs. Jones even seeks out student ideas using "what if" questions. Student judgments are also requested. Clearly, Mr. Smith and Mrs. Jones are quite different in their styles of questioning.

Teachers like Mr. Smith have traditionally developed knowledge level thinking while openly stating the value of higher level mental performance; the inconsistency is evident. If students are to understand what is taught at a variety of levels of thought, questions at a variety of cognitive levels must be used. Teachers, like Mrs. Jones, who use higher level questions in their instruction tend to elicit higher level questions from their students. These teachers are actually modeling desired student behavior. Since many studies have shown that teachers use primarily knowledge and comprehension level questions, it is expected that student understanding of the material will more than likely remain at these lower levels of cognition. In order to aid students in performance at the higher levels, questions must frequently be used at these levels; thus, if teachers incorporate questions at a variety of cognitive levels, students will be aided in thinking and performing at a variety of levels. Perhaps Mr. Smith's students would have an opportunity to perform at higher levels if he would provide greater structure and development in some of his questions.

As you read through the next section on classifying teacher questions, try to recall some of the questions used by Mr. Smith and Mrs. Jones. By learning more about the classification of teacher questions, you will come to appreciate the skills displayed by Mrs. Jones. The ability to ask good questions does not develop naturally. Mrs. Jones has obviously done a great deal of preparation in developing this aspect of her instructional style.

2.2. Classifying Teacher Questions

Many attempts have been made to develop a classification system for teacher questions which accurately characterizes the thought level required of the student answering the question. One of the most functional systems was developed by Gallagher and Aschner (1963). This observation system, based on Guilford's model for the structure of the intellect (Guilford, 1959), is used for analyzing what is termed the quality of thinking in classrooms. The major categories of this observation system were (1) cognitive-memory,

(2) convergent thinking, (3) divergent thinking, (4) evaluative thinking, and (5) routine. The question classification system advocated in this text is a modification of those categories generated by Gallagher and Aschner. This system is not offered as a panacea to solve all question-asking problems of teachers but as a means of studying and analyzing one's own questions. In this modification, only the levels, or types, of questions dealing with the cognitive domain are considered: *COGNITIVE-MEMORY, CONVERGENT, DIVERGENT,* and *EVALUATIVE.* The four levels constitute a hierarchy; that is, they are ranked, with cognitive-memory being the lowest and evaluative being the highest. A basic assumption of this classification system is that a question asked at a given level will produce thought and subsequent response at the same level. The teacher who asks a cognitive-memory question will get a cognitive-memory response. Each of the four major categories are discussed in the following paragraphs.

Cognitive-Memory Questions

By definition, cognitive-memory questions require a recall of previously learned and memorized knowledge. This represents such a low level of thought involved in responding to the question that responses often require only single-word answers. Even more lengthy responses to this type of question do not require creative thought; student answers tend to sound alike and are predictable. Cognitive-memory questions typically require such behaviors as *RECALLING, RECOGNIZING,* and *REPORTING.* The following are examples of questions at this level of cognition:

- What is the sum of two plus seven?
- Why did we say that Indians are sometimes called the native Americans?
- Who painted the Mona Lisa?
- How many cogs are on this gear?

Convergent Questions

As the previous examples indicate, cognitive-memory questions involve the recall of factual knowledge or an explanation of a past experience or observation. Convergent questions, on the other hand, refer to a broader type of questioning which requires the respondent to put facts or concepts together in order to obtain the single correct answer. To classify a question correctly as convergent, it must be assumed that the respondent has not merely provided a memorized response. Thus, many convergent questions are responded to in the students' own words. The respondents provide the single correct answer resulting from their interrelating of different facts or concepts. Convergent questions may require students to *MAKE COMPARISONS*, to *EXPLAIN FACTS OR CONCEPTS, STATE OR DESCRIBE RELATIONSHIPS*, or *SOLVE PROBLEMS* using learned procedures. The following are examples of convergent questions:

- How many sandwiches would you have left at the end of the day if you came to school with three and only ate one?
- What is the relationship between crude oil and plastic?
- How are amphibians and reptiles alike?
- How are present methods of communication different from those used in the past?

Divergent Questions

The third category of this question classification system describes those questions which expand on the convergent category by allowing more than one possible correct answer. In other words, the respondent is expected to engage in a divergence of thought and produce a response which is original for that respondent. Students answering such questions carry on higher levels of thought by organizing elements into new patterns. As teachers enter this broad questioning level, predictability in student response is reduced. Student responses, by the very nature of this level, should be unique and novel. Questions classified as divergent may require students to *PREDICT, HYPOTHESIZE,* or *INFER*. Expressions such as "what if" are quite common to questions classified as divergent. The following are examples of divergent questions:

- What do you think our society will be like in one hundred years?
- If you were in charge of the school, what is the first thing you would do?

- What kinds of problems might occur if the use of DDT were legalized in this country?
- What would our class be like if we couldn't use our desks anymore?

Evaluative Questions

The highest category of thought is termed evaluative; in responding to evaluative questions, the student must make judgments based on logically derived evidence. The evidence is derived from the use of the levels of thought described in the other three categories. Students must defend their judgments based upon criteria that they designate or which have been established by others. In either case, reasons for judgment must be implied or explicitly stated. Response to evaluation level questions, in effect, represents a two-part intellectual procedure. First, a decision must be made or a stance identified. Second, the reason supporting the decision or stance must be communicated. Evaluative questions require students to *MAKE JUDGMENTS*, as well as to *DEFEND THEIR POSITIONS*. The following are examples of evaluative questions:

- Should we change to electric cars in this country? Why?
- Which is the better numeration system — the Roman or Arabic system? Why do you think this?
- Which is the best nursery rhyme we have heard? Why?
- Do you think that people are more inquisitive today than in the past? Why do you think this?

We strongly recommend that you occasionally classify your questions according to appropriate cognitive levels using the classification system advocated. An audiotape made during a classroom discussion will reveal valuable information that can be of great assistance to you when analyzing your ability to ask questions at the different levels. Analyzing questions in such a fashion is certainly not the only means of improving instructional efforts, but the reward in doing so, in terms of better planning and increased student achievement, will be well worth the effort.

To determine if you are prepared to effectively analyze your own questions, classify each of the following questions as either cognitive-memory (CM), convergent (C), divergent (D), or evaluative (E).

1. What is four divided by two?
2. Which do you think is more important to life, clean water or clean air? Explain.
3. Suppose that from this point on all poets were men, how might poetry be different in the future?
4. Who discovered the vaccine for polio?
5. What is one secondary color?
6. In what ways are living in a big city and going to a big school the same?
7. How do you think our country would be different if there were three major political parties instead of two?
8. If you could go anywhere on a vacation, where would you go? Why?
9. What do you think it would be like to live under a dictator rather than a president?
10. What is the difference between soccer and rugby?
11. What punctuation is used at the end of an interrogative sentence?
12. What are some things man still needs to invent?

ANSWERS: (1) CM, (2) E, (3) D, (4) CM, (5) CM, (6) C, (7) D, (8) E, (9) D, (10) C, (11) CM, (12) D

Hopefully, you got at least ten of the twelve questions correct. If you did not do well, it would be beneficial to review the definitions and examples which were provided. If by chance you are still having difficulties, study the definitions and examples once again and keep in mind that the goal is to learn to plan and use questions at the various cognitive levels. The ability to classify the questions of others in isolated situations is perhaps not as crucial.

2.3. Planning Questions

Asking students who are unfamiliar with a lesson topic large numbers of divergent and evaluative questions could prove to be quite fruitless because, in order to reach these levels, careful preparation is needed. Students must have experiences with the topic at the lower levels before they will have the necessary background experiences to really profit from higher level questions. Thus, teachers should plan a variety of questions in advance of class discussion.

For example, if you were to plan a lesson on "General Ecology," it would be a good idea to plan questions at each cognitive level to help guide your presentation. Of course, it would be unwise to try to plan all questions in advance; this could lead to an inflexible, stilted approach where you would merely read questions, pausing only long enough for brief student responses. You should allow opportunities for student response and build upon these as the lesson progresses. All that is needed in advance is a few questions at the various levels to stimulate your thinking as the discussion progresses so that a logical questioning sequence may be followed. For the topic "General Ecology," you could plan questions such as the following:

Cognitive Memory:
In what year was the first federal legislation passed to protect our environment?

Convergent:
What is the difference between ecology and conservation?

Divergent:
What might happen to the world if people stopped being concerned about ecology?

Evaluative:
Which do you think is more important, our environment or our industrial growth? Why?

Write at least one question at each of the four levels using a topic of your choice. Try to think of questions that you might actually use if you were going to lead the discussion. Compare the questions you write with those of a study partner or consult with your instructor.

2.4. Guidelines For Effective Questioning

Planning questions according to cognitive levels, of course, is only one aid in improving the quality of classroom questions. A teacher should also consider such characteristics of questions as clarity, sequence, and frequency. Figure 3-3 presents some of the "do's and don'ts" of good questions and questioning strategies as an aid in identifying effective characteristics. Examination of these important points will help in developing successful questioning strategies.

Formative Evaluation: Section 2[*]

1. Classify each of the following questions as Cognitive Memory (CM), Convergent (C), Divergent (D), or Evaluative (E).

   _____ What role does photosynthesis play in the growth of plants?

   _____ On the average, how long can a person live without food?

   _____ What is the name of one poem written by Robert Frost?

   _____ What is the largest city in the United States?

   _____ Who do you think has the most difficult job, the painter or the carpenter? Why?

   _____ Given all possibilities, what has been man's greatest invention? Why?

   _____ How does a telescope work?

   _____ What is the name of this numeral?

   _____ If you found yourself on a deserted island, what possessions do you think might be helpful to have with you?

   _____ How many millimeters are in a meter?

2. Assume you were going to teach a lesson on the topic "American Revolution." What questions might you preplan? Write two examples of questions at each of the four levels.

3. Describe three each of the "do's" and "don'ts" of effective questioning.

---

[*]See the Appendix for suggested answers to these questions.

DO's	DON'T's

DO's

Write out beforehand, in a logical sequence, the key questions to be asked during the lesson.

Listen to student answers carefully and phrase subsequent questions accordingly. Be flexible and deviate from the planned sequence as necessary.

Ask questions at a variety of cognitive levels, not just low (cognitive-memory, convergent) or high (divergent, evaluative). In addition, strive to include variety in the phrasing of questions.

Provide ample time for students to respond, especially to those questions requiring higher levels of thought. Rowe (1969) studied the problem of giving students enough "wait-time" to answer questions and found that the average wait-time before the teacher rephrased the question, asked another student to answer, or answered the question for the student was *LESS THAN ONE* second. This is clearly not long enough to develop quality answers.

Consider the ability and maturity levels of students in deciding what questions to ask. Students with lesser ability will only be frustrated by a question which is *FAR* above their ability. However, challenging questions can sometimes provide the necessary motivation for able students to encourage them to achieve at the higher cognitive levels.

On occasion, repeat or rephrase students' responses. Such behavior serves to reinforce their efforts. However, avoid overdoing this; students may begin to ignore listening to one another while expecting the teacher to repeat all important information.

Systematically record classroom questions; use these recordings to analyze and develop questioning skills. Such recording and analysis encourages the development of this essential skill for effective instruction.

DON'T's

Do not ask questions which encourage a choral response such as: "Why did the President order an embargo, class?" It is often better to address a single student by name following a question to avoid a choral response.

Do not make extensive use of rhetorical or leading questions. Such questions serve little purpose, and they occasionally confuse the students.

Do not ask fill-in-the-blank type questions such as "The formula for density is *WHAT?*" These questions tend to catch students unaware and create confusion. It is much better to initially phrase the question clearly and unambiguously; for example, "What is the formula for density?"

Do not make frequent use of questions which call for a "yes or no" answer such as "Was Sitting Bull an Apache chief?" Such questions could encourage guessing by allowing students a fifty-fifty chance of arriving at the correct response; these responses could provide the teacher with inappropriate feedback concerning the students' progress.

Do not ask questions using complex language which causes ambiguities.

Do not ask questions which are actually two questions in one such as "Who discovered America and where was he from?"

Do not use questions which actually allow a variety of correct responses when only one correct response is desired. Such a question as "Which is our largest state?" might be confusing in that either geographic size or population could be thought of by the student.

Figure 3-3. Do's and don'ts of effective questioning.

REFERENCES

Biehler, R., and Snowman, J. *Psychology applied to teaching* (4th ed.). Boston: Houghton Mifflin, 1982.

Bloom, B. *Human characteristics and school learning.* New York: McGraw-Hill, 1976.

Gallagher, J., and Aschner, M. A preliminary report of the analysis of classroom interaction. *Merrill-Palmer Quarterly,* 1963, (9), 183–194.

Good, T., and Brophy, J. *Looking in classrooms.* New York: Harper and Row, 1973.

Guilford, J. Three faces of intellect. *American Psychologist,* 1959, (14), 469–479.

Hoetker, J., and Ahlbrand, U. The persistence of recitation. *American Educational Research Journal,* 1969, (6), 145–167.

Hunt, J. The implications of changing ideas on how children develop intellectually. *Children,* 1964, 11(3), 83–91.

Piaget, J. *Science of education and psychology of the child.* New York: Orion Press, 1970.

Rosenshine, B. Enthusiastic teaching: A research review. *The School Review,* 1970, (78), 499–515.

Rowe, M. Science, silence, and sanctions. *Science and Children,* 1969, 6(6).

Taba, H., Levine, S., and Elzey, F. *Thinking in elementary school children.* U.S. Department of Health, Education, and Welfare, U.S. Office of Education, Cooperative Research Project No. 1574, San Francisco: San Francisco State College, 1964.

CHAPTER FOUR

THE TEACHER AS
AN INSTRUCTIONAL STRATEGIST

Planning the procedures portion of any lesson, regardless of the type of information to be communicated (e.g. facts or concepts), requires that the teacher select or develop appropriate strategies to accomplish the lesson objectives. This chapter examines several specific instructional strategies from which a teacher might develop learning experiences which are both varied and stimulating. It is felt that there are many good strategies that can be used in instruction; nevertheless, each strategy has identifiable characteristics which may make it more effective in some instances than in others. Strategy selection should be based primarily on the correlation of objectives to be completed with the readiness of the students. Readiness may be thought of in a very broad sense to include mastery of prerequisites, motivation level, and developmental stage. Of course, the teacher must also consider such factors as time requirements, resources available, and cost demands of each strategy. In order to choose an instructional strategy for a given objective or set of objectives, the effective teacher must be aware of the salient characteristics of each strategy as well as its most appropriate area of application.

Instructional strategy, as used in this text, refers to the general, planned teaching procedure utilized by the teacher to aid students in the accomplishment of stated objectives. It is important to note that procedures which are not purposely planned should not be really referred to as instructional strategies. The spontaneous change of instructional procedure in mid-lesson should only be referred to as an instructional strategy if the change is accompanied by purposeful planning on the part of the teacher. This important flexibility is frequently called into operation instantaneously.

115

Effective teachers are prepared for these moments; while they often do change their instructional procedures, their changes are still made with initial instructional purposes in mind.

Strategies may be classified into two broad categories: those which involve individual students and those which involve groups of varying sizes up to and including the entire class (see Fig. 4-1). However, the purpose of each strategy, whether individual or group, remains the same: to aid the learner in accomplishing stated objectives.

GROUP STRATEGIES		INDIVIDUAL STRATEGIES
Guided Inquiry	Lecture	Instructional Contracts
Demonstration	Discussion	Learning Activity Packages
Panel	Laboratory	Learning Centers
Field Trip/ Guest Speakers	Game	Independent Study Projects
Drill		

Figure 4-1. Types of instructional strategies.

Other means of classifying strategies are often used. For example, overall strategies involving frequent lectures, demonstrations, and teacher-led discussions have been classified as direct instruction (Barr & Dreeben, 1977). This type of instructional endeavor has received much recent acclaim. Regardless of how one chooses to classify strategies, an important point to be made is that a variety should be considered and an eclectic approach which involves the selection of the best strategy for the students involved should be utilized.

The use of instructional media has not been described as a discrete instructional strategy because media could and, really, should be incorporated in virtually all strategies. The use of media serves as a variation in the learning stimulus and tends to improve student motivation and subsequent achievement.

After studying this chapter, you should be able to complete the following performances:

1. Design the procedures portion of a lesson using any *one* of the following group strategies: guided inquiry, lecture, demonstration, discussion, panels/debates/committees, field trip, drill, laboratory, or instructional game.
2. Design procedures for a lesson using *two* of the above group strategies.
3. Develop an instructional contract.
4. Plan a Learning Activity Package for a selected unit of instruction.
5. Describe procedures for the incorporation of learning centers or individual student projects in a unit of study.

SECTION 1. GROUP INSTRUCTIONAL STRATEGIES

Group instructional strategies are those approaches involving at least two students and may include the entire class; group size usually varies considerably depending on the nature of the objectives and the rate of progress common to the learners involved. The strategies enumerated and described in the following paragraphs are, by no means, exclusive nor exhaustive. For example, a typical teacher-led discussion may have elements of inquiry and lecture within the same lesson. By the same token, a combination of strategies might be thought of as a discrete category. Therefore, virtually any listing of strategies is not exhaustive of all possibilities.

It has become obvious to educators attempting to classify strategies that a single best all-purpose strategy does not exist. For example, an inquiry lesson in a mathematics lab may have the effect of producing a very stimulating set of learning experiences, including observation and manipulation of materials, that results in desirable student achievement. On the other hand, a brief lecture in that same class could also be stimulating and culminate in many positive learner outcomes. Inquiry and lecture lessons tend to be quite different due to role expectations for both students and teachers. Moreover, any two lessons that seem to be similar in structure and role expectation may produce vastly different learning outcomes.

1.1. Guided Inquiry

As a strategy relevant for students of all ages, the guided inquiry approach is the only strategy considered here which may be best defined in terms of what the students do rather than specific teacher behaviors. When used with very young children, care should be given to adjust expectations to the intellectual level and attention span of the learning group. In this approach, the role of the students is to engage in problem solving: beginning and conducting investigations of phenomena. While doing so, students not only learn about the topic being investigated but, at the same time, learn how to learn on their own. The inquiry process is often described as being made up of the following procedural steps: (1) statement of the problem, (2) development of a hypothesis, (3) collection of relevant data, (4) analysis of data, (5) interpretation of results, and (6) reporting of conclusions and generalizations. The teacher's role is primarily that of a guide using effective questioning techniques, giving good directions, and providing quality resource assistance. The teacher is also responsible for helping the students, when appropriate, with the investigation, selection, or development of problems and/or situations to investigate. Teaching through inquiry is, then, a process of developing and testing ideas and, as such, should be approached systematically. Figure 4-2 presents an outline of the major steps of a guided inquiry strategy and indicates the associated teacher responsibilities.

The following is an example of how a teacher might incorporate the steps outlined in Figure 4-2 into the introductory lesson of a unit of instruction which incorporates the guided inquiry strategy:

> Mrs. Green often uses a guided inquiry method in her fourth grade classroom. One of her favorite lessons is based on the problem: What are the French people like? She gives the students an opportunity to form hypotheses, then gives them French coins and stamps to examine. Her first eliciting

STEPS	TEACHER RESPONSIBILITIES
1. Statement of the Problem:	aid in problem selection, clarify problem(s) through a question/answer session, help make problem(s) meaningful and managable.
2. Development of Hypotheses:	elicit hypotheses through questioning, accept all relevant hypotheses, help clarify hypotheses, aid students in focusing on a managable number of hypotheses.
3. Collection of Relevant Data:	serve as a resource for the development of data collection methods, guide students to other sources of data, provide references to the extent possible, allow classroom time for students to collect data if necessary.
4. Analysis of Data:	use questions to clarify data, investigate the different sources of data utilized, organize all data collected.
5. Interpretation of Results:	identify relationships among data collected, conduct data interpretation session(s), aid students in the development of conclusions and generalizations related to the original hypotheses.
6. Reporting of Conclusions and Generalizations:	provide a system of reporting (e.g., data gathering committees present oral reports) or help students determine what types of conclusions and reporting are necessary for their problem.

Figure 4-2. Steps in the guided inquiry strategy.

question — "What do you see?" — encourages the students to enumerate the data. The students then write down everything they see on the stamps and coins. Mrs. Green then asks the students: "How would you group this information?" The students then look at their data and put them into categories, after which Mrs. Green leads the students to label these categories (e.g. symbols, people, buildings). Finally, the students are encouraged to form generalizations about the French people. Mrs. Green asks the students to tell the class what they think the French people are like based solely on the data found on their national currency and postage stamps.

Following such an introductory lesson, Mrs. Green's students have developed tentative hypotheses of what the French people are like. Either as groups or individuals, Mrs. Green will send the students into further areas of investigation to include such subtopics as religion, politics, family life, and industry. Once this investigation is complete, Mrs. Green will bring the students back together and assist them in testing their hypotheses and in forming realistic conclusions and generalizations.

Young people are natural inquirers; they wish to learn. The preceding statement is true, although formal schooling will, all too frequently, have a negative effect on some student's natural inquiry. The typical rote memory approach to education (e.g. "Who discovered America?") tends, at best, to stifle the natural curiosity of the learner. What is needed is a strategy, such as guided inquiry, which incorporates these natural tendencies and utilizes them to the advantage of the learner. Teachers, like Mrs. Green, incorporate a guided inquiry approach and tend to move beyond the "facts" to work with "bigger ideas" and thus provide students with an opportunity to display their natural tendencies to inquire. The modeling of a systematic approach to the solution of problems through guided inquiry provides valuable experience for students. This will enable the students to become better at solving problems and making related decisions. Clearly, if learners become involved with something that interests and challenges them, they will become motivated to deal with other problem situations, particularly if the guided inquiry procedures used by the teacher are designed to produce success.

A guided inquiry approach may be used when the lesson's goal is to have the student investigate a particular situation and form generalizations. It may also be used to encourage interest in the subject matter. This strategy is probably not appropriate for lessons which focus at the knowledge and comprehension levels of cognition. Lessons which require the learner to apply, analyze, synthesize, or evaluate are the lessons which should be used to foster inquiry behavior in students. An inquiry lesson is best thought of as an experience *in* the subject matter, rather than an experience *about* the subject matter. Therein lies its greatest strength; learners are apt to develop a much more realistic conception of the subject matter at hand. Another strength of the guided inquiry approach is the opportunity provided the learner to use the higher levels of thinking (application-evaluation). In doing so, a set of thinking skills develops which is, to some degree, transferable to other subject matter areas. The guided inquiry approach also has a definite advantage in that it builds interest in the subject matter being considered as well as interest in learning in general. It motivates the learner to think: an often rewarding and always necessary process.

A consideration, not to be taken lightly, when using this strategy is that it is demanding. Teachers may find it much easier and more convenient to go into the classroom and page through a typical textbook or set of worksheets with their students and concentrate on factual material. In inquiry, you must develop effective questions and directions to guide students through the lesson. Problems and situations to be investigated must be selected with care and attention given to the previous cognitive development of the learner (i.e. cognitive readiness) and the abstract nature of the lesson to be learned. Teacher questions must also be preplanned in the same manner. While teachers may find it easy to ask many questions, the object in guided inquiry is to ask questions which aid the learner in understanding, applying, and internalizing the inquiry process along with the content under study. Questions at all cognitive levels are needed, rather than just those at the lower or even the higher levels.

An additional characteristic that makes guided inquiry a complex approach is that it is not intended for the delivery of large amounts of material at the knowledge and comprehension levels of cognition. Such material is, however, often necessary, for it provides the foundation for future inquiry and learning; accordingly, inquiry allows time for assimilation of these facts and concepts for the development of new thoughts. If time is needed in class to provide large amounts of material, then guided inquiry would not be an appropriate strategy. A more effective means of accomplishing such a task might be an expository presentation such as the lecture strategy. Essentially, you, the teacher, will have more control over the amount of information that each learner is exposed to and the rate at which the information is delivered when the lecture approach is used as opposed to guided inquiry. The following checklist, adapted from Sugrue and Sweeney (1969), may prove to be helpful in analyzing your approach to guided inquiry teaching.

AM I AN INQUIRY TEACHER?

	Yes	No
• I focus on lessons involving exploration of significant ideas, concepts, or problem areas that can be investigated at many levels of sophistication.	____	____
• I prepare for a broad range of alternative ideas which the students may raise related to a central topic.	____	____
• I select materials and learning experiences to stimulate student curiosity and support student investigation.	____	____
• I make available a wide variety of resources and materials for student use.	____	____
• My introductory lessons present some problem, question, contradiction, or unknown element that will maximize student thinking.	____	____
• My aim is for students to react freely to the introductory stimulus with little direction from me.	____	____
• I encourage many different responses to a given introductory stimulus and am prepared to deal with alternative patterns of exploration.	____	____
• The students talk more than I do.	____	____
• Students are free to discuss and interchange their ideas.	____	____
• When I talk, I "question," not "tell."	____	____

- I consciously use the ideas students have raised and base my statements and questions on their ideas.   _____ _____
- I redirect student questions in such a way that students are encouraged to arrive at their own answers.   _____ _____
- My questions are intended to lead the students to explore, explain, support, and evaluate their ideas.   _____ _____

1.2. Lecture

The lecture approach is clearly a much more direct strategy than inquiry. It involves telling students that which you wish them to learn; that is, information is presented orally by the teacher in its final form. Whether it is the first grade teacher telling the class about the zoo, or the secondary teacher explaining the relationship between proper punctuation and good communication, the emphasis is on the teacher telling students what they need to know. Students must learn the information just as it is presented to them. An adage, of unknown origin, may serve to further define the lecture strategy:

Tell 'em what you're gonna' tell 'em,
Tell 'em
Then, tell 'em that you told 'em.

In this fashion, the lecture strategy typically involves the teacher making a formal presentation to the entire class with minimal involvement by the students. Informative lecturers often illustrate their lectures through the use of varied audiovisual aids such as models or overhead transparencies. Some teachers also make extensive use of the chalkboard. When this is the case, the term *"chalk-talk"* is sometimes used to describe such lectures. Illustrating the lecture serves the important purpose of aiding in the maintenance of student interest.

Most teachers can plan and organize the content of a good lecture. However, to insure effectiveness, they must also have the content very firmly in mind and organized to such a degree as to be intelligible and interesting to all members of the class. Teacher clarity becomes a vital issue. As stated earlier, the primary strength of the lecture strategy lies in the fact that large amounts of material can be delivered in a short period of time. Occasions exist, at all grade levels, when this may be both necessary and desirable. Such occasions are fewer in number with young children, however. Although this strategy is used extensively in higher education settings, keep in mind that such settings are not always the best source of good instructional strategies to meet individual needs. In other words, avoid the "teacher as professor" syndrome; extensive use of lectures can be counterproductive at the public school level.

When preparing a lecture presentation, a number of important considerations should be kept in mind. Most authorities agree that the following is the role of the teacher when presenting a lecture.

The teacher should:
1. Relate the presentation of new information to that which the students have already learned
2. Begin the lesson with an "attention grabber" (see Chap. 3)
3. Project confidence in understanding the material
4. Present the selected content for instruction in a logically ordered sequence
5. Solicit verbal feedback through questioning
6. Monitor student nonverbal behavior to determine receptivity
7. Use voice inflections and animated body movements
8. Be receptive to student questions during the presentation
9. Use audiovisual aids to provide appropriate stimulus variation

If poorly planned or inappropriately used, the lecture strategy can definitely lack stimulation for learners. This, obviously, is an important consideration when preparing to use this approach. Students, particularly those in the elementary and middle grades, prefer active involvement. Contrarily, the lecture strategy relegates the learner to a distinctively passive role. This tends to limit the amount of teacher-student interaction which is needed for a complete evaluation of the instructive process. In general, the lecture approach is more appropriate for older learners pursuing large volumes of lower level cognitive material. This observation reinforces a very important characteristic of the lecture strategy; it is generally limited to the knowledge and comprehension levels of cognition with greater emphasis at the knowledge level. Only infrequently, students are accorded an opportunity to develop higher levels of thought. If inappropriately employed, a lecture may go from the teacher's notes to the learner's notebook without ever passing through the "mind" of either individual. Nevertheless, some (e.g. Ausubel, 1968; Ausubel and Robinson, 1969) have suggested that lecture is the most efficient method of instruction with abstract thinkers if the teacher can clearly tie the new information being presented to information the students have already learned.

1.3. Demonstrations

Unlike a lecture, which is essentially telling students that which you wish them to learn, a demonstration primarily involves showing. For example, the kindergarten teacher demonstrating how to tie the laces on a shoe, the elementary teacher demonstrating proper substraction procedures on the chalkboard, or the secondary teacher demonstrating how to put a new ribbon in a typewriter are all instances of teachers using this showing approach. If done properly, a good demonstration can be like a picture— worth a thousand words. In a demonstration, students are afforded the opportunity of looking at something instead of merely talking about it. In practice, a demonstration is what often takes place when teachers actually intend to conduct an experiment. True experiments require the guided inquiry strategy, not the demonstration approach. Regrettably, few real experiments are done in public schools. Most are classroom demonstrations wherein the expected outcomes are already known in advance by the teachers and often by the students. Be that as it may, students are often better able to make a visual analysis in route to understanding the concept or modeling the expected behavior after watching a demonstration.

Effective demonstrations require very careful planning; adequate preparation should include practicing the demonstration prior to making the classroom presentation. Such practice of the demonstration serves to determine if the procedure actually works or provides the expected results. The teacher also has an opportunity during the practice session to compose more fully an appropriate narrative and set of questions to guide the students through the lesson. Although demonstrations are mostly showing, verbal communication by the teacher is of utmost importance. Most effective demonstrations have extensive guiding questions which accompany a narrative produced by the teacher. It may even be necessary and appropriate in some demonstrations, particularly those dealing with abstract concepts, to include written guide sheets or other materials to be used by the students.

Teacher demonstrations fall into two basic categories: (1) those concerning the demonstrations of phenomena or events which students are unable to do for themselves and (2) those which are of an explanatory-directive nature which require the student, at a later time, to complete the demonstrated task resulting in a product or an improvement in a process or skill.

A basic strength of an effective demonstration is that it provides a concrete example. Facts may be illustrated and verified for students. Obviously, some abstract concepts can be made more meaningful (e.g. molecular structure, appropriate telephone manners, or factoring) and thus understandable by demonstrating concrete instances of the concept. Also, through illustrative demonstrations, students may sharpen observational skills such as effective listening. Moreover, a demonstration has the characteristic of being a strategy which may substitute for students actively doing something for themselves. In this instance, the teacher may provide a demonstration of that which may be too dangerous or time consuming for students to do for themselves or for which sufficient materials are lacking. Indeed, through demonstrations, teachers may more expediently build concepts for students rather than letting them, alone, acquire the information. All points considered, demonstrations are also usually very economical in terms of time, materials, and effort.

A key consideration when selecting the demonstration strategy is the somewhat passive role assumed by the student. As mentioned previously, many students prefer active involvement, and there is evidence that more meaningful learning does take place when learners are actively involved. A continuing concern about demonstrations is that viewing problems are also frequently evident. To be effective, everyone must be able to see the demonstration; this is not always easy in a classroom of twenty to thirty students. This disadvantage may be alleviated somewhat by the use of instructional media such as the overhead projector or videotape recorder. If facilities and equipment are available, the teacher may wish to videotape a demonstration that is difficult to see. This technique has the advantage of providing the means for individual student viewing, or reviewing of the demonstration, and of keeping a successful demonstration for future classes as well as for students who missed the initial demonstration. A further limitation of a demonstration becomes evident if the strategy is poorly correlated with ongoing instruction. Students may, in this case, perceive the demonstration as merely a "show" or diversion. It is essential that teachers conscientiously deal with this problem and, through effective planning and explanation, insure the relevance of all demonstrations. Even when this is done, the best-planned demonstrations sometimes fail and do not communicate the intended results. This is particularly true of the classroom "experiment" type of demonstration; the intended event simply may not occur as expected. Wise teachers usually take advantage of this situation, in that opportunities are now generated for student inquiry by asking the question, "Why did it not work out as we expected?"

Figure 4-3 presents an outline of the major responsibilities of a teacher conducting a demonstration.

1.4. Discussion Sessions

The teacher-led discussion session is probably the most commonly used strategy at all levels of elementary and secondary education. Therefore, discussion sessions must be planned carefully to complement other strategies. Although some class discussions are essentially off-task conversations, the true class discussion is a type of purposeful interaction designed to achieve stated objectives and is characterized by active student verbal participation.

```
THE TEACHER SHOULD:

    1.  arrange seating so that everyone can see and hear,

    2.  begin with a short overview,

    3.  outline the main points in handouts, on the
        chalkboard, or on the overhead projector,

    4.  elicit verbal or physical participation by students,

    5.  conclude with a short question/answer session to
        clarify main points, and

    6.  provide immediate practice opportunities for
        maximum effect.
```

Figure 4-3. Major responsibilities of a teacher conducting a demonstration.

While this strategy may contain elements of both inquiry and lecture, extensive student-initiated interaction and participation is its defining characteristic. Discussion sessions work best if students feel free to participate and believe that their input is valued by their teacher and classmates. These feelings are engendered by teachers who acknowledge the importance of other views, who refer to others during the discussion, and who are overtly authoritative.

Teachers often select this strategy because it aids in the development of certain positive learner attributes: open-mindedness, flexibility of thinking, and objectivity. A good discussion session has several other advantages. It can quickly tie student interests and personal experiences to the subject under discussion. This serves not only to increase the value of student experiences but to enhance interest in the academic subject and encourage participation. A further strength of the strategy is that it allows for the development of higher level thought processes by students. When students are encouraged to publicly present their ideas and feelings, they receive the feedback necessary for effective analysis of their own thinking processes. Teachers can facilitate this process by carefully planning their questions in advance in order to move students from lower to higher levels of thinking (see Chap. 3). Reflective analysis of one's thought processes tends to lead to improvement. The more thought processes are analyzed, the more sophisticated these processes are apt to become. Figure 4-4 presents the responsibilities of the teacher when planning for effective instruction during a class discussion.

THE TEACHER SHOULD:

1. Prepare objectives and organize content to structure the discussion

2. Provide background information and resources

3. Use key preplanned questions to guide

4. Encourage student-to-student interaction (e.g. arrange seating in circle)

5. Accept student contributions as worthwhile

6. Expand upon student contributions

7. Encourage non-volunteers to participate (without them feeling threatened)

8. Keep digressions to a minimum (return to the topic as soon as possible)

9. Use short summaries throughout to maintain focus

Figure 4-4. Guidelines for effective discussions.

A procedure often used to facilitate discussion sessions is called *BRAINSTORMING*. The purpose of brainstorming is to generate a large variety of ideas concerning a specific problem/situation in a short time period which are then typically used in the discussion. The teacher, using brainstorming procedures, acts as a facilitator by making sure that certain basic procedures are followed as outlined below.

The teacher:

1. Identifies a problem/situation (perhaps with the help of the students)

2. Explains the purpose of the session and encourages everyone to participate regardless of their ideas
3. States that ideas are not to be discussed or evaluated during the session
4. Writes contributions as they are presented using the chalkboard or overhead projector
5. Encourages a rapid pace and completes the session in a short time period (usually less than 10 minutes)

After the brainstorming session, the teacher helps the class to categorize and clarify the ideas and contributions for the discussion to follow.

When you use the discussion strategy, you should remember that it may become very time consuming. In fact, the discussion is thought by many to be more time consuming than most other strategies, with the exception of inquiry. A teacher must decide, while considering the objectives and other parameters of the learning environment, if the time spent is worth the anticipated gains in student motivation and learning. Following this decision, it is felt that, in almost all cases, regardless of the strategy used, effective teachers will involve their students in some discussion episodes.

1.5. Panel Discussion

A panel discussion frequently involves four to five students (one of whom generally serves as chair of the panel) who have completed study on a topic and are to share their information with the remainder of the class. The role of the teacher is similar to the one assumed when using guided inquiry, in that the teacher must assist with guidelines in the research process and assign various responsibilities to individual students. After guidelines have been established, individual students then gather information and present it, as members of a panel, to their classmates. Panel members usually make a short presentation concerning their assigned areas of study after which the panel, as individuals or a group, may respond to questions through the guidance of the chairing member. Due to the fact that young learners may lack the necessary communication, thinking, and study skills to participate successfully in the panel discussion, this strategy may be more appropriate for the upper elementary and secondary grade levels.

In order to use this strategy well, it is necessary to consider guidelines which will prevent a panel from aimlessly meandering from one member's opinion to another's. Since students often lack extensive experience in conducting and participating in well-organized discussions, they need to be prepared so that their ideas are properly specified and structured. It is suggested that a pre-panel orientation session be orchestrated by the teacher so that all panel members will have carefully identified their problems and selected and organized all important information. The teacher also should carefully choose a leader for the panel who has definite leadership qualities and cue the leader to questions that either should be anticipated from students or should be posed to other panel members. After the panel members have concluded with their remarks, the teacher, as a skillful guide, should follow up on the discussion by highlighting the salient points presented insuring closure through enumerating all important items. Figure 4-5 outlines suggestions for planning and conducting a successful panel discussion.

THE TEACHER SHOULD:

1. Identify four to six students for the panel

2. Assign responsibilities for the chairperson and others according to abilities and interests

3. Suggest and guide the development of a major topic

4. Assist students in dividing the research efforts

5. Suggest appropriate time schedules

6. Monitor students closely during their work

7. Provide summary remarks which relate to the instructional objectives

Figure 4-5. Suggestions for planning and implementing panel discussions.

Panel discussions are particularly useful for "current events" or "issues" topics such as political campaigns, censorship, and nuclear power generation. Selected topics may not only be complex, requiring considerable out-of-class preparation, but may also frequently be controversial. By dividing responsibilities among several panel members, complex and controversial topics can be more effectively discussed. A limitation of the panel discussion lies in the number of panel members; usually, few students are involved in this strategy at one time. One may find that the panel plus three or four verbal students represent the only students actually involved. In such circumstances, it is the teacher's role, as a guide and facilitator, to encourage more active involvement of the remaining students in the class. Lack of involvement may be avoided if the teacher closely adheres to the suggested guidelines previously identified.

In planning to use debate teams, it is useful to consider two types of debates: formal and informal. The formal procedure uses the same basic team makeup as two panels. In essence, you would have two chairpersons, one on each debate team, who coordinate the research on the instructional topic. During the debate, the teacher serves as moderator allowing equal time for presentation of views and rebuttals. The student chairperson leads the team and directs members to make presentations and rebuttals. The informal debate could possibly involve larger numbers of students and allow, perhaps, the entire class to participate. Once a debate topic is selected, all individuals could be assigned to opposing viewpoints after researching the topic. Thus, one-half of the class would present one viewpoint and the other half of the class another. During the debate, students volunteer to speak on the topic from the podium with each team taking turns. The teacher serves as moderator and allows each team equal time for presentation and responding to questions from the other team. Like the panel discussion, the use of debates, whether formal or informal, require considerable planning and preparation by the students and the teacher.

Another logical extension of the panel discussion strategy is that of committee work. If you are already using students in small groups for such activities as the panel discussion, you may easily incorporate committee work procedures into your instruction. To use committees successfully, a key consideration is, of course, to make the committees' task clear. You must carefully plan those areas you wish the committee to consider. As is the case with panel discussions, if you carefully structure committees according to student abilities and interests, you will have a greater chance for success. Committee members must not only be aware of the groups' charge (or task) but also be aware of the reporting procedures. The primary options for reporting are written and oral reports. A committee member could present the committees' report or the entire committee may be required to participate. The latter reporting procedure serves to involve greater numbers of students in instruction and is recommended.

1.6. Laboratory

In the laboratory strategy, students manipulate objects or equipment under the direction of the teacher. Manipulation may also refer to calculations wherein one manipulates concrete materials to solve mathematical problems as is frequently the case in the elementary classroom. A laboratory is often defined to include demonstrations as well, but a useful distinction between the two strategies is that a laboratory usually involves several small groups (e.g. teams or lab partners) working on an activity, while a demonstration, on the other hand, is typically presented by the teacher to all of the students at the same time. It should be noted that the two strategies may be combined, in that a teacher may choose to demonstrate effective laboratory techniques.

The typical laboratory activity may serve to address one or more of the following purposes:

1. To secure new knowledge and information
2. To apply previously learned concepts
3. To develop new skills and processes
4. To serve as reinforcement or verification of previously learned knowledge
5. To serve as appropriate practice to reinforce objectives already mastered

In addition, some laboratory sessions aid in clarifying the nature of the subject matter in a manner that would be possible with no other strategy. For example, science may be more realistically approached as inquiry through the effective use of laboratory experiences in which data are organized and conceptualized into unique concepts and generalizations. Figure 4-6 outlines suggestions for teacher planning and implementing a successful laboratory strategy.

An advantage of the laboratory strategy lies in its versatility; it can serve both a variety of important functions as outlined above as well as various subject matter areas (e.g. physical education, social studies, and foreign language). In addition, students are typically motivated by laboratory work because it is often a change from typical class routine and provides an opportunity for them to participate more fully in their own learning endeavors.

A definite disadvantage in some laboratory strategies is cost. If multiple copies of expensive equipment are needed, the cost of the laboratory activity may become prohibitive. Space requirements can also be a deciding factor when considering the use of a laboratory activity. In order to properly conduct laboratory experiences, you clearly need both adequate equipment and space so that active student involvement is possible. In such circumstances where adequate space and materials cannot be provided, you would be well advised to purchase only one piece of apparatus and utilize the demonstration strategy rather than deleting the experience from your students' curriculum. Extensive time required for organizing and structuring the laboratory environment, along with the considerations of space and materials, may prove to be an important influence in the eventual use of this strategy.

1.7. Field Trips/Guest Speakers

While such strategies as demonstrations and laboratories are intended to bring a portion of the "real" world into the classroom, the field trip strategy takes students out into the real world to see things for themselves. Field trips require the teacher and students to leave the classroom in order to become involved in a learning experience. Such trips may merely be to the school grounds out-

THE TEACHER SHOULD:

PRE-LABORATORY ACTIVITIES:
1. plan activities to correlate with instructional goals and objectives,
2. use demonstrations of techniques or equipment utilization as necessary,
3. provide necessary content background,
4. delineate roles and expectations for students,
5. select or develop laboratory guides,

LABORATORY EXPERIENCE:
1. allow students to work in teams of two or three,
2. serve as a facilitator and guide answering questions as needed,
3. provide adequate time for completion of the laboratory,
4. direct students to maintain records of their activities,

POST-LABORATORY ACTIVITIES:
1. once again correlate the laboratory experience with instructional objectives,
2. conduct follow-up discussions,
3. allot time for the presentation of reports/findings as necessary, and
4. evaluate the objectives if this was not built into the laboratory exercise.

Figure 4-6. Suggestions for planning and implementing a successful laboratory strategy.

side the classroom or may be more extended and involve transportation to areas far removed from the immediate school facility. The length of the trip can also vary from ten to fifteen minutes on the school grounds to an all-day or, perhaps, overnight excursion to other locales.

Since field trips may serve to introduce or conclude a unit of work and motivate students, they require extensive planning well in advance of the activity. In particular, in elementary classes where students are not as able to deal with abstract concepts, it is recommended that the teacher plan concrete experiences, such as field trips, to introduce units of instruction. Pre- and post-trip activities must be planned in order to fully capitalize on the educational significance of the trip. Other factors such as cost, transportation, and scheduling must be considered along with appropriate measures to evaluate both student outcomes and the success of the experience. As with any other strategy, the use of the field trip should be based on its relationship to the accomplishment of identified objectives. Figure 4-7 outlines the teacher's responsibility in planning and implementing a successful field trip.

Like demonstrations, field trips have the advantage of providing concrete, real-world experiences not usually available in the classroom. In addition, field trips typically generate high student interest. It is hoped that this level of motivation has not been precipitated by a strategy viewed only as an opportunity to "escape" formal classroom instruction but as a result of an opportunity to experience a relevant, concrete learning activity. An important characteristic of field trips is that they provide experiences which students could not have otherwise. A tour of a powerplant to learn, firsthand, how electricity is produced is an example of such an experience. While these visits are usually not available to the general public, school group visitations are often encouraged. Some field trips share a disadvantage with certain laboratory sessions: they may be costly. For example, if students are to be transported over fairly long distances, the expense may become prohibitive. Extended (at least one-half day) trips have another disadvantage, particularly in secondary school settings, of interfering with ongoing instruction in other classes; a field trip in one class may necessitate a student being absent in another. The amount of time devoted to planning a successful trip must also be considered. The conscientious teacher must plan carefully to insure the safety and supervision of students on a field trip. Some of the noninstructional characteristics of the field trip strategy that must be planned for, when necessary, are as follows: transportation, adult supervision, meals, advance scheduling, and on-site arrangements.

Well-conducted field trips often are good for community relations.

PRE-TRIP ACTIVITIES

Plan Instructional Components:

1. Correlate the field trip with goals and objectives.
2. Develop necessary background information.
3. Decide on safety information.
4. Define role expectations.

Plan Non-Instructional Components:

1. Secure transportation.
2. Secure adult supervision.
3. Develop schedule.
4. Calculate cost.
5. Secure permission from parents.
6. Secure sanction of the school.
7. Coordinate with on-site personnel.

Present the Instructional Components along with the essential Non-Instructional Information

TRIP ACTIVITIES

1. Serve as guide and director.

2. Assist students in information gathering.

3. Provide new information as needed.

POST-TRIP ACTIVITIES

1. Conduct a follow-up discussion or other activity to correlate field trip experience with goals and objectives.

2. Evaluate instructional objectives using student reports or the more typical testing situation.

Figure 4-7. Responsibilities in planning and implementing a field trip.

If these are coupled with an occasional guest speaker from the community, the gains in community relations can be quite substantial. Of course, community relations are not the only reason for obtaining the services of a guest speaker. Guest speakers can make instruction realistic and help to motivate students. Students are able to see applications of their instruction to real-world people and jobs. The guest speaker may also serve as a source of expertise for a topic in which the teacher does not feel adept. The use of guest speakers usually works best if students are involved in the process of obtaining and introducing the speaker. Greeting and introducing a guest speaker is also a valuable learning experience. Students should be prepared in advance with any necessary background information and encourage the speaker to allow interaction. A question-and-answer session should take place at the end of the presentation. The teacher should also provide a short discussion session to summarize the guest speaker experience with the students. Students might then be encouraged to write and mail thank-you notes to the speaker.

It is pointed out that community projects such as cleanup campaigns also have substantial rewards in the area of community relations. If individuals within the community see students and teachers taking such an interest in the community, their interest in the schools might very well be heightened. This can only lead to better school/community relations.

1.8. Instructional Games

Instructional games may be classified into two major categories: simulation and non-simulation. In simulation games, as the name implies, students simulate authentic roles and experiences (i.e. role play). By doing so, they become involved in a variety of situations before they encounter a similar real-life situation. It should be remembered that many simulation activities do not have winning or losing as an objective; the activities are designed to provide students merely with opportunities for vicarious experiences which approximate real-life situations and roles. Non-simulation games, on the other hand, do not involve role playing as an integral part of the game. Monopoly, a popular commercial board game, is a legitimate example of a non-simulation game because assuming highly specialized roles in specific situations is not required. Many non-simulation games are commercially available and various ones may be used effectively for instructional purposes. A teacher may also wish to construct a board game following procedures such as those outlined by Bedwell (1977) (see Fig. 4-8).

Simulation games have three basic components: player profiles, a scenario, and rules of procedure. The development of these components around specific objectives may be a time-consuming and complex activity requiring a great deal of lengthy preparation by the teacher. Teachers should be aware that simulation games for instructional purposes are also commercially available.

Active involvement of students, at least those directly involved in the simulation game, is a definite advantage of this strategy. Through these procedures, students realize that learning can be interesting and enjoyable and thus are typically more motivated to become actively involved. Instructional games, particularly those of a simulation nature, provide extensive opportunities for students to practice and improve their communication and decision-making skills. In such strategies, students are often required to communicate their viewpoints and listen to the ideas of others. The use of well-planned games may be a successful strategy to help clarify abstract concepts. For example, if a student is required to role play the values of another person, abstract values such as *LOVE* and *HATE* may be further clarified for that student as well as for others participating in the simulation.

A common criticism of instructional games is that they merely mimic reality; real-life situations usually are not quite as simple as instructional games might portray. This may be particularly true when games are used to clarify controversial issues. One soon realizes that there are many sides to any controversial issue; precisely, this is what produces the controversy. An additional consideration in the use of instructional games is that games can be rather time consuming, requiring both considerable planning time and a great deal of class time to complete. Beyond this difficulty, many instructional games involve only a limited number of students at a given time. Teachers sometimes find it difficult to monitor the game activity while, at the same time, attempting to guide the instructional activities of non-participating students. Due to the fact that instructional games require large amounts of

To begin developing a non-simulation game for a game
board, first select the topic, issue, or problem
to be studied and follow the steps outlined below.

Step 1. Develop Learner Objectives

Quality planning for board games is no different than other
types of quality planning; it is based on carefully prepared
learner objectives.

Step II. Prepare Evaluation Procedures

Appropriate evaluation procedures must be prepared in order
to determine both the progress of the students and the effectiveness of the game. The procedures may consist of merely
listening to students playing the game or may be a more
formal procedure such as a paper and pencil test or quiz.

Step III. Complete the Game Components

A series of questions should be prepared and printed on question cards. The answers to the questions should also be provided in some form such as on the reverse side of the cards.

Problem cards should also be prepared by writing such phrases
as "go back three" and "move ahead four".

The board itself should be prepared on durable paper or card-
board. It should consist primarily of a multi-colored path-
way for the students to traverse.

A set of rules may be developed by the teacher or in mutual
cooperation with students in the class.

Step IV. Tryout

A trial run of the game should be completed with a small group
of students, perhaps after class, and revisions based on this
experience should be completed before the game is used as part
of the curriculum.

Step V. Evaluate and Revise

Using student test scores as well as subjective impressions,
revise and improve the game for future use.

Figure 4-8. Developing a non-simulation game for a game board.

planning and organizational time, too frequently teachers spend instructional time "covering" textbook materials rather than exploring this potentially exciting approach.

Instructional games may be unsuccessful because their implementation is poorly planned. To be effective, the teacher must plan both pre- and post-game activities to facilitate learning. Such activities before and after the game are as important as playing the game (See Fig. 4-9).

THE TEACHER SHOULD:

PRE-GAME STAGE:
1) relate the game to instructional goals and objectives (students must realize that the game is a part of their on-going instruction),
2) outline the game, whether it is a simulation (role-play) or non-simulation (e.g., board) game, explaining the purpose and procedures,

DURING THE GAME:
1) firmly establish ground rules at the beginning of the game in order to avoid confusion at a later point. (Duplicated copies of the ground rules are very useful),
2) serve as a monitor and source of directions for the game or actively participate in the game (The latter is recommended whenever possible),

POST-GAME STAGE:
1) serve as a discussion leader in relating the game experience back to the original goals and objectives, and
2) conduct formal or informal evaluation keyed to the instructional objectives if it was not built into the game.

Figure 4-9. Guidelines for conducting instructional games.

1.9. Drill

The final group instructional strategy to be discussed perhaps should not be thought of as a separate strategy at all but as a component of virtually any strategy for students of all grade levels. If you expect your students to learn, not only must the stimulus material be presented but also sufficient opportunities for appropriate practice must be provided. Drill refers to actually repeating the performances described in the objectives after they have been demonstrated by the student. This strategy provides an opportunity for the student to obtain feedback—a necessary component of effective instruction (Good and Brophy, 1980; Bieler and Snowman, 1982). In fact, feedback has been described as an essential event of instruction (Gagné, 1970) and, as such, should be incorporated, to some degree, in all other strategies. Analysis of homework assignments, a common practice, can provide teachers and students with necessary feedback concerning progress. Or, a portion of class time may be set aside for an organized drill session in order that students, as well as the teacher, may obtain more immediate feedback.

If done properly, the drill strategy has the important advantage of aiding in retention through the provision of immediate feedback to the student. If students understand a concept and are able to apply it through appropriate drill, the material will be remembered longer and more completely than if students are not afforded the drill opportunity for feedback. Numerous educators, moreover, take the position that drills provide an "overlearning" which eventually aids in the retention of factual material.

It is often difficult for teachers to decide when drill in a particular area is appropriate. Drill is being used inappropriately if its main purpose is only to keep students active (i.e. "busywork"). Obviously, this is not an efficient use of instructional time. An appropriate use of drill is to provide students with an opportunity to develop competencies as described in the instructional objective. An important consideration for the teacher is the readiness level of the students to engage in a drill activity. The teacher runs the risk that students will only be practicing their errors of understanding if they lack the proper background to prepare them to do drill exercises. Figure 4-10 provides guidelines to help insure a successful drill strategy.

THE TEACHER SHOULD:

1. insure that students have an understanding of the significant concepts or skills before drill is assigned,

·2. match the practice with individual attention spans,

3. match the practice with learning abilities,

4. make certain that the drill does not seem punitive to the students,

5. when possible, move through the classroom in order to monitor progress and answer questions, and

6. provide corrective feedback as soon as possible.

Figure 4-10. Guidelines for the drill strategy.

1.10. Summary

An effective teacher is characterized by an ability to use any of the aforementioned strategies. Obviously, these strategies should not be used at random but only after careful analysis of lesson purposes, student characteristics, and instructional constraints (e.g. time, cost, and availability of materials). Frequently, teachers find it necessary to use an eclectic approach, which requires the use of multiple strategies. Figure 4-11 provides the teacher with a summary of the major considerations of those group strategies that have been presented.

Formative Evaluation: Section 1*

1. Design the procedures portion of a lesson using the discussion strategy. The lesson should deal with the following

---

*See the Appendix for suggested answers to these questions.

INSTRUCTIONAL STRATEGY	MAJOR CONSIDERATIONS
Guided Inquiry	-provides an opportunity for students to display natural tendencies to inquire -interests and challenges learners -develops higher level thinking -requires considerable planning time and expertise -does not deliver large amounts of information quickly
Lecture	-adapts easily to all content areas -delivers large amounts of information quickly -depends upon high levels of clarity in the presentation for effectiveness -requires a basic "performing" talent on the part of teachers -focuses on the knowledge and comprehension levels of thinking -can be boring if poorly presented -limits active student involvement
Demonstration	-capitalizes on the visual modality of learning -results in occasional viewing problems -is economical in terms of time, material, and effort -replaces a student's direct experiences with dangerous materials -sharpens listening and observational skills -provides concrete examples -relegates students to a somewhat passive role
Discussion Session	-compliments all other strategies -allows extensive student interaction and participation -aids in development of positive learner characteristics -aids in development of higher level thought -may be very time consuming -reduces the breadth of material which may be explored
Panel Discussion	-leads to stimulating coverage of "current events" or "issues" topics -involves, on occasion, only a limited number of students -enables students to share information with one another -aids in the development of student research skills

Laboratory

-capitalizes on active student involvement
-encourages group sharing of ideas
-clarifies the nature of the inquiry process
-can be very motivating for students
-requires extended teacher preparation
 and organization time
-is versatile in adapting to various
 instructional objectives
-may prove to be costly

Field Trip/Guest Speakers

-brings a portion of the real world to the
 student's attention
-provides experiences not normally available
 to the learner
-requires extensive planning
-offers concrete experiences
-generates high interest
-can be costly

Instructional Game

-may simulate authentic roles and
 experiences
-motivates through active student
 involvement
-enhances communication skills
-can oversimplify reality
-requires considerable planning and
 instructional time

Drill

-provides practice opportunities
-aids in retention through the provision
 of immediate feedback
-risks the practicing of errors
-is conducive to over use

Figure 4-11. Group instructional strategies.

objective: given the names of twenty common animals, identify the habitat of at least eighteen.

2. Design the procedures portion of a lesson on the same objective using a different group strategy.

3. Write an objective and design the procedures portion of a lesson plan incorporating a blend of at least two different group strategies.

SECTION 2. INDIVIDUAL INSTRUCTIONAL STRATEGIES

Individual instructional strategies are those that promote individualized instruction and are designed to be used by individual students, not groups. A review of the literature in this area reveals that individualized instruction has been defined in many different fashions by many different people; it is apparently impossible to get all educators to agree upon a single definition. Thus, regardless of its definition, true individualized instruction is an ideal to strive for and, as such, is probably difficult to attain. Nevertheless, as an ideal, it may be thought of as having the following definition: *individualized instruction is that type of instruction which is designed so that individuals are involved in learning which is commensurate with their own rates, styles, and abilities of learning.* In other words, individualized instruction may be thought of as an attempt to develop perfect instruction for each individual in the classroom. It is self-evident that to plan such instruction is difficult at best. It is perhaps more productive to consider, instead, the degree to which individualization can be obtained. Considered this way, instruction neither "is" nor "is not" individualized. Instead, some instructional endeavors are more individualized than others.

To determine the degree to which any given instructional sequence is individualized, assessment of student entry levels must be considered along with an examination of the materials provided and the variation in student time allotted for completion of the instructional objectives. A successfully individualized instructional strategy may also provide students with some choices in the resources and activities they will use to accomplish the objectives. While students may have the opportunity to choose certain activities, the making of these choices is not the final determiner in the instruction being referred to as individualized. For instruction to be individualized, each learner's style, rate, and ability must be addressed. This may or may not involve student opportunities to select content and activities to be undertaken. Therefore, instruction can be considered as individualized even though the teacher places definite limitations on student choice of both learning activities and subject matter to be mastered.

The amount of time required for achieving the objectives must also be allowed to vary to some degree among the students in the class. This is sometimes termed the "self-paced" aspect of individualized instruction. A variety of instructional materials and procedures for each objective should be provided in order to assure that learning styles and abilities of individual students are appropriately accommodated. An effective individualized instructional program does not necessarily involve each student working alone. This is a popular misconception of the individualized instruction approach.

The individual instructional strategies enumerated and described in the following paragraphs are provided as examples of strategies through which one might approach the ideal of providing for true individualized instruction.

2.1. Instructional Contracts

An instructional contract is an agreement between two or more parties, usually one teacher and one student, formed to bring about specific learning outcomes (Wiseman, 1983). The student may agree to complete contract activities as the teacher has designed them, or sit with the teacher and negotiate certain portions of the contract with alternatives being suggested. The teacher may even be presented with a student-prepared contract to approve, disapprove, or modify through negotiation.

Contracts generally involve student consideration of what may be called learning alternatives. Alternatives are learning experiences which the teacher feels represent the contract area to be studied. Typically, the student is given the opportunity to make selections related to alternatives to complete. Following a grading formula previously established, the student contracts for a specified grade. This depends upon how many, or perhaps which, alternatives are selected. It should be noted that the contract approach in no way limits the leadership role of the teacher. It merely provides an alternative form of instruction which is accompanied by a high level of student participation. Whether teacher, student, or jointly designed, the teacher gives final approval before any contract is accepted for use.

Instructional contracts are characterized by a set of basic parts which cover the entire learning procedure. The elements, together with an indication of their purpose or content, are as follows:

1. TITLE: To draw the students into the experience—should be exciting, intriguing.
2. INTRODUCTION: An explanation of what may be found in the contract—an overview of the content.
3. INSTRUCTIONAL OBJECTIVES: A list of what is to be known, performed, or accomplished through the contract activities.
4. LEARNING ALTERNATIVES: Varied choices should be provided which include opportunities for active participation in the learning experience.
5. RESOURCES AND MATERIALS: Materials necessary for the successful completion of the contract should be listed.
6. REPORTING PROCEDURES: An identification of means by which the student will show what has been accomplished.
7. CLOSING AGREEMENT: A clear listing of what grade is being contracted for, which alternatives will be completed, and any other conditions. Of course, the grade contract portion is typically omitted in early childhood settings.

In a very real sense, the use of contracts in teaching represents an effort toward individualization. You should analyze the major factors related to the use of this strategy prior to classroom implementation. Consider the following questions with their accompanying responses:

1. Who should be given a learning contract?

   Adding variety to the traditional classroom, getting to know all of the students in a more personal way, thinking of students as individuals, and involving students in curriculum decision-making activities are all worthwhile outcomes regardless of the academic level of the class. Instructional contracts can be used with all students, provided that individual learning styles are taken into consideration.

2. How long should a contract last?

   A basic guideline to follow might be that if the contract approach is new to both the teacher and students, the length of time devoted to the contract should be relatively short. As a starting point, allow perhaps a two-week maximum length for contracts to be completed, or even less for elementary students (e.g. 1 week).

3. Can contracts be broken?

   The contract must allow some form of decision-making activity on the student's part. As this is the case, changes are possible. A time will come, however, in the contracting activity where changes are no longer practical nor profitable. At some point, decisions made should be considered as final.

4. If the contracts are used in some subjects, should they be used in all subjects?

   There is no need for a teacher who elects to use contracts in one class or subject to feel that all other classes or subjects taught during the day must use contracts. All content does not lend itself to the contract strategy.

5. Who determines the guidelines for the instructional contract?

   Although the teacher has the final decision to make regarding the guidelines for this strategy, student ideas must be considered since it is presented as a means of increasing student involvement in the learning process.

The contract is an endeavor wherein student success in an engaging form of instruction is clearly possible. Learning alternatives should represent assignments which nearly all students can complete. If the contract has a hidden agenda, it is in providing relevant decision-making and confidence-building experiences. Consider the following contract designed for upper elementary level students as a model which you may refer to in constructing your own instructional contracts.

The primary strength of the contract approach is that the teacher can readily provide opportunities for student choices and a rather high degree of individualization. In addition, contracts tend to

TITLE: Why Eskimos Don't Wear Bikinis

INTRODUCTION:

Have you ever wondered what it might be like to live in an igloo? Would you like to live in a climate where the only clothing needed was a loincloth? What causes climates to be different? This contract is designed to acquaint you with the different climates and how they affect human lives.

INSTRUCTIONAL OBJECTIVES:

This contract is a Grade Contract, meaning your decision concerning the learning alternatives you choose will determine your grade for this experience.

  1. Following independent investigation, describe the influence of climate on the human life-style.

  2. Given reading, writing, and participating activities, identify the relationships between temperature, precipitation, and climate.

LEARNING ALTERNATIVES:

The following learning alternatives relate to the objectives for this contract. Those alternatives marked with an asterisk (*) must be completed. You will be graded according to the number of alternatives you select (A = 6 alternatives, B = 5 alternatives, C = 4 alternatives, D = 3 alternatives).

  1. Pretend you are taking a trip to Greenland. Make a list of the following: (a) the items you might take with you, (b) what you would expect to see during your visit, (c) the countries through which you would pass on your trip.

  2. Look at the slides on geographic areas. Write a paragraph telling how you think people living in each of the areas might make their living. Support your answers.

  *3. Choose one of the world climate regions and make a poster or collage describing that region.

  4. Find pictures of people who live in different climates and make a scrapbook. Label the climate region in which they live.

  5. Make a diagram of the sequence of mild, severe, and polar regions in relation to the equator.

  6. Find and read a short story about Eskimos, nomads, or natives who live in the tropics. Make a report to the class or put your report on a cassette tape.

  7. Write a two-page paper identifying the world climate region in which you would like to live. Tell why you would like to live in this particular region.

  *8. Write a paragraph describing the relationship of temperature and precipitation to climate.

RESOURCES AND MATERIALS:

National Geographic, newspapers and magazines, slides (geographic areas), *Follet's Atlas, Skills for Understanding Maps and Globes*

REPORTING PROCEDURES:

Your teacher will check the items you have selected and enter the date you completed them on a checklist. This will be done on conference days. At the beginning of a conference day, arrange a time for the teacher to listen to the tapes you have made.

CLOSING AGREEMENT:

I do hereby agree to fulfill the requirements for the following learning alternatives: _____. It is my understanding that by completing these alternatives I will be awarded the grade of _____ for my work on this learning contract. Number of learning alternatives selected: _____.

CONTRACT DUE DATE: SIGNED:

_____   TEACHER _____

                                     STUDENT _____

                                     DATE _____

provide more opportunities for student activities, with the teacher acting more as a planner and facilitator and less as the fountain from which all knowledge springs. Further, students using the contract approach are allowed to work at different rates; to this degree, contracts are self-paced.

Contracts, however, require more and different resources than some of the more traditional forms of instruction; this could prove to be costly if teachers choose to include expensive materials in each and every contract. Increased teacher planning and organizational efforts are also important considerations in using the contracting procedure. The planning and organizing required represents increased teacher responsibilities. Furthermore, in this strategy some students may have difficulty in using their time wisely due to their inability to function without close adult supervision. You must remember that the ability to be self-paced does not develop naturally in all learners. For this reason, it is suggested that you spend time, before individualizing is attempted, to develop the students' abilities to stay on task and to pace themselves in their work. Figure 4-12 outlines the basic responsibilities of the teacher using the contract strategy.

INTRODUCTION:	-present the contract to all students while establishing procedural rules and delineating student responsibilities,
STUDENT INTERVIEW/CONFERENCE SESSION I:	-set aside time to meet with each student individually to discuss which learning alternatives are to be selected and which grade the student is contracting,
STUDENT EXPLORATION PERIOD:	-provide a period of student exploration to allow the student to "get into the contract" and see what is there,
STUDENT INTERVIEW/CONFERENCE SESSION II:	-continue to monitor student progress closely and make final decisions regarding learning alternatives and grading procedures,
STUDENT WORK PERIOD:	-allow for a somewhat large segment of time during which the student completes most of the work on the learning activities selected, and
CONTRACTS HANDED IN/WRAP-UP:	-provide a closing counterpart to the introduction which allows the entire class a chance to get together once more for the purpose of reacting to the contract experience.

Figure 4-12. Basic responsibilities for a teacher using a contract strategy.

2.2. Learning Activity Packages

A learning activity package (LAP) is a structured, self-contained and activity-based instructional strategy. The LAP contains all of the basic information which students are expected to master and is assembled in a self-instructional manner allowing learners to proceed at their own pace. Thus, a LAP may completely replace the textbook for some students studying a given topic. As described, each LAP follows a format similar to that outlined in Figure 4-13.

1. OBJECTIVES: The first part of a learning activity package should
                 be stated in performance terms to indicate to students
                 what they will be able to do following their study,
                 the conditions under which they will have to perform,
                 and the quality of expected performance.

2. PRETEST: The pretest following the objectives is designed to
                 identify those objectives which the student may have
                 already mastered. Therefore, the test is keyed to
                 specific instructional objectives. The student may
                 be directed to consider enrichment activities for
                 objectives already mastered or to work only on the
                 remaining objectives.

3. LEARNING ACTIVITIES: Learning activities are designed to provide
                 students with appropriate and necessary experiences
                 for mastery of identified objectives. They should
                 include a wide variety of multi-sensory activities
                 and materials and should be presented through a
                 variety of media such as games, experiments, and
                 video and audio tapes. Suggested enrichment activ-
                 ities for each objective should be included. Activ-
                 ities may be organized for independent, small group
                 or even large group work, but all students are
                 expected to complete the LAP.

4. SELF-TESTS: When the students have completed the necessary
                 learning activities, they are then directed to the
                 self-test to determine if they are ready for the
                 final evaluation on the LAP. The self-test also
                 serves to redirect the students' learning through
                 revised activities or tutorial assistance by the
                 teacher.

5. EVALUATION: The final evaluation is designed to assess the degree
                 to which the student has mastered the objectives.
                 Unsuccessful students are re-directed through portions
                 of the LAP sequence or are presented with additional
                 learning activities by the teacher.

Figure 4-13. Sample learning activities package format.

As you can see in Figure 4-13, the LAP has the following major
components: (1) *OBJECTIVES,* (2) *PRETEST,* (3) *LEARNING AC-
TIVITIES,* (4) *SELF—TEST,* and (5) *EVALUATION.* Because of their
importance, each of these elements will be examined at some length.
Like other approaches recommended in this chapter, the LAP approach begins with a statement of desired instructional *OBJEC-*

TIVES. These objectives are typically determined by the teacher after systematic diagnosis of student interest, need, learning style, rate, and ability. Based on this diagnosis, every student in a typical classroom may not receive the same instructional LAP and, therefore, may not be working toward the same objectives. Additionally, you must remember that student diagnosis might reveal that one, or a cluster, of objectives are relevant for a group of students rather than a single individual. When this is the case, numerous students may be studying in the same LAP; these students would be working on the same objectives but at their own individual rates.

The importance of the *PRETEST* before beginning the LAP activities cannot be overstated. The pretest provides a valuable final check as to whether or not all LAP objectives are appropriate for a particular student. It is possible that the pretest will reveal that some objectives have already been mastered by other means. When this is the case, you should cite these and communicate to the student that study toward these objectives is unnecessary. If, following the pretest, some students are identified as already possessing the competencies related to all of the LAP objectives, their study in this particular LAP should be reconsidered. In essence, the pretest helps to insure that your students will not be spending their time studying content which they already know. While review is at times important, wise use of instructional time should always be considered with the use of any teaching strategy.

A thoroughly prepared LAP includes numerous, varied *LEARN-ING ACTIVITIES* correlated with each instructional objective. This allows a particular learner or group of learners, a number of alternative ways in which to address the study of the objectives. All students need not develop mastery of an objective through the same type of study. Some learning activities may be, in a very precise way, directed toward only one objective; of course, others may address two or more. In the preparation of any LAP, the teacher should determine what different activities are available which would help students meet the identified LAP objectives. This determination could result in a variety of possible learning activities relevant to the instructional objectives identified. In selecting relevant learning activities, the self-pacing and self-contained characteristics of this strategy must be kept in mind. If every activity proposed in the LAP needs to be directed by the teacher, the LAP has not been properly conceptualized and designed. Directions must be complete to the degree that the teacher can maintain the role of guide or facilitator.

Once required activities have been completed by the student, the *SELF— TEST* is then taken. The purpose of the self-test, which is similar to the final LAP evaluation, is to identify whether or not the student is actually ready for the final assessment. When students successfully complete the self-test, you can conclude that the final evaluation should be taken. If the reverse is true and they do not successfully complete the self-test, it is an indication that the students are not ready for the final evaluation and that further study is necessary. At this point, you will need to review which learning activities students have completed and then reassign or redirect them to others. A rather special type of instructional programming occurs at this point. If one learning activity did not produce success, an alternate should be ready to take its place. If, after the second learning experience, students are still not ready for the final evaluation, a third learning activity, or set of activities, should be provided. The LAP strategy, in this fashion, matches students to learning activities until success on the final evaluation, predicted through self-test performance, is expected.

The *EVALUATION COMPONENT* provides a final assessment for the LAP indicating a measure of student performance. Because the LAP is an individual strategy with a self-pacing characteristic, different students will complete the final evaluation at different times. As with evaluation in any strategy, the assessment must be related to the originally identified objectives and measure only those which have been previously designated. While the self-test, prior to the evaluation, will serve as a rather accurate indicator of student performance on the final evaluation, some students may do well on the self-test but not be successful on the subsequent final evaluation. Treated as any other instructional approach, poor performance on a final evaluation creates an important decision-making situation for the teacher. When confronted with such a decision, two courses of action are possible: (1) the student may be guided to further learning activities to help improve performance, or (2) the teacher may conclude that sufficient time has been spent on the LAP and allow the final evaluation to stand. In regard to this learning endeavor, such a situation requires a professional decision based on many influencing factors. It is important to note that it is not a misuse of the LAP approach to allow the final evaluation to stand as is even when it indicates less-than-desired student performance. It is essential, however, that prior to making this decision the teacher has considered, once again, such points as the overall importance of the objectives of the LAP, the learning activities which remain available, and the degree to which the current LAP acts as readiness material for future activities. The LAP is an individual instructional strategy, but its use should be incorporated smoothly into the rest of the curriculum. Few teachers have total freedom to blend, carte blanche, self-pacing strategies into the conventional school schedule. Therefore, you must remain flexible in your development of instruction so that the activities chosen to further learning are both diverse and appealing. Moreover, you must plan instructional activities which are compatible with existing time constraints.

Figure 4-14 is provided as an outline of considerations for the development of learning activity packages.

An important strength of the LAP approach lies in the evaluation components. Students are provided with pre-tests and self-tests as well as the typical end-of-instruction assessment. These components, coupled with the fact that students are provided with both enrichment and remedial activities, tend to increase the probability that students will actually master the individual objectives. The LAP does, however, require extended teacher time and effort to prepare. Since teachers have many duties and extensive demands on their instructional time, some of which are non-instructional in nature, this problem becomes an important consideration concerning the LAP approach. Like the contract previously discussed, a LAP requires many varied materials, which could prove to be expensive. Furthermore, the LAP approach requires the learner to read independently and work on tasks without close teacher supervision; this type of learning is often not characteristic of low ability students. Many educators suggest

THE TEACHER SHOULD:

1. determine if the objective is stated properly in precise behavioral terms,

2. make sure that necessary materials are available,

3. provide a variety of learning activities which are multi-sensory in nature,

4. assure student access to the required materials,

5. insure that all evaluation components match the objective(s),

6. design the self test such that it enables the students to determine what they do or do not know,

7. generate a final evaluation instrument which will tell the student and the teacher where learning break-downs occurred, and

8. provide enrichment activities for students who show an interest.

Figure 4-14. Considerations for the development of LAPS.

that this strategy is best used in the upper elementary grades and higher. Teachers in early elementary grades often use learning centers to achieve the same type of instructional benefits.

2.3. Learning Centers

The use of a learning center can be an extremely productive enterprise for the student as well as the teacher. A learning center is defined as an area designated and designed by the teacher (sometimes with the help of students) for the purpose of providing students with an opportunity to participate in individualized, student-centered instruction so that differing styles and rates of learning can be accommodated. Further, learning centers create a situation where students become active participants in their own education. With such active involvement, the use of learning centers increases the possibility that all students will achieve the desired learning objective(s) and, at the same time, demands that they accept a greater responsibility in the learning endeavor.

Learning centers are of primarily three types: (1) those that promote and reinforce skill and content development, (2) those that allow for student exploration and interest development, and (3) those that provide content enrichment. Each type has its own appropriate place in the classroom. *SKILL AND CONTENT DEVELOPMENT CENTERS* are useful because they are designed for use after initial instruction by the teacher and reinforce the skills or content being developed. Once the teacher has introduced the skill or content to be learned, students proceed to the center to practice at their own rates and eventually to master the material. The teacher should provide a diverse selection of materials to aid students as they work on their tasks. As the name implies, *ENRICHMENT CENTERS* serve to enrich and expand the student's knowledge and interest about a particular area of study. These centers provide a number of alternatives that may stimulate an individual's curiosity and allow for the various interests that exist to be expanded and clarified. While skill and content centers provide many effective ways for students to reach mastery of instructional objectives, the activities are generally prescribed as being essential, and, as such, each student must demonstrate competence with respect to the material being studied. Enrichment centers, on the other hand, provide for more variability in student achievement because there is opportunity for students to proceed in any number of directions. *INTEREST CENTERS* are created to allow students the opportunity to pursue their own personal interests. These centers are often initiated by students. The subject matter introduced by this type of center is not necessarily part of the required curriculum. Interest centers provide the best opportunity for student input in developing learning activities. While it is expected that there will be some student assistance generated in the creation and expansion of skill and content or enrichment centers, realistically, it is assumed that the teacher will be the major force behind them. Interest centers, however, allow students to specify their own interests and objectives and pursue them.

Learning centers can be set up in any area of a classroom or building and can range from a very elaborate design to one that is extremely simple. Centers can be arranged in a variety of ways in a variety of places (e.g. tables, walls, closets). While often believed to require wide, spacious facilities, learning centers can be quite functional in limited physical areas. There can be numerous centers in the classroom, each promoting different skills or interests that reinforce and expand upon the material presented in the text, class lecture, or discussion. An effective teacher considering the use of this approach should keep in mind a number of important responsibilities (see Fig. 4-15).

THE TEACHER SHOULD:

1. provide each center with complete instructions and objectives that complement a captivating title which is used to generate student interest,

2. establish a set of clearly designed learning activities,

3. provide learning activities that are diverse in terms of varying student abilities, rates, and learning modalities,

4. develop activities which follow a logical sequence (e.g., concrete to abstract, familiar to unfamiliar),

5. create activities which provide the opportunity for students to clarify what they have learned by applying what they know to new situations,

6. establish and communicate procedures for assessment prior to student work in the center, and

7. plan such details as: how many students may be in a center at one time, how long students will be allowed to remain in a center, who decides which center a student may attend, and what students are to do while not working in the centers which are available.

Figure 4-15. Teacher responsibilities in planning and implementing learning centers.

Learning centers provide the teacher with the opportunity to:

1. Expand the curriculum
2. Foster active learning on the students' part
3. Make content more relevant to student concerns and interests
4. Provide increased alternatives for learning

At the same time, consequently, the implementation of learning centers will require more work and organization than a traditional approach to teaching. For this reason, teachers who already feel overburdened with work may not be immediately receptive to this concept. It should be considered, however, that while the initial effort may seem Herculean, the hard work eventually "pays off" in terms of providing more time for instruction and requiring less time for "busywork." In addition, the teacher may be assured that, when implemented properly, students are learning more, probably having a better time doing it, and, above all, are learning to learn on their own.

2.4. Independent Study Projects

Independent study projects have long been used by teachers in a variety of ways and for many purposes. Often, an entire unit of instruction is presented through the use of independent study projects. Independent study projects are those activities, initiated by the student with the teacher's guidance or assigned by the teacher, which culminate in a student-prepared product. This product usually consists of a student report (written and/or oral) which is often accompanied by an example of the student's creative efforts (e.g. models, illustrations, collections). Regardless of the type of product prepared, an important feature of this strategy is that students have an opportunity to display their results. This provides positive rewards for those doing the projects and makes numerous learning situations available for other students in the classroom.

To plan such a strategy, the teacher must develop a "menu" of project ideas which correlate directly with planned instructional objectives. The purpose is to aid the student in the selection of worthwhile, relevant projects which will help in mastering stated objectives. Of course, the teacher must also prepare evaluation measures for these objectives to determine if they are mastered by the students.

Consider the following possibilities in the use of the Independent Study Project approach:

> Mrs. Brown, a fourth grade teacher, teaches a unit around a grouping of objectives related to the study of the *FAMILY.* Mrs. Brown has identified five potential Independent Study Projects available for study in this unit. This may be thought of as Mrs. Brown's "menu" of projects from which students may select.
>
> 1. Design a family mobile with no less than five parts and display it in class for no less than one week.
> 2. Cut at least twenty pictures from magazines and make a family collage poster. Display the poster in class.
> 3. Interview at least three family members (brothers, sisters, aunts, uncles, parents, grandparents) about what things they like to do best as a family. Prepare a written report on your findings.
> 4. Do some research in your text or from the library and compare families found in a foreign country (e.g. China, Japan, Germany, Sweden, Brazil) with your own family. Write up your findings and give an oral report to the class.
> 5. Prepare a diorama depicting families in different periods in history. Use "the frontier family," "today's family," and "the space-age family" as three periods to illustrate how families change over time.

Mr. Taylor's tenth grade math class is studying the topic *MEASUREMENT.* Here are some Independent Study Projects which he has made available to his students.

1. Prepare a scale model of the basketball court using a one-inch to thirty-six-inch scale.
2. Make a growth chart using both standard and metric units for the growth of a bean seedling over a two-week period.
3. Make a drawing comparing the size of the gym to the size of your classroom using measures to the nearest square foot.

4. Observe the numbers of foreign and American-made cars passing through the intersection in front of the school from 3:00 to 4:00 for a one-week period. Make a bar graph to illustrate the results of your observations.
5. Prepare a line graph based on one week of observation in the school lunchroom during your lunch period. Graph your observations of the relationship of students purchasing their lunch from the "fast food" service to those purchasing from the "full meal" service.

A major strength of this approach is that it permits students, because of the unique interest developed, to become more fully involved in their own instruction. Sometimes, students who do poorly in typical classwork procedures produce excellent projects because of their increased interest in the activity. Thus, projects may be very motivating inasmuch as students are necessarily active in their work. Figure 4-16 outlines major teacher responsibilities in the planning of independent study projects.

Although student projects do not consume as much of the teacher's planning time as contracts or learning activity packages, a characteristic of this strategy is that it frequently requires a great deal of classtime for the completion and reporting of project activities. Students might tend to flounder along feeling that they do not know exactly what to do, at least during the early stages of the unit of instruction, and need considerable individual direction and assistance from the teacher.

A critical problem that many teachers have faced when selecting this strategy deals with the originality aspect of the student product. For example, numerous teachers have received projects that were, beyond doubt, the results of efforts of an individual other than the student. In order to address this problem, teachers should be concerned with legitimate content considerations for the given grade level of the students as opposed to merely the aesthetic quality of the product. This may help the teacher avoid such problems which arise when student projects are evaluated. In addition, to help insure quality and originality in the student-developed project, the teacher must relinquish adequate classtime for the monitoring and guiding of the *STUDENTS'* work.

THE TEACHER SHOULD:

1. establish instructional objectives related to the goals of the unit being studied,

2. prepare evaluation measures based on objectives,

3. develop a "Menu" of project ideas,

4. guide students in selecting projects,

5. clearly delineate expectations for student products and evaluation criteria to be used.

6. provide students with guidance and assistance while they develop their projects,

7. collect written reports and/or hear oral reports,

8. lead a discussion on the major points developed in the reports, and

9. evaluate all aspects of the project as related to desired student outcomes.

Figure 4-16. Major responsibilities in planning and implementing independent study projects.

2.5. Summary

To be effective, a teacher must analyze each strategy to decide which will be most appropriate in the given learning environment and use those which seem to have the greatest promise based on the nature of the material to be taught and the learning styles, rates, and abilities of the students involved. Figure 4-17 should aid in completing this analysis and in summarizing some of the important aspects of this section.

INSTRUCTIONAL STRATEGY	MAJOR CONSIDERATIONS
Instructional Contract	-provides an opportunity to develop independent study habits -provides extensive opportunities for student choice -generates high interest and involvement -creates an environment where students possibly may not use study time wisely -requires considerable and varied resources -requires considerable teacher planning and organizational skills -creates difficulties in the identification of suitable resources
Learning Activity Package	-provides an extensive testing component for instruction -provides an opportunity to develop independent study habits -contains enrichment and remedial activities -requires extended teacher planning time -increases the expense factor in material acquisition -is often not well suited for low ability students -is usually best for upper elementary levels and above -requires considerable teacher planning and organizational skills
Learning Center	-encourages movement and interaction -adapts to limited space requirements -provides an opportunity to develop independent study habits -provides teachers an opportunity to expand the curriculum -fosters active involvement and increases relevance -provides alternatives for learning -requires considerable teacher planning and organizational skills
Independent Study Project	-gives students an opportunity to display their work -provides an opportunity to develop independent study habits -permits students to become fully involved in instruction -requires extended classtime for task completion and reporting -creates the possibility that teachers may encounter unoriginal work -makes objective evaluation difficult -requires considerable teacher planning and organizational skills

Figure 4-17. Individual instructional strategies.

Formative Evaluation: Section 2*

1. Develop an instructional contract for an objective of your choice.
2. Outline the components for a learning activity package for a unit of instruction of your choice.
3. Select an objective and briefly describe how you would develop instruction using either learning centers or individual student projects.

REFERENCES

Ausubel, D. *Educational psychology: A cognitive view.* New York: Holt, Rinehart and Winston, 1968.

Ausubel, D., and Robinson, D. *School learning: An introduction to educational psychology.* New York: Holt, Rinehart and Winston, 1969.

Barr, R., and Dreeben, R. Instruction in classrooms. In L. Shulman (Ed). *Review of research in education,* Volume 5. Itasca, IL: Peacock Publishers, 1977.

Bedwell, L. Developing environmental education games. *The American Biology Teacher,* 1977, 39(3), 176–177, 192.

Biehler, R., and Snowman, J. *Psychology applied to teaching* (4th ed.). Boston: Houghton Mifflin, 1982.

Gagné, R. *The conditions of learning* (2nd ed.). New York: Holt, Rinehart and Winston, 1970.

Good, T., and Brophy, J. *Educational psychology: A realistic approach* (2nd ed.). New York: Holt, Rinehart and Winston, 1980.

Sugrue, M., and Sweeney, J. Check your inquiry-teaching technique. *Today's Education,* 1969, 50(5), p. 44.

Wiseman, D. Using instructional contracts in the middle school classroom. *Middle School Journal,* 1983, 14(2), 13–15.

---

*See the Appendix for suggested answers to these questions.

CHAPTER FIVE

THE TEACHER AS A MANAGER OF STUDENT BEHAVIOR

Classroom management is that aspect of teaching which seems to be of greatest concern to most beginning teachers. In fact, even experienced teachers spend considerable time discussing many of the problems associated with controlling the behavior of certain students. Moreover, classroom management concerns are not limited to teachers; school administrators are also extremely aware of the significance of classroom management problems as are the parents of students. Actually, parents often judge the overall quality of a school and its faculty by the behavior of students. Dealing with the tendency of the public to complain vigorously when teachers fail to control the deviant behavior of students is clearly one of the major activities of school administrators. Educational leaders simply cannot afford poor public relations with the community. Because of this, genuine concern is made clearly evident when a teacher is characterized as being unable to manage student behavior. Having a classroom that is constantly in a state of disruption can, without doubt, quickly jeopardize a teacher's position. Today, more teachers than ever before either resign or are released from their teaching positions because of their inability to maintain classroom environments which are orderly and task oriented.

We do not take the position that classroom management skills are the most important competencies a teacher can possess. However, it is readily acknowledged that teachers who cannot control the behavior of their students are certain to find much unhappiness in their work and are likely to have a short tenure in the teaching profession. Since it is difficult to imagine how a teacher could ever be effective in a classroom where the students are continually disruptive, it is felt that classroom control skills are among the most important abilities an effective teacher can possess.

Throughout this chapter, the term *CLASSROOM MANAGEMENT* will be used as opposed to the term *DISCIPLINE*. There is a very important reason for this selection of terms. *DISCIPLINE* tends to have a connotation of being after the fact. *CLASSROOM MANAGEMENT,* on the other hand, implies not only the ability to deal with problems that arise but, also, the ability to organize the classroom environment in such a way as to prevent the occurrence of deviant behavior. The ability to avoid behavior problems is one of the most important competencies which can be possessed by any teacher. Regardless of how adept the teacher may be at getting a group of students under control after a disturbance has arisen, that teacher is running a risk of losing overall control of the class simply because the disturbance has been allowed to take place. This risk would not have taken place if the teacher had been able to prevent the disturbance from happening. Good and Brophy (1973) have appropriately noted that successful classroom management is primarily a matter of preventing problems before they occur. However, it would be erroneous to assume that behavior problems will never emerge in an effective teacher's classroom. Behavior problems will occur because, if for no other reason, some students have a great deal of trouble adjusting to the social milieu of the typical classroom. Because of the importance of preventing problems before they occur and the need to solve behavior problems after they emerge, the current chapter is organized in such a manner as to allow you the opportunity to examine both of these important areas.

Specifically, after careful study of this chapter, you should be able to complete the following performances:

1. Explain why a classroom should be considered both a psychological and a sociological environment.
2. Outline the major characteristics of five theoretical models of classroom management; compare selected models in terms of teacher and student roles.
3. List and describe seven important categories of management behaviors which are often characteristic of good managers.

4. Outline the events in a retreating episode and outline six suggestions for avoiding retreating problems.
5. Describe actions a teacher could take to help prevent management problems in general.
6. Use a checklist to analyze personal management characteristics.
7. Describe the three major control strategies, compare and contrast remunerative and coercive strategies in terms of potential, harmful effects on students, and outline the pros and cons of using punishment in the classroom.
8. Define and provide an example of each of seven specific classroom control problems, suggest possible causes, and outline preventive measures a teacher could take to avoid each of the problems.

SECTION 1. MAJOR THEORETICAL MODELS OF CLASSROOM MANAGEMENT

No discussion of classroom management would be complete without the inclusion of the major contributions made by those who have developed specific theories of group management. These theories of group management are often referred to as MODELS because they attempt to serve as examples for imitation or as a description of possible cause-and-effect relationships which would help the teacher to better visualize procedures for managing students. Since there are several different models, there is, likewise, no complete agreement among theorists as to how best to manage group behavior. Some theorists examine the classroom from a psychological viewpoint, resulting in models different from those who tend to analyze it from a sociological perspective. Nevertheless, though they differ, much can still be learned from an examination of these models. Following this review, you will be able to form a unique concept of classroom management that is suitable both to your personality and teaching style. This unique concept can be developed by selecting components from the different models and combining them to form a comprehensive, personal approach to management. Such synthesizing will help you to stay in a position where new ideas and techniques can readily be added to further refine your classroom management skills.

1.1. Viewing the Classroom Setting

In terms of managing student behavior, at least two distinct views of the classroom setting may be conceptualized; these can be termed the *SOCIOLOGICAL VIEWPOINT* and the *PSYCHOLOGICAL VIEWPOINT*. It is reasonable to suggest that the vast majority of research and writing focused upon the topic of classroom management has been from the psychological viewpoint. Schlechty (1969), a well-known educational sociologist, has labeled this phenomenon as the psychological bias of education. That is to say, a bias has been formed as most teachers are trained to view classroom situations as psychologists, to the exclusion of the sociological viewpoint. The psychologist tends to view the classroom in terms of such constructs as individual learner behavior, individual teacher behavior, and the gain of insight on the part of individual students or teachers. The constructs may then change depending upon whether the psychologist is a follower of the behaviorist, cognitive-field theorist, or has some other outlook on behavior. Regardless of the type of psychology being supported, however, the psychological view concentrates on individuals as opposed to the total group. Sociologists, on the other hand, tend to study a different set of constructs; for example, they might examine the role expectations of teachers and students, group interaction patterns, group sociometrics, and leadership-follower dynamics. The sociologist, instead of examining the different individuals within a group, attempts to develop a detailed analysis of the group as a unique unit.

The psychological viewpoint has clearly made a significant contribution to the field of education in general and to the specific analysis of classroom management skills in particular. There is no question about the importance of such skills when it is necessary to shape the behavior of a deviant student. Psychologists have provided teachers a wealth of information concerning the motivation of student behaviors as explained through knowledge of reinforcement manipulation and need-directed drives. However, as important as psychological research has been to the study of classroom management, the sociological viewpoint must also be considered. Essentially, it is impossible to interact with one student in a group without having an effect on other group members. When a teacher punishes one student or reinforces another, the teacher's actions may very well influence the behavior of the entire class. From a sociological viewpoint, the classroom is a dynamic setting characterized by much interaction between and among the students and the teacher. Teachers who feel that they can interact with any student, or small group, in isolation from this complex interaction system are in danger of making a serious miscalculation. Teachers who are unaware of the social order of the classroom (i.e. the influence that some students have over others) and are not cognizant of the fact that any group will have its own unique set of characteristics are apt to lack and, therefore, not utilize important information needed to prevent management problems.

The relationship between the two views of the classroom as has been identified is most significant. The principles of psychology provide needed direction as teachers design strategies to shape the behavior of individual students who may be exhibiting undesirable classroom behaviors. These principles are valuable to teachers in helping to determine the individual learning, motivational, and developmental characteristics of a learner in order that the student's behaviors can be better understood and a meaningful curriculum can be provided. Sociological principles, on the other hand, provide the teacher with an equally important but different perspective of managing behavior. From these principles, the teacher learns that the behavior of an individual must be examined in terms of total group dynamics; a student's behavior can often be explained in terms of interaction with peers. Also, an individual student's behavior is frequently influenced by social status in the group. The teacher should be aware, for example, of whether students are very popular with their peers, members of a small fringe group on the periphery of the total group, or social isolates having little significant interaction with other group members. Most importantly, the teacher must be conscious of the fact that when an instructional leader corrects the deviant behavior of one student in the group, this action will often affect the behavior of other students who witness the interaction. Kounin (1970) has referred to this phenomenon as the *RIPPLE EFFECT.*

Thus, you, as the teacher, must be aware of both the psychological and sociological viewpoints when analyzing and forming strategies to correct misconduct in classrooms. Understanding the principles of learning theory, human development, and group dynamics will help you develop rational and consistent leadership behaviors needed to manage the classroom. Teachers who develop this level of understanding will exhibit their own unique set of leadership characteristics.

1.2. The Dreikurs' Model

The Dreikurs' model for classroom management is based on the work of Rudolf Dreikurs, a noted psychologist and behavior analyst. Dreikurs' background in psychoanalytic theory permeated his theory of group management. Dreikurs (1968) and Dreikurs and Cassell (1972) stated that children develop certain significant defense mechanisms designed to protect their self-esteem; Dreikurs felt that these protective mechanisms were needed by some students because of harmful, early relationships with members of their families (i.e. parents and siblings). Dreikurs suggested that all student behavior has a specific underlying purpose. When behaving inappropriately, the student is doing so in pursuit of a goal. The mildest form of misbehavior is done to *SEEK ATTENTION.* The next most severe form of misbehavior has as a goal the *SEEKING OF POWER.* A form of misconduct designed to get *REVENGE ON ANOTHER INDIVIDUAL* is the next most severe. Finally, the gravest type of misconduct is designed to obtain *SPECIAL TREATMENT FROM THE TEACHER THROUGH AN OVERT DISPLAY OF INFERIORITY.* Dreikurs noted that students exhibit these deviant behaviors because they do not have the ability to make the necessary personal adjustments needed to co-exist in the interpersonal structure of a peer group. This inability is due to self-esteem problems rooted in the students' early family life.

The primary role of the teacher in the Dreikurs' model is to analyze the misconduct of a given student and then, in a one-to-one conference, help the student to understand the goals behind his own behavior. To help the student understand the need to avoid the above-mentioned goals for deviant behaviors, the student must experience what Dreikurs referred to as the natural consequences of his own misconduct. Students should be encouraged to help the teacher establish rules for acceptable behavior and the consequences of misconduct. Teachers should not deal with punishment per se; group control is the concept that natural, unpleasant consequences will always be the result of misconduct.

As Charles (1981) explained, the Dreikurs' model is based on four major ideas. First, students must learn that they are responsible for their own actions. Second, students must develop self-respect while, at the same time, developing a respect for others. Third, members of the group have the responsibility to influence their peers to conduct themselves properly. Finally, students are responsible for knowing the rules for appropriate behavior and the consequences of misconduct.

The psychoanalytic background of Dreikurs surfaces in his model for behavior. In order to fully utilize this design, you, as the teacher, must be able to analyze the group behavior of students and determine the goals motivating such behavior. You must, moreover, have the interpersonal skills necessary to help students understand their goals in order to change their behavior when necessary. Naturally, this type of complex analysis and communication requires skill that usually comes after considerable practice and training.

1.3. The Glasser Model

Glasser (1965, 1969) has provided a general model for classroom management that he has labelled *REALITY THERAPY.* Glasser has a wide following among teachers in this country, and there are data which indicate that the model can have positive effects when applied appropriately (Good and Brophy, 1980). There is one significant, obvious commonality between the models of Glasser and Dreikurs; students are responsible for their own behavior and must accept any negative consequences that might result. Glasser, like Dreikurs, also stated the importance of students helping in the establishment of rules for proper conduct. In contrast, Glasser indicates that these rules should be established through a specific process — the class meeting.

The class meeting, a gathering together of the teacher and all students, is central to the Glasser model. During the class meeting the teacher is a democratic stimulator of discussion, not an authority figure. All decisions are arrived at through majority rule. Any time that the rules and regulations must be adjusted or unique situations evolve, the group meets again and decisions are revised by vote. The class meeting, therefore, is a recurring event during the school year.

There are, of course, other important characteristics of Glasser's model. An overriding principle of this approach is that the student must learn that in order to remain in the classroom, agreed-upon rules for appropriate behavior must be followed. Removal from the group occurs only after repeated behavior violations and is accomplished through a sequential process. First, the student is simply isolated from the total group and asked to devise a plan to insure that the rules for proper conduct are followed in the future. If positive results are still not forthcoming, the next step is described as in-school suspension; the student now must deal with the principal, not the teacher. A further plan must be devised to insure that misconduct will no longer take place. If this does not achieve the desired results, the student's parents must come to the school and take the student home. This removal is temporary in the hopes that the student can return to school shortly and begin anew. Finally, if the above steps all fail, the student is completely expelled from the school.

This technique can be very profitable providing you can accept a democratic leadership role. If you feel it necessary to make totally unilateral decisions, you will have a difficult time following Glasser's suggestions. This model is very systematic and relates well to most classroom situations; however, in order to fully function within the boundaries of Glasser's suggestions, you will need specialized training and an opportunity to observe other professionals who use the techniques in a classroom environment.

1.4. The Skinnerian Model

The present model will not be referred to as *SKINNER'S MODEL* because B. F. Skinner did not actually develop an approach which he labelled a model for classroom management; however, many of his concepts, as discussed later in this chapter under the heading *REMUNERATIVE STRATEGIES*, have been drawn together by other psychologists to form a model often referred to as behavior modification. The behavior modification model distinguishes between punishment and negative reinforcement, and punishment is not used. Negative reinforcement refers to a situation where students are removed from an unpleasant situation as a reward for exhibiting desired behavior.

The key principle of behavior modification is that students will repeat behaviors for which they receive reinforcement and will stop exhibiting behavior for which they receive no reinforcement. Therefore, the basis of this model is focused upon the positive (rewarding appropriate behavior) as opposed to concentrating on the negative (punishing inappropriate behavior). As a student begins to change to exhibiting more acceptable behavior, the teacher will need to reinforce each time proper behavior is exhibited. However, as the acceptable behavior pattern becomes more commonplace, it can then be maintained through occasional reinforcement on an unpredictable, less systematic schedule.

There are several systems of behavior modification that vary, from an informal approach, where the teacher simply waits for students to exhibit desired behavior, to more structured systems, where the teacher elicits desired behavior through the systematic use of tangible rewards. In order to modify a student's behavior, the teacher must closely observe the selected student to determine the degree to which that student exhibits the unacceptable behavior. The teacher can use this entering or baseline behavior to determine whether the student is making progress toward changing to more acceptable behavior patterns. Following the identification of this baseline, the teacher then may establish a schedule of reinforcement for rewarding the student for proper conduct. The schedule may be based on time (e.g. a reward for every five minutes of appropriate conduct) or may be based on frequency (e.g. a reward for every two examples of appropriate conduct).

This model has been praised by many behavioral psychologists (Biehler and Snowman, 1982) while, at the same time, criticized by other psychologists and educators (Travers, 1977) on the basis that this manipulation of reinforcements may be focusing on symptomatic behavior without considering the causes of the maladaptive conduct. Nevertheless, a substantial amount of evidence that behavior can be shaped by the manipulation of rewards has been generated. There has, however, also been disagreement about the effectiveness of such a system as it relates to working with normal children (see the discussion under *REMUNERATIVE STRATE-GIES* in this chapter) and to the appropriateness of reward systems being given to specific students in a group because they are exhibiting desired behavior patterns which other students exhibit without ever being rewarded. As with most highly systematic models for classroom management, the use of behavior-modification techniques can only be competently accomplished after professional training has been received.

1.5. The Kounin Model

Kounin's model (Kounin, 1970), which seems to focus more on total group characteristics than on individual teacher and student personalities, has contributed greatly to the study of effective group management. As described by Charles (1981), five key ideas characterize this approach. First, when teachers correct the misbehavior of one student, this correction can have an effect on the total group. Kounin referred to this phenomenon as the RIPPLE EFFECT. Second, teachers must have the characteristic of WITHITNESS; this means that the teacher must always be aware of what is taking place in all parts of the classroom. Third, teachers must also be concerned about the flow of the lesson. Transitions between learning tasks and momentum within the tasks must be smooth. Teachers must avoid rushing into an activity with little preparation (Kounin called this a THRUST) as well as avoiding such behaviors as spending too much time on one topic or activity. Optimum pacing must be maintained which will keep the students on task; busy students are, as was stated earlier, much less likely to cause management problems. This leads to the fourth key point: teachers should have as a goal the maintenance of GROUP FOCUS, which is achieved by keeping all students alert and accountable for learning the concepts under study. It is important here that every student feel the teacher is aware of each person's individual level of progress. Therefore, before students will feel the need to be alert and accountable for learning, the teacher must develop a system for consistently monitoring student progress. Finally, teachers must make every effort to structure the curriculum with general as well as specific learning tasks to avoid student boredom. Kounin suggested that this can best be done by adding variety and diversity to the kinds of activities the students undertake and by placing individuals within a scope and sequence of academic events which assures all students the opportunity for success. Students who are bored or feel that progress is unlikely are prone to create management problems.

Kounin's model is valuable in that it focuses upon leadership qualities related to group dynamics. The primary emphasis is on the teacher's ability to prepare a good learning environment where all students receive adequate feedback and perceive themselves as making academic progress. This emphasis on group characteristics becomes evident through such concepts as the *RIPPLE EFFECT* and *WITHITNESS;* Kounin's model is based on a very realistic view of classroom life. Most teachers, regardless of their teaching styles, could benefit from an understanding of the components of this model.

1.6. The Gordon Model

Gordon's model (Gordon, 1974) of classroom management is referred to as teacher effectiveness training (TET). Teacher effectiveness training is, perhaps, the most popular model today in terms of the number of workshops and training sessions being conducted for the dissemination of classroom management skills (Good and Brophy, 1980). Gordon's philosophy of control is based on gestalt psychology similar to that of Carl Rogers. Rogers is noted for his technique of nondirective counseling.

Central to TET is the position that teachers must give up their role as powerful authority figures. Teachers should be able to discuss their differences with students in a free and caring way. Students should not be coerced to behave in any manner. The teacher must discuss the unacceptable behavior with the student in what Gordon calls a *NO LOSE* situation. If teachers demonstrate a concern and caring attitude toward students, those students, in turn, will demonstrate the same type of respect for their teachers.

When problems occur in the classroom, teachers and students must first determine to whom the problem belongs: the teacher, the student, or both. Problems that belong to the student involve such inhibitors to learning as fear and anxiety. Teacher-owned problems, on the other hand, involve behaviors such as student misconduct, which tends to frustrate the teacher because it interrupts the instructional flow. When the problem is owned by students, the teacher must *ACTIVELY LISTEN* to the students in order to be able to help them arrive at their own solutions. Essentially, active listening involves encouraging students to talk about their frustrations while showing them that the teacher does, in fact, see the problem as being serious. The teacher should never take a student's problems lightly, even in an attempt to reassure the student that everything will eventually be worked out. Feedback to students must be offered in an attempt to help them solve their own problems. Conversely, as Good and Brophy (1980) explain, when the problem is the teacher's, the teacher must take the initiative and send messages to the disruptive students in order to change their behaviors. Therefore, the person who owns the problem must be the one who talks about it.

Gordon believes that teachers are likely to have difficulty in changing students' behavior when they approach their students by confronting them with criticism; such confrontations are labelled *YOU MESSAGES* in this model. Gordon suggests that the best way to change students' behavior is through what he refers to as *I MESSAGES*. An *I MESSAGE* is developed in three distinct parts. The first segment delineates the deviant behavior, the second describes the effect that such behavior has on the teacher, and the final part tells how such behavior makes the teacher feel. An example of an *I MESSAGE* would be as follows: (1) when someone comes into class late, (2) it disrupts the flow of the lesson and disturbs the learning activities, (3) and I become very frustrated. The *I MESSAGE* is a central concept to teacher effectiveness training; it gives the teacher an opportunity to change student behavior without having to become involved in a power struggle or the use of coercive strategies.

The use of *I MESSAGES*, which focus on behaviors—not the student as a person—is based upon the assumption that all students can understand communications which are sent in what some linguists would consider to be elaborate codes (Bernstein, 1960). That is, the teacher is attempting to persuade students to change their behavior by giving them a rational explanation of the effects of their negative behaviors. It is suggested that some students, especially those from low socioeconomic conditions, do not understand nor positively respond to such elaborate communications. These students frequently come from what Bernstein has called *CLOSED SYSTEMS*, where control strategies tend to be based on the authoritarian power of the adult in charge. Such students have, in the past, often responded to brief commands without being given an explanation of the command nor a chance to voice their opinions. When placed in the middle-class environment of the classroom and given elaborate communications designed to help students subjectively empathize with their teacher, these students are likely to misinterpret the communication. They may not associate such elaborate messages with the teacher's desire for them to change their behavior. In simple terms, lower socioeconomic status students may not be accustomed to authority figures using such rational, democratic control methods; they tend to be more familiar with a direct, authoritarian method.

Formative Evaluation: Section 1*

1. Explain why a classroom should be perceived as both a psychological and a sociological environment.
2. Outline the major characteristics for each of the theoretical models of classroom management.
3. In what ways are the Dreikurs' and the Glasser models alike?

---

*See the Appendix for suggested answers to these questions.

4. Select two of the theoretical models and compare and contrast them in terms of teacher and student roles.

SECTION 2. CHARACTERISTICS OF
EFFECTIVE CLASSROOM MANAGERS

Good classroom managers represent a relatively heterogeneous group of teachers; that is to say, it is somewhat difficult to develop a list of very specific characteristics common to all effective managers. This difficulty is partly due to the fact that many ineffective managers also exhibit some of these same effective management behaviors. It is possible, however, after analyzing both effective and ineffective managers, to develop a listing of broad categories of behaviors which are characteristic of teachers who have the ability to control the behavior of their students. Nonetheless, it must be noted that effective classroom managers will vary in the degrees to which they exhibit any one or all of these behaviors. It is suggested that you examine each category of behaviors carefully in order to rate yourself in terms of whether or not you can model the behaviors under discussion. Figure 5-1 will facilitate this rating process after an examination of each of the characteristics.

2.1. Thorough Preparation

An effective classroom manager is aware of the fact that most deviant student behavior emerges when learners are not on task. Students who have nothing to do because they have finished their work early or have to wait idly for long periods of time because the teacher has not given them an assignment may tend to exhibit some type of unwanted behavior. Conversely, students who are meaningfully occupied with their studies have less opportunity to become involved in misconduct. For this reason, good managers tend to exhibit behaviors which keep students on task and involved in some aspect of the learning enterprise. Effective managers plan ahead of time exactly what will happen during all instructional sessions. As a result, time is not wasted at the begin-

MANAGEMENT CHECKLIST

Characteristics	Exists Satisfactorily	Needs to be Improved	Personal Notes
Thorough Preparation			
Development of Routines			
Calm and Confident Behavior			
Professional Demeanor			
Recognizing Inappropriate Behavior			
Avoidance of Retreating			
Preventing Problems			

Figure 5-1. A checklist for classroom managers.

ning of the lesson, nor is it likely that students will be left with nothing to do at the end of the instructional period.

Until the teacher is confident in planning adequately for a given time allotment, it is advisable for that teacher to plan more than could possibly be accomplished. It is, by far, better to over-plan than to under-plan for instruction. A teacher who has left students without anything meaningful to do is creating an environment conducive to student misconduct. Most assuredly, effective managers are organized and realistic in their planning for instruction.

2.2. Development of Routines

Another important aspect of organization is the ability to develop a comfortable, customary procedure for handling the daily, ongoing affairs of the classroom. Students are much less likely to exhibit misconduct when they know exactly what to do and can, in effect, function almost by habit. That is, good managers tend to structure the classroom environment in such a way as to lessen the opportunity for confusion. These routines must take place at all grade levels. One example might be the biology teacher who has set procedures for the distribution and collection of laboratory equipment and manuals. Another example is the kindergarten teacher who has structured the manner in which children wash their hands and line up before leaving for lunch. The classroom is an interesting, exciting social arena; teachers can expect and need to plan for student loss of self-control when the student either does not know what is about to take place or what is expected. Through this development of routines, the effective manager attempts to structure daily activities in such a way as to promote a calming effect on students.

2.3. Calm and Confident Behavior

The teacher's own behavior is an essential aspect in the development of a calming social environment. Effective managers tend to exhibit leadership styles characterized by calm, confident behavior.

As teachers lose confidence in themselves as managers and come to feel that they cannot control their classes, panic is a typical end result. Often becoming defensive, such teachers frequently are unable to think rationally when confronted with misconduct. Teachers who are not calm and confident are apt themselves to exhibit behaviors that destroy the productive atmosphere of a classroom.

Effective leaders rarely display loss of temper because they know that this behavior could lead to arguing and bickering with students. Out-of-control behavior makes the teacher appear weak and insecure in the eyes of the students. Teachers who maintain an air of confidence are less vulnerable and more likely to be in charge. They are less likely to make mistakes in judgment because they do not panic when confronted by the unexpected. Too, students have greater respect for a leader who seems calm and confident than one who has emotions which are easily manipulated.

2.4. Professional Demeanor

A professional demeanor is one of the most important attributes of the teacher who desires to command the respect of students. Conduct in a professional manner is a somewhat abstract idea; PROFESSIONALISM is, no doubt, defined in several acceptable ways. A professional in the classroom, regardless of the definition, is one who accepts the role of leader seriously. A teacher must gain and maintain the respect of all students through consistent and fair treatment. Such a teacher treats all students with due respect and never holds a grudge against students for past misbehavior.

Beyond the rather obvious characteristics of fair play and respect for students, professional conduct implies that teachers must be aware of their overall duties and responsibilities and carry them out in a dignified fashion. Teachers must additionally have respect for the profession; for example, they should dress, speak, and act professionally as they are guided by the expectations of society and colleagues. Effective managers tend to develop relationships with their students which could be characterized as being similar, in a sense, to a parent-child relationship. Rarely is it found that an effective manager tries to develop a peer-like relationship with students. Teachers who want to have the respect of their students must consistently put themselves in positions where students look to them for leadership. This is not to imply that teachers should be inflexible, despotic leaders. On the contrary, teachers should lead with concern and respect for students while, at the same time, remembering that they are the adults in charge. Finally, a professional is one who strives to develop competency in teaching skills and is willing to make changes directed toward personal improvement without feeling threatened.

2.5. Recognizing Inappropriate Behavior

One of the most important skills a good classroom manager can possess is the ability to determine when student behavior is truly inappropriate at the time and place that it occurs. Behavior that is inappropriate at one time may be best ignored at another; indeed, an effective manager realizes the importance of analyzing each situation to determine the best action to take. Many teachers often disrupt class by stopping instruction in order to reprimand a student for doing something which, in fact, is not causing a disturbance or interfering with anyone's learning. For example, the teacher who is involved in a very stimulating lesson should not interrupt such a positive learning environment by focusing everyone's attention on two students who briefly whisper in the rear of the classroom. Simply put, a good manager tends not to react to everything that occurs; sometimes it may be best to *PRETEND* not to see everything that happens. This is not to imply that teachers can ignore true disturbances and hope they will soon go away. Actually, when left alone, real disturbances tend to worsen, not diminish. The important point to be remembered is that teachers must not treat innocuous student behavior as if it were truly inappropriate. Such action on the teacher's part can frustrate students and can have the effect of disturbing the flow of an effective lesson, which will result in the distracting of many students and potentially causing even more misbehavior. Effective managers, when correcting student misbehavior, tend to react only to behavior which clearly impedes learning, endangers one or more students, or is socially unacceptable.

The ability to recognize innocuous behavior only solves part of the perplexity of identifying inappropriate behavior. Effective leadership also necessitates the ability to determine which student behaviors require an immediate corrective response from the teacher. Teachers who often have problems with classroom control typically make the mistake of assuming that they need do nothing about classroom disturbances and still can be effective instructors. Naturally, teachers cannot afford to ignore true disturbances in the learning environment. Those who fail to meet such disturbances with determination and corrective measures are likely to find themselves surrounded by chaos.

2.6. Avoidance of Retreating

Although it has been illustrated that some teachers are guilty of creating disturbances by reacting unnecessarily to some student behaviors, too often, other teachers allow real disturbances to continue and, in turn, destroy their credibility as leaders. At no other time do teachers seem so incompetent as when they stand before a chaotic group trying to teach when few, if any, of the students are paying any attention to the instruction. Such teachers usually leave the profession due to their own anxieties or are relieved of their positions by administrators whose evaluations document the teacher's inability to demonstrate competence in this critical area. Perhaps, no other characteristic can be more damaging to a teacher's reputation than the inability to control undesirable student behavior. Hunt and Bedwell (1982) have stated that a single behavior seems to be common to teachers who have trouble controlling their students; this behavior is referred to as retreating. It is important to note that while retreating is characteristic of poor leaders, it is rarely a behavior exhibited by teachers who can control their classes skillfully.

Retreating, as described by Schlechty (1976), is a complex social behavior common to small groups where the leadership of the person in charge is being undermined by one or more group members. Specifically, it occurs in the classroom when the teacher backs down from student rebellion. The retreating sequence takes place when the teacher issues a directive intended to influence the behavior of one or more students with the result being that students ignore the teacher in such a fashion as to let it be known that they are not going to comply. At this time, if the teacher ignores the rebellious behavior of the students, the teacher is, in fact, retreating. Consequently, retreating occurs when the teacher ignores the fact that students are continuing to exhibit unwanted behavior after they have been asked to stop. Clearly, a critical point occurs in the management episode immediately after the teacher gives a directive to change the deviant behavior of one or more students. The teacher must follow through on the established directive to students.

No other behavior so clearly separates the effective from the non-effective manager as does retreating. Thus, the teacher who avoids retreating is more apt to avoid management problems before they reach the critical stage. Teachers whose behaviors are characterized by a series of retreating patterns, on the other hand, are likely to find themselves in situations where control is lost, never to be recaptured. Once the teacher retreats, the rebellious effects of a few students are likely to run through the entire group. The teacher, who has already demonstrated weakness in leadership, is now in a situation that the best of teachers would find difficult to remedy.

Obviously, the best plan of action is to avoid retreating; the avoidance of such behavior is likely to result in the teacher's being able to prevent future classroom disruptions. Hunt and Bedwell have made the following suggestions to help teachers avoid such management problems:

1. Give directives to students only when necessary (i.e. only when student behavior is harmful, disturbing, or impolite).
2. Observe student behavior immediately after a directive has been given since this is the most critical instant during the management episode.
3. Know what will follow if the students rebel — this helps the teacher feel prepared and less threatened.
4. Remember that leaders must enforce their authority — do not become involved in a confrontation unless it is known that the leadership position can be sustained.

5. Deal with rebellious students outside of the total group — the chance of negatively affecting the group is thereby lessened.
6. Stay calm and confident when dealing with a control problem — the poised teacher is much less likely to retreat.

The teacher who follows these rules and avoids retreating is well on the way to preventing many classroom management problems before they ever occur.

2.7. Preventing Problems

Unless problems occur in the classroom, the teacher will never have to be concerned about confrontations and retreating. Because of this, the ability to avoid problems before they occur is the most important leadership quality a teacher can possess. Due to the complexity and importance of this characteristic, it is felt that prevention of behavior problems should be discussed at length in this and subsequent sections.

Above all else, teachers who desire to prevent management problems must consistently conduct themselves in a controlled fashion so as to model the type of behaviors described earlier in this section. Being a good, effective leader requires much forethought. Teachers simply cannot *LEAVE IT TO CHANCE* that they will be able to control students and function successfully in the classroom. Management problems are contagious; a few problems today tend to balloon into excessive problems in the future. Conversely, the absence of behavior problems today will increase the likelihood that there will be few behavior problems in the future. The avoidance of behavior problems becomes, in itself, a measure of prevention.

Under the best of conditions, it would be unrealistic to expect that all behavior problems are preventable. Problems do arise for all teachers. However, some teachers have many more management problems than should be expected. Charles (1981) has suggested seven key steps to be taken in the prevention of behavior problems. These steps are concerned with the (1) physical setting, (2) curriculum, (3) attitude of the teacher, (4) expectations of the teacher, (5) support systems, (6) plans for the unexpected, and (7) performance of teaching.

The physical setting can definitely influence the behavior of the students involved. Students who are too hot, overcrowded, unable to see or hear the teacher well, or in some other way uncomfortable are most likely to become inattentive and create disturbances. The setting should be arranged to diminish the number of possible distractions that might occur due to noise or movement outside of the room. A wise teacher is aware that some students are likely to become distracted if they sit too close to one another. Therefore, a formal seating arrangement is sometimes crucial. Many teachers also find it best to seat easily distracted and inattentive students near their desk in order that the teacher's nearness will decrease the probability of a disturbance (Additional attention was given to this topic in Chapter 1 as related to learning styles.)

The curriculum must match the needs, abilities, and interests of each of the students if they are all expected to remain task-oriented throughout instruction. When the curriculum becomes so difficult that a student becomes fatigued or, even worse, begins to fail at most or all tasks, that student is apt to become disenchanted with learning and rebel. The student who meets learning endeavors with success is much more likely to remain on task. A busy, industrious learner rarely disrupts the classroom. On the other hand, the learner who is not being challenged by a curriculum that is too easy or lacks relevance is probably going to talk or move around disturbing other learners because he is bored or has nothing to do.

The attitude with which a teacher enters the classroom is most important. If a teacher feels that controlling a class will be impossible, that teacher very likely will fail. However, teachers who enter the classroom feeling that they are the leaders in charge are probably going to communicate this feeling to the students; the result is apt to be a prevention of control problems. Good and Brophy (1973) have noted that the essential attitudes of an effective manager are (1) respect and affection for the learners, (2) consistency which leads to credibility, (3) responsibility for all students learning, and (4) enjoyment of learning which leads to the students valuing education.

Expectations for behavior should be decided upon and delineated from the beginning of the school year. Charles (1981) suggests that the teacher should decide upon five or six rules that are nonnegotiable, explain their rationale to the students, and write these rules down in order that they will be questioned by no one. It is the teacher's responsibility to determine how behavior will be rewarded or corrected in relation to these rules. Charles emphasizes that it is important to have criteria for rewarding good behavior in relation to rules. Emphatically, expectations should not be thought of only in terms of negative consequences associated with nonconformity.

The effective teacher, in order to prevent behavior problems, considers the development of a support system to help sustain the management plan. The principal must be aware of the teacher's plan, and the teacher should fully understand the extent to which the school administration is willing to offer support or backing. Parents also must be fully aware of the teacher's intentions. Of course, the teacher must be aware of the extent to which each parent is willing to cooperate with the established plan and the administration. Often, a group of parents will vary in the extent to which they will actively support a management plan.

Teachers must be prepared to handle unexpected events that can take place during the school year. Students should know how to conduct themselves if, for example, a substitute teacher replaces the regular teacher or if the classroom has unexpected visitors. When teachers try to enumerate all of the possible unexpected events which could take place and prepare the class for them, it is less likely that the students will show confusion at an inopportune moment.

Charles' steps for prevention also consider the actual teaching act. He further divides teaching performance into four categories: (1) management of teaching, (2) teacher on stage, (3) *THE GOLDEN TONGUE*, and (4) acceptance for everyone.

Management of teaching actually refers to two unique concepts: classroom routines and the delivery of lessons. Classroom routines, as discussed earlier, act as parameters for structuring student movement in the classroom environment. The routines are the organized, consistent procedures that take place in the school setting. When students know there is one accepted way to ask permission to leave the room, sharpen pencils, hand in papers, or line up, much less confusion is likely to occur during such events. A lesson which is delivered in an interesting fashion and which has no large time lapses is one which will keep the students' attention on task; as a result, this type of lesson delivery will help to prevent control problems.

The teacher who has a *GOLDEN TONGUE* is one who speaks to students with respect, not with sarcasm or disdain. The importance of communicating with clear, supportive messages was discussed in Chapter Two in great detail. Students are likely to exhibit courteous behavior when the teacher makes a practice of speaking to them with respect.

Stage presence deals with the teacher's ability to form a close relationship with the students by holding their interest through the use of dramatic and novel gestures and voice inflections. Simply put, a dry, unexciting teacher will not be able to hold the interest or the attention of the students for a length of time. When this is the case, students may be more interested in non-academic endeavors (i.e. disruptive behavior) than in the content of the lesson being presented.

Many educators have pointed out the importance of accepting all students so that they, the students, will feel important and valued within the group. Students obviously have a need to feel accepted; students who see themselves as existing at the fringe of the social group or, worse yet, as isolates from the group are less likely to follow the rules and expectations for behaviors within the classroom. Teachers must draw such students into the mainstream of the social and academic endeavors of the classroom.

Certainly, Charles' thoughts on prevention of management problems are worthy of any teacher's scrutiny. Good and Brophy (1973), in their discussion of prevention, added one further suggestion concerning how a teacher can improve classroom management through effective delivery. These authors noted the importance of variation in questioning patterns. The teacher who randomly calls upon students, never allowing the students to know who will be called upon next, is more apt to hold certain students' attention and keep them on task. This is to say that while routines are important, too strict routines in questioning styles can lead to undue predictability resulting in a greater possibility of management problems.

Waller (1932), in his classic analysis of the classroom social system, noted that a student having feelings of inferiority is likely to exhibit disruptive behavior. Teachers must be aware of the fact that in many cases, those students who are academically unsuccessful are often the same students who frequently behave in such a way as to disrupt the classroom. The child who has a low self-concept typically is very unhappy at school, especially when academic activities are being conducted. While the teacher must show acceptance for all learners, undoubtedly, the notion that all students should be treated equally is erroneous. Some learners are very successful in the learning environment of the classroom; their success leads to reinforcement from teachers and acceptance and respect from peers. Other students cannot share this envious position. School can become a hated place for students who constantly fail and are ridiculed by their peers for their ineptness. There is little wonder why some students rebel against the school, its curriculum, and its authority figures. Rebellion, in this sense, is a type of defense mechanism used to maintain sanity. Not to rebel would mean to accept a system which daily crushes self-worth. Such students must be treated with patience and understanding, even when it seems they are doing everything in their power to disrupt classroom activities. To treat these students with forceful disdain is to provide a poor model of behavior which results in an augmented feeling of inferiority and an increased likelihood of continued, defiant behavior in the future.

Teachers who go into the classroom with a plan for preventing problems before they occur are well on their way to becoming effective classroom managers who not only communicate confidence but develop in their students the characteristics of well-behaved learners who know what to do and expect in their classroom. Figure 5-2 summarizes some major ideas that a teacher must remember to prevent behavior problems.

Personal Consideration	Instructional Consideration	Environmental Consideration
-conduct one's self in a calm, confident fashion	-able students must be challenged	-the classroom must be a clean, comfortable setting
-teachers must be prepared for unexpected events	-low ability students should not be placed in frustrating situations	-the classroom should be void of major distractions to learning
-teachers must praise positive behavior	-instruction should be both exciting and enjoyable	-a few rules for acceptable conduct should exist.
-teachers must show respect and affection for learners	-a variety of questioning patterns should be utilized	-parents and administrators must offer support
-teachers must treat students in a consistent fashion		-the atmosphere should be one of acceptance

Figure 5-2. Considerations for the prevention of management problems.

Formative Evaluation: Section 2*

1. List and describe seven important categories of management behaviors which are often characteristic of teachers who have the ability to manage the behavior of their students.
2. Outline the events that take place in a retreating episode.
3. Describe at least five actions a teacher could take to help prevent management problems.
4. Use the checklist in Figure 5-1 to rate yourself as a classroom manager or potential manager. Describe your rating.
5. Outline six suggestions for avoiding retreating problems.

SECTION 3. CONTROLLING DISRUPTIVE BEHAVIOR

There are three main categories of leadership strategies which can be used to control the behavior of others: normative, remunerative, and coercive (Schlechty, 1976). You should be aware that the type of strategy chosen will, to a significant degree, affect the learning environment of the classroom. There is also reason to believe that all teachers cannot use each strategy with equal success. That is to say, a given teacher may be able to control students by using coercive strategies while being unable to establish control through the use of either normative or remunerative strategies. Moreover, a given student may comply to the influence of normative and remunerative strategies but, at the same time, not readily comply to coercive strategies. Because of this, it is important for you to be cognizant of both your own personal characteristics as a leader as well as the characteristics of your students as followers. We will discuss each of the three strategies at some length in this section, with special attention given to the topic of punishment.

---

*See the Appendix for suggested answers to these questions.

3.1. Normative Strategy

The normative strategy develops naturally as a result of the teacher having the characteristics of an effective manager as discussed earlier in this chapter. When teachers use this strategy of control, students are expected to conform due to respect for the teacher's role. When normative control is applied, all are expected to comply to the teacher's directives because it is expected that when teachers give commands, students will follow them. Obviously, this is an ideal type of leadership. When students comply to normative control, the group is relatively easy to manage. If a disruptive situation arises, the teacher simply makes a request for the unwanted behavior to stop. In this case, as a result of the teacher's request, students are influenced to comply. They stop the unwanted behavior.

This type of control is based upon the students' respect for the teacher or the teaching position. This type of respect, gained through interaction, is earned by the teacher, it does not come automatically. Unfortunately, some teachers do not understand the relationship between their own actions and levels of ability to influence students through the normative strategy. Teachers who are not well prepared, not well organized, not calm and confident, not characterized by a professional demeanor, not able to recognize inappropriate behavior, not able to avoid retreating, and not able to prevent problems before they occur will more than likely have trouble influencing student behavior through the normative strategy. On the other hand, teachers who take their leadership roles seriously and strive to conduct themselves in a manner conducive to effective classroom control will find that students are much more frequently influenced normatively.

For an assortment of reasons, the normative strategy does not work for every teacher in every situation. Some students, due to their inability to adjust to the social complexity of the classroom group, find it virtually impossible to comply to normative control in a consistent manner. For this reason, normative compliance requires students to be well adjusted to their roles, just as normative control requires that teachers be well adjusted to theirs.

3.2. Remunerative Strategies

Control through remunerative strategies is used to influence the behavior of students by the manipulation of a reward system. Rewards, it is noted, are those things which are reinforcing and not normally systematically received. For example, if students typically receive a fifteen-minute break, it is not a reward when the teacher allows students to go on their break because they have finished all of the assigned work. But, if the teacher increases the break time to twenty-five minutes because all the students finished their work, the reward for everyone finishing would be the extra ten minutes. For this reason, remunerative strategies are viewed as positive, in that the teacher concentrates on and reinforces desired behavior.

The operant conditioning theory of B. F. Skinner has been applied to the shaping of desirable behavior in the classroom.* Behavior modification is the name given to the systematic application of operant conditioning as used in the classroom setting. Since the latter part of the 1960s, behavior modification has been a major part of many teacher training programs (Travers, 1977). Behavior modification is based on the assumption that only observable behaviors are significant. Teachers should carefully observe the behaviors of given students and record the frequency that they exhibit deviant behaviors. The goal then becomes to lessen the frequency of the unwanted behaviors. Teachers, taking each unwanted behavior separately, then design a schedule of reinforcement to reward the student for exhibiting proper behavior. In turn, the frequency of proper behavior will increase because it has been reinforced, while, at the same time, the frequency of unwanted behavior will diminish because of the lack of reinforcement.

The concept of behavior modification is based upon a principle of conditioning which has a long history of supportive research — the principle is that behaviors recur to the degree that they are reinforced. Although numerous behavioristic psychologists strongly

---

*The reader is referred to a more complete discussion under the heading THE SKINNERIAN MODEL earlier in this chapter.

recommend the use of behavior modification as a remunerative control strategy, other social scientists and educators have been critical of its use. Travers (1977) has taken the position that the stated values of behavior modification have dubious validity and that the commercial training kits available are too expensive and often lacking in a substantive base. He went on to state that there is little research to support the notion that behavior modification is effective when working with normal children in the typical classroom setting. Kounin (1970), who seems to analyze the classroom more from the sociological viewpoint, also warned that such remunerative strategies can be ineffective when overly used and may have negative effects on the other students.

This is not to suggest that behavior modification is an ineffective method of control. When used properly in a systematic routine, it is a very powerful method of management. Many teachers, as noted by Charles (1981), have found it to be the answer to their management problems. The emphasis on reward instead of punishment and on "good behavior" instead of "bad behavior" makes life in the classroom more enjoyable for teachers as well as students.

A most important point for all teachers to remember is that leaders often inappropriately use remuneration to reinforce behaviors because they are not aware that they are giving rewards. For example, a teacher may allow a disruptive student to go on an errand in order to get the student out of the classroom. This strategy may gain the teacher a few minutes of peace and tranquility, but more problems will be caused in the long run. Without being aware of it, the teacher has used a type of remunerative strategy. The student received a reward (being allowed to go on an errand) for exhibiting something the teacher did not mean to reinforce: disruptive behavior. If the theory is sound, the student is likely to relate such *DISRUPTIVE BEHAVIOR* to *BEING ALLOWED TO LEAVE THE ROOM*. This would result in the augmentation of similar disruptions. Teachers must constantly and systematically analyze their own behavior to determine if the reinforcements they provide are really for those behaviors they want to see repeated.

All instructional leaders, at some point, use certain remunerative strategies to control the behaviors of their students. Frequently, as noted above, teachers actually reward behaviors that they would like to see extinguished. Since remuneration is such a powerful tool in the management of behavior, teachers must use it systematically, not randomly. When rewards are given in an unsystematic fashion, they lose their effectiveness and tend to have a negative effect on the total group.

3.3. Coercive Strategies

Coercive strategies are punitive in nature. They are designed to react directly to the disruptive behavior being exhibited. Coercive strategies are being used when a teacher does one of the following: (1) strikes a student, (2) takes away a student's belongings or privileges, or (3) threatens to do either of the preceding. Consequently, coercion is leadership by force. When a teacher decides to use coercion in order to influence the behavior of students, that teacher is telling the students they must do what they are told to do because the teacher is a powerful person whose strength and influence must be feared. Coercive strategies, therefore, rest upon a power base which must be sustained. The degree to which a teacher appears strong and in control is the degree to which that teacher can expect to influence students through coercion.

One is reminded, when thinking of threats and their effects, of the analogy of the town marshal and the gunfighter movies about the "Old West." In this analogy, the marshal's ability to control the town is based on his strength and skill with a gun. The outlaw comes to town, and the marshal's ability to maintain order is based upon the fact that he must be able to either scare the deviant away or defeat him in a contest of strength. The marshal begins by issuing a threat to the gunfighter (these threats often work on less adventurous, more timid people but never seem to influence the professional gunman). After listening to the marshal's threat, the outlaw rebuffs the lawman in no uncertain terms. At this point, the marshal has but one course of action left open: he now must back up his threat with action. The two characters now meet in the street to have their "showdown" with the eyes of all the citizens upon them. As events have pushed both protagonists into a situation nearly beyond their control, the marshal knows he must fight because to back down would be tantamount to giving up all control of the town forever. The marshal also realizes his ability to control is based on his power and strength; conversely, to display weakness would lessen his ability to control some of the citizens of the town who, in the future, would see if they too could back down the authority. In most old movies, the marshal successfully defeats the outlaw, and the citizens go back to their daily tasks confident that the control of their society rests in the hands of an invulnerable leader.

The teacher who relies on coercive strategies is, in many respects, like the marshal just described. A student may disrupt order in the class, just as the outlaw disrupted order in the town, and the teacher may issue a threat to frighten the student, just as the marshal attempted to frighten the gunfighter. Threats did not always work for the marshal, and they do not always work for teachers who sometimes receive rebuffs from their students. Just as the marshal had to back up threats with action, so do teachers. The teacher who uses coercive strategies to control the group is just as certain to have "showdowns" as was our fictitious marshal. Moreover, like our lawman, the teacher knows that retreating is a poor option because all eyes are focused on the event. If the teacher allows the deviant student to continue the misconduct without backing up the previous threat of punishment, other students in the group are likely to attempt a similar power play in the future. Unfortunately, this is where the analogy ends; real life is often very different from old movies. In real life, many marshals were either shot by gunmen or backed down from the danger. In the classroom, teachers, too, may retreat and lose confrontations. Although it is rare that such a loss results in physical danger, teachers can suffer from such defeats and can be hurt even more when they choose to retreat from the confrontation. The type of damage done to the teacher is that which is manifested in an inability to control future disruptions. Such a teacher has been "outgunned."

The teacher who chooses to use coercive strategies must be prepared to maintain a strong power base from which to operate. If anything ever happens to erode the teacher's power, the ability to influence students through coercion will quickly wane. Teachers who abuse the use of coercive strategies (i.e. use them to excess) put themselves in leadership positions that are oftentimes difficult to maintain. Essentially, this means that a teacher who enters the classroom with the intention to manage the setting with a *FAST GUN* and an *IRON FIST* must have the strength of character and leadership skill necessary to maintain the position of authority. The teacher who tries to coerce and cannot sustain a position of authority through strong action is likely to retreat and appear vulnerable to many of the students. Such a teacher usually finds it difficult or impossible to regain leadership by turning to remunerative and normative strategies. It is advisable for teachers to enter the classroom with the notion that control can best be maintained through normative and remunerative approaches.

3.4. An Example of Coercion: Use of Punishment

Although you should try to maintain control in other ways, a time will come when you will face a situation where one or more students are disturbing your class on a regular basis. Punitive measures (a type of coercion) may be the only alternative. If this does come (and it is hoped that it would come only infrequently), you must have a precise plan of action. Accordingly, such coercive strategies should only be used after considerable forethought.

When the teacher decides that punishment is in order, it is of utmost importance that the punishment fit the individuals involved as well as the infraction committed. With this in mind, it must be remembered that punishing seven-year-olds is a very different matter than punishing seventeen-year-olds. Also, punishment, to a great extent, is actually a state of mind; that which seems severe to one individual may not even bother another. In a social setting such as a classroom, punishment must appear due and fair to both the students being punished as well as to the other students in the classroom. It is nearly impossible to use coercive measures with one student and not affect the attitudes and behaviors of all the other students as well.

It is recommended that punishment never take the form of striking a student or withholding affection. There are simply too many risks involved to ever justify this course of action. Naturally, the striking of another human being brings rise to certain ethical questions; such questions must be solved in the minds of each individual involved. It should be pointed out that corporal punishment of a child by a parent is a significantly different question than corporal punishment of a student by a teacher. The possibility that such teacher behavior could result in litigation is a reality. Punishment, then, will be discussed here as it refers to restricting students, taking away one or more of their privileges or belongings, or talking to students in a derisive way.

It must be admitted, even by those who feel strongly against the use of coercive strategies, that research evidence supports the contention that the intensity and duration of punishment is positively related to the rapidity and the degree of suppression of unwanted behaviors (Walters and Grusec, 1977). In other words, if a teacher wants a student to stop exhibiting some behavior, that teacher can punish the student, and the student will stop the behavior if the punishment is severe enough. In fact, the longer and harder the punishment, the more likely the behavior will be suppressed. Therefore, it is not a question of utility being considered in the use of punishment; punishment can stop undesired behavior. The question of concern is, in essence, an ethical one. Should punishment be used? Does punishment have harmful effects on students' personalities? Walters and Grusec have suggested that non-physical punishment and those types which avoid ridicule and other attacks on the student's self-esteem are not harmful and can actually aid in the socialization process. The authors went on to suggest that the student who receives punishment will not necessarily associate negative reactions with the teacher if the teacher is also seen as a reinforcing agent, not just a punishing agent.

It seems clear that punishment can produce the desired results: suppression of unwanted behavior. However, not only does the use of coercive strategies require a strong power base in the social setting, the teacher must be aware that punishment can have negative psychological effects if the student's self-esteem is attacked. Punishment must be administered only when the students involved have a clear understanding of why they are being punished. Although there is reason to believe that the misuse of punishment can do more harm than good, it is not necessary to conclude that because of this, coercive strategies should never be used to influence the behavior of students. Punishment, when used in a proper, humane fashion, can be an invaluable socialization strategy in the classroom setting. The teacher should always adhere to certain reasonable guidelines concerning the use of such strategies. They should never be used recklessly.

Personal attacks on students must be avoided; punishment should center on the unwanted behavior, *NEVER THE STUDENTS.* In order to function productively, students must feel that they are an important part of the classroom group. If the teacher makes a habit of scorning certain students or making jokes at their expense, these students are likely to lack any feeling of belonging. Moreover, personal attacks weaken students' self-concepts. Any lowering of self-esteem may lead to poor academic performance and an augmentation of disruptive behavior. Personal attacks on students by a teacher are generally viewed as unfair and inexcusable by all students, not just the students being ridiculed. Clearly, any chance that the teacher has to develop normative control strategies will be seriously jeopardized. Students in this predicament are not likely to be normatively influenced by a teacher who practices personal attacks against them.

At all cost, teachers must avoid embarrassing students in front of their peers. This type of behavior is destructive, in that it will void future attempts at developing normative strategies and will increase the likelihood of subsequent student rebellion. In fact, especially in the case of students in the upper elementary and secondary grades, students often feel they must rebel against a teacher who belittles them in front of their peer group. For example, an adolescent who is told by the teacher to "Take a seat or I will put you in one!" has no alternative left open. If this student takes the seat, his peer group may tease him because he allowed the teacher to put him down in such a rude fashion. Consequently, the student, who may really prefer to take his seat and avoid the problem, often feels compelled to rebuff his teacher. Now, of course, the teacher is truly in a difficult position. In situations such as this, it is easy for the teacher to be put in a position where retreating is imminent. What does the teacher do if the student feels pushed enough to tell the teacher to back up the threat?

Coercive strategies should not be used to influence students through fear of public embarrassment. If students are not treated with a certain amount of dignity, the teacher is not likely to be viewed as a professional worthy of respect. This type of abusive behavior on the part of a teacher, then, will create an image that students can learn to detest. Students often rebel against such a teacher out of revenge. The avoidance of embarrassing, personal, public attacks on a student is an absolute maxim of effective classroom management.

When the teacher finds it necessary to use punishment, it is important to explain clearly to the student why the punishment is being administered. Giving the student a rationale for the use of punitive measures not only helps the student relate his behavior to that of the teacher but also creates an image of fair play on the teacher's part. Obviously, this image of fairness can be used as a foundation for the development of subsequent normative control strategies. The development of a rationale for punishment can also be very beneficial to teachers. If the teacher takes the opportunity to create such a rationale, it will become much easier for that teacher to deal with subsequent disruptions and to decide upon a punishment which is suitable for the circumstances involved. Teachers frequently misinterpret the disruptive behavior of students. After developing a rationale for the punishment of students, the teacher will come to a point where the students' behavior is seen in a more realistic light. As a result, the behavior and the students can both be reacted to more justly.

Punishment should be administered in such a way as to allow students soon to redeem themselves with the teacher. In the meantime, the teacher should not hold grudges against students after the punishment has been administered. Since a major objective of any coercive strategy is for the student to associate the disruptive behavior with some negative consequences, it is imperative for the student to understand that punishment is not being administered due to a personality conflict with the teacher. It should be remembered that all group members have a need to be cared for and to feel as if they belong. When someone as significant as the teacher shows disapproval, students may feel so threatened that it becomes difficult to function in a meaningful way. Such students need to be given an opportunity to receive some type of positive display of approval from the teacher. Upon receiving approval from the teacher, students can then ascertain that it was the unwanted behavior, not a personal dislike, which caused the teacher to use punitive measures. Students who feel that the teacher still respects them are much more readily influenced by normative strategies than are students who feel that their teacher dislikes them and wishes they were not part of the group.

For the safety of both the student and the teacher, the teacher should avoid any overt display of anger or emotion when administering punishment. Due to the fact that coercive strategies are to be used only after much forethought and wise judgment, the teacher should avoid any type of angry outburst that could result in a "snap" decision. As stated earlier, the calm, confident teacher is much less likely to make a mistake in judgment and, therefore, is much more likely to develop an image necessary for the successful use of normative strategies. Moreover, anger and emotion on the part of the teacher may foster such behavior, in return, on the part of the students. By the teacher remaining even-tempered, however, a calming effect will develop among the students which will generally result in the diminishing of further difficulties. Finally, as the teacher works to develop a more productive relationship with parents, it is important to avoid any emotional displays in the classroom that might lead to the deterioration of such a relationship. It is difficult for parents as well as administrators to support teachers who continually lose their tempers with students.

Punishment, although it can suppress unwanted behaviors, often has a tendency only to be temporary in its effectiveness. Too frequently, punishment tends to focus on merely one isolated behavior. Coercive strategies often fail to center upon the actual cause of disruptive behaviors. Punishment, therefore, must be seen as a means to *TEMPORARILY* deter particular student behaviors that are creating an immediate classroom disturbance. The teacher may regain control of the classroom and continue instruction, but disturbances frequently recur because the underlying cause of the problem still exists. As a result, punishment must be used only as a small portion of a larger strategy designed to change disruptive behavior by alleviating its cause.

Punishment, then, should be administered infrequently as a

reaction to repeated misbehavior. If a student repeatedly exhibits disruptive behavior, the teacher has two problems to address. First, the teacher must immediately regain control over the group in order that instruction may continue. Second, the teacher must help the pupil deal with the cause of the misbehavior because, even if the disturbance no longer exists within the classroom, there may be disturbances within the student which make it impossible for the learner to successfully function in a social setting. Punishment may very well help the teacher control the first problem, but coercive strategies will never help to alleviate and may even exacerbate the second. If the deviant behavior continues and is accompanied by repeated punishment, the student's self-concept may be damaged in such a way that even more defiant activity will characterize future behavior. It is easy to see that punishment can produce an effect opposite from that which the teacher desires. If a student is being disruptive because of anger or fear, punishment might even aggravate the situation causing further disruption.

The use of punishment has been a very controversial topic. Many educators and psychologists alike feel that punishment should never be used to influence a student's behavior. Hill (1981) suggests that this is probably so because reinforcement is more pleasant and produces a closer and friendlier relationship between teacher and student than does punishment. Teacher use of punishment seems to be associated with negative behaviors such as hitting and revenge. In this light, it is likely that educators and psychologists prefer positive reinforcement over punishment because of humane values, not because positive reinforcement is relatively more effective at changing behavior. The misuse of punishment has several weaknesses, as does the misuse of positive reinforcement. In spite of this, most teachers use some type of coercive strategy when students repeatedly display disruptive behavior.

Formative Evaluation: Section 3*

1. Describe the three major types of group and personal control strategies.

---

*See the Appendix for suggested answers to these questions.

2. Compare and contrast the remunerative and coercive strategies in terms of potential harmful effects on students.
3. Outline the pros and cons of using punishment in the classroom.

SECTION 4. COPING WITH SPECIFIC CONTROL PROBLEMS

All specific control problems should be approached with the long-term goal of solving the cause of the problem. Such an approach will take time and effort on the part of the teacher, but the benefits should make the effort worthwhile. Suggestions concerning the treatment of several common management problems follow. You should be reminded that all such problems must be reacted to with consideration given to the make-up of the total group and the personalities of the students involved. It would be a mistake to suggest that all students exhibiting a common behavior problem exhibit this behavior for the same reasons. For example, all inattentive learners are not inattentive for the same reasons. Charles (1976), while discussing a study by Ritholz, reported that the seven most commonly mentioned examples of misbehavior are as follows: (1) *INATTENTION*, (2) *DISRUPTIVE TALKING*, (3) *UNRULINESS*, (4) *AGGRESSION*, (5) *ATTENTION-SEEKING*, (6) *DEFIANCE*, and (7) *DISHONESTY.* Each one of these behavior syndromes will be examined individually.

4.1. Inattention

Inattention is usually manifested in such behaviors as staring into space (or daydreaming), doing unrelated work, and doodling or playing with objects on the desk (e.g. pencils or rubber bands). This type of behavior is typically disturbing to teachers for several reasons. Primarily, if attentive students decide to copy such inattentive behavior, the teacher will find it virtually impossible to conduct instruction. In situations such as these, the teacher is always concerned when observing inattentive students because the conscientious teacher desires that all students profit from the instructional process. Frequently, there is another reason teachers become disturbed when observing inattentive behavior. Teachers often take offense when students are inattentive. They feel the students are communicating that they, as teachers, are boring and ineffective. This personal criticism, whether realistic or not, generally places the teacher in a defensive position.

What are the underlying causes of inattentive behavior? Inattention can be caused by a number of influencing factors, including both poor teaching and curriculum construction. If the teacher's instruction is characterized by a repetition of long, dry episodes where students are given little opportunity and encouragement to participate actively, many students are apt to become bored and, as a result, inattentive. Lessons that last for long periods of time while focusing on the same activity also frustrate learners to the point where they simply lose interest and are no longer attentive. Aside from these factors, certain personal characteristics of the teacher can contribute to student inattentiveness. The monotonic voice that drones on, for example, has become a symbol of the stereotypical bore; a teacher with such a voice quality should not expect students to become excited listeners. Teachers who fail to use gestures or other movement to supplement their verbal communication often lose the students' attention. To complement gestures, effective teachers must also be cognizant of the positive impact of occasional humor in the classroom. Effective teachers frequently insert a humorous anecdote or joke at the precise moment the learners are beginning to allow their minds to wander. Probably, the most significant consideration in the analysis of student attentiveness is the level of student participation allowed. Classrooms where students are given the opportunity to actively participate in the lessons, as well as the planning of activities and selecting of materials, constitute environments that foster learner attentiveness.

Naturally, the source of an attention problem could be found in the students as opposed to the teacher or the curriculum. Some students may become inattentive even when the teacher is doing an excellent job and the curriculum is dynamic. In addition, students may have problems outside of school which are so serious that the classroom instruction simply represents insignificant demands. As a result, teachers must become acquainted with their students in order to better understand them and their problems. Some students, unfortunately, have been allowed to be inattentive so frequently that they have made a habit of letting their minds wander. In fact, students may have short attention spans simply because they have never been encouraged, reinforced, or even required to be attentive. Regardless of the cause, inattentiveness is a behavior which seems deviant to many teachers. Solutions must be found to aid the inattentive student in developing a longer attention span.

Fortunately, there are ways a teacher can help inattentive learners. Developing an effective question-asking strategy is frequently beneficial in addressing this problem. Too, teachers may need to repeatedly ask questions of those students who have the habit of not paying attention to class discussions. Drawing the learners into the lesson and making it necessary for them to remain alert are the purposes of these questions. In this regard, it often is helpful to ask the question first and then call upon the student. If the student is called upon before the question is asked, other students in the classroom may not pay attention to the question. Another major consideration for the teacher is whether or not reinforcements are being used effectively. Just as it is important to reward students for being attentive, it is also necessary to withold reinforcements when students are being inattentive. For example, when directions are given and students do not pay attention, teachers are only reinforcing inattentiveness when they continually repeat the directions. When teachers make it easy for students to be inattentive, they are not only reinforcing the inattentive learner but they are also communicating to the entire group that it is not really necessary to listen carefully. Careful listening is a learned behavior. Students who are inattentive are not likely to become careful listeners in one or two days; their behavior must be molded over time. It is the teacher's responsibility to be careful always to reinforce such students when they are attentive; moreover, teachers must review the importance of careful listening with the group and insure that no one will be reinforced for being inattentive.

4.2. Disruptive Talking

Disruptive talk is that type of verbal communication which is viewed as unacceptable by the teacher. Of course, different teachers set their own standards for acceptable talk at different levels. It is possible that no other standard for acceptable behavior varies as much among teachers as the one that serves to define acceptable talking. Since many teachers change their level of acceptable talk from one day to another, these changes may very well be due to the teachers' change of mood. As might be expected, students often find it confusing when their teachers fluctuate in the amount of talk allowed. In an effort to avoid such confusion, teachers must always be consistent and aware of the danger of punishing a student today for a behavior which was acceptable previously. Talking can often disturb the learning process for students who are attempting to attend to instruction. Even more than being disruptive, the student who is constantly involved in idle talk is not likely to be achieving the desired learning outcomes. Furthermore, as was the case with inattentive students, teachers frequently take personal offense when students talk when it is felt they should be listening. Teachers tend to interpret this behavior to mean that students think their instruction is unexciting or unimportant.

Students become involved in disruptive talk for several reasons. Even though these reasons are both numerous and varied, the teacher can control the environment to the extent that much of what can be viewed as the causes for such talk is eliminated. Disruptive talk often takes place because students do not understand the instruction or directions of their teacher. That is, when teachers are not clear in their communication, students are likely to become confused and ask one another for clarification. Teachers should observe this type of student behavior and determine the need for further elaboration. Unfortunately, teachers frequently punish students when they are asking one another for help because the teacher erroneously assumes the talk is not related to the instruction. Another cause for idle, disruptive talk is boring lessons. Teachers will be able to diminish much unwanted talking by developing instruction which holds the interest of the learners. Many problems associated with disruptive talk and inattentiveness can be solved by teachers simply projecting enthusiasm about the content under study and by adding some variety to the type of instruction taking place. Teachers will often profit greatly from a re-examination of what they perceive as being *DISRUPTIVE TALK*. It is not uncommon for students to become so excited about their work that they share their ideas with each other. The teacher should be pleased to see such interest and should be aware that verbal interaction is an invaluable aid to learning. Students may become engaged in unwanted talk because they have become excited over some unexpected event or special occasion. Happenings such as ball games, assemblies, birthdays, and classroom visitors frequently create a stir of emotion resulting in what may be interpreted as disruptive talk. Finally, disruptive talk can be a problem resulting from certain student traits. For example, the outgoing, verbal student who completes assignments early may develop a habit of using all spare time visiting with other students. Talking to one's friends can be a most enjoyable pastime and a difficult habit to overcome. Added to this, conversation is almost "contagious," in that if some students begin to talk freely, others will see and hear them and begin to talk with their neighbors as well.

Prevention of disruptive talk must begin with the teacher. If students are to be quiet during a given time period, they must have assignments which are both stimulating enough to hold their interest and adequate enough to keep them occupied for the entire instructional period. Students who have an ample amount of work to complete at the proper level for instruction (i.e. neither too simple nor too difficult) are not likely to become involved in idle conversation. It is important that teachers also remind students about the proper conduct to be exhibited when unexpected events take place, such as visitors coming to the classroom or going to special assembly programs. Teachers should be aware that these interruptions in the typical schedule have the potential to arouse the interest and excitement of the students. If the teacher would take a moment to talk with the group about these events and to answer their questions concerning the event, the class should quickly calm down. Effective teachers do not try to fight to suppress this normal curiosity and excitement. If the teacher knows about these events before they happen, prior adjustments can be made to prepare the students instead of waiting until the last minute when the level of excitement is apt to be at its highest. Students who chronically exhibit disruptive talk may need to be isolated from the source stimulating their disruptive behavior. All that might need be done is to create seating arrangements that separate those students who insist upon talking to each other. Another effective method of controlling disruptive talk is the placing of talkative students in an area of the room which will usually be in close proximity to the teacher. When seated close to the teacher, students, regardless of their talkative traits, are less likely to continue unwanted talking.

When events occur which arouse unwanted chatter, the teacher might discuss the problem and its cause with the total class afterwards. The technique of the class discussion, sometimes referred to as the class meeting (discussed earlier in this chapter), has received much acclaim as a method of approaching such problems. While it is difficult for students to objectively examine their own behavior when they are excited, they can look back upon their behavior at a later point and determine what they did which was inappropriate and how best to avoid future recurrences.

A final word of warning is appropriate. You should never have a classroom atmosphere where all student-to-student talk is discouraged. Students need to interact both with their peers and their teachers if optimal learning is to take place. Although teachers cannot allow students to chat with each other in such a way as to diminish their own learning as well as the learning of their classmates, it would be ill-advised to set such rigid rules that students are afraid to ask questions or make appropriate remarks during a lesson. Much has been said about excessive talking; however, remember that the student who never speaks may have a learning problem due to the lack of the ability to communicate ideas to others. It would be a serious shortcoming if teachers developed classroom environments which fostered such a lack of open communication.

4.3. Unruliness

Unruliness is defined as a state of general misbehavior where students seem to lack any control over their own actions. Examples of such behavior are *PUSHING OTHER STUDENTS, LAUGHING LOUDLY, GETTING OUT OF ONE'S SEAT WITHOUT PERMISSION,* and *PLAYING PRACTICAL JOKES.* The unruly student is not necessarily aggressive or defiant; such a student simply is conducting himself in a way that is not desirable. These students may exhibit this type of behavior on a regular basis. Charles (1976) reported that teachers feel the most serious offensive behavior that students could manifest is heterosexual behavior. Actually, this in not a behavior exclusive to secondary students as might be thought. Elementary school students satisfy a natural curiosity by mutual exploration of the body. It is interesting that teachers find this type of behavior the *MOST* offensive of all possible behaviors. Evidently, the social mores concerning public sexual behavior are so powerful that many teachers react quite strongly to a set of behaviors which psychologists have come to simply label as normal behavior. Teachers, of course, are much more concerned with group control and socialization than are many psychologists. Unruly behavior, then, is a group and situational-related concept. That which may be acceptable in certain groups or in certain situations might not be acceptable in others. No doubt, to the degree that a student's home and community adopts the same standards of behavior that the school adopts, that student's behavior will be seen as being compatible with and in conformity to the role expectations for a public school student. In essence, a student who comes from a background which does not reinforce the middle-class standards of the school is much more likely to exhibit behavior seen as being unruly than is the student who has been rewarded for such behavior in his home and community. This factor places the teacher in a difficult situation. When correcting the behavior of an unruly student, the teacher must avoid making statements that attack individuals who exhibit such behavior. For example, if a student curses and is told by the teacher that only evil and sinful people do such a thing, that student may become alienated if those in his home and community use such language. It is important to separate, at all times, actions from people when reacting to unruliness. In reference to the previous example, the teacher could inform the student that such language is not to be used in the classroom without referring to the individual as being bad or evil because he used such words.

Because general misconduct can be manifested in a number of different forms, the causes of unruliness are varied. Obviously, the learning tasks assigned to a student can be so difficult or non-challenging that the student becomes either overextended, frustrated or bored. Such a learning environment frequently puts so much stress on students that they become unruly and difficult to control. Teachers who fail to create an appropriately stimulating learning environment for the students are setting the stage for this state of general misbehavior. Unfortunately, unruliness, as is the case with most types of misbehavior, is both *CATCHING* and habit forming. Students who observe their peers involved in inappropriate conduct are prone to participate in unruly behaviors themselves. As a result, when left unchecked, this type of general misconduct becomes commonplace, making it even more difficult for students to stop their improper behaviors. Naturally, teachers can expect a certain amount of a lack of self-control from all students under some circumstances. Elementary students can become very excited over special events like holiday parties and magic shows just as older students do when it is time for an important ball game or prom night. Teachers should not expect young people to always exhibit self-control and restraint; adults certainly do not always exhibit such qualities under similar social conditions. It is advisable for teachers to remember that such special events can activate unwanted conduct on the part of overstimulated students.

In controlling unruliness, teachers must plan ahead in order to be prepared for these special events so that the students' emotional reactions do not go beyond reasonable limits. Effective teachers talk to the students beforehand to help them become ready for upcoming events and to make them aware of what type of behavior is to be considered acceptable. When dealing with students who are consistently unruly, the teacher must assume that the learning environment is lacking something which would make their social adjustment easier. Too frequently, students who consistently display this sort of general misconduct are unhappy with school because they cannot achieve a desired level of satisfaction from their academic progress. Such students are having learning difficulties which are being manifested in an overt behavior which allows them to exist in an environment that provides them little reinforcement and satisfaction. The teacher, upon identifying such a student, should *FIRST* view the student as one who is in need of a better placement within a more stimulating learning environment, not as a student in need of discipline. Teachers often forget that unruly behavior can be the symptom of an inappropriate learning activity and to attack the unruliness is only to attack a symptom, not the cause, of misconduct. Unruly students are often those who are easily overstimulated or have short attention spans. Such students frequently need more structure in their activities and movement, especially until they have fully learned what is expected of them. These students probably are less successful working on their own than under the supervision of a teacher because they are too easily distracted. Classwork is often more productive when students are seated in a section of the room where their peers cannot interfere with their learning; sometimes it only takes a casual comment from a peer to distract these individuals enough to get them off task and involved in some undesirable behavior. Total isolation from the group may be necessary if they become stimulated to the point where proper conduct is unlikely. Such isolation should be in a *NONSTIMULATING* area, and students should see it as an opportunity to be calm and under control more than as punishment. Consequently, this isolation should be a direct result of the students' unwanted behavior and never a form of reward. The student who has developed a habit of unruliness must receive reinforcement for segments of desirable behavior. As already noted, such a student often obtains very little positive feedback. Reinforcement for desirable behavior will often help the teacher get close enough to the learner to discover the real cause of the students' misconduct.

4.4. Aggression

Aggression on the part of students can present the teacher with immediate and serious problems. When students talk out of turn or are inattentive, the teacher can take some time to analyze the behavior and try to determine how best to deal with it. However, when students are being overly aggressive, the teacher may well have to react quickly and decisively. The teacher has the responsibility of protecting the safety of every student in the classroom; aggressive students, frequently, can threaten the safety of others or even themselves. It is important for the teacher to remember that aggression is marked by a lack of emotional control. Students who are involved in fights or temper tantrums are not in the proper state of mind to reason or discuss problems. Moreover, when such students are approached by the teacher, they are very likely to be so upset that they will verbally or even physically attack. Students like these obviously need to be calmed by the teacher as quickly as possible; whereas, verbal retorts by the teacher will only increase the students' level of frustration and increase the likelihood of even more severe aggression. *AGGRESSION*, then, is a much more intense behavior problem than is *UNRULINESS*. An unruly student is usually bothersome and often distracting to other students, but the aggressive student, on the other hand, can be physically or emotionally harmful to other students. Aggression cannot, under any circumstances, be permitted in the classroom.

The causes of aggression can often be extremely complex. In fact, some students who chronically exhibit aggression probably will only learn to curb their emotions after they have received professional help. Some students may have problems that are so deep-seated that they are actually emotional *TIME BOMBS* who find it virtually impossible to function in a highly active social setting such as a classroom. Fortunately, the number of these highly unstable students who should be removed from the school is very few indeed. Most agressive behavior results from momentary outbursts as a consequence of tense frustration. Aggression can be modeled. Therefore, students who come from homes and communities where aggression is a relatively common behavior are likely to exhibit hostile behavior because they have seen others do so consistently. Aggression can also result from the intense frustration that is caused by repeated academic failures. Some students have such difficult and unsuccessful learning experiences that they actually rebel against the school and teacher by overt, aggressive behavior. Oddly enough, this type of aggression is often seen by psychologists as a healthy release of inner frustrations that would be much more serious if it were held within. Teachers, however, cannot allow this type of behavior to exist in the social structure of the classroom. Student aggression, besides its potential for personal harm, is a true threat to the teacher's leadership role.

In dealing with aggressive students, teachers must first try to calm them down before attempting to solve the actual problem. Unfortunately, this can rarely be done by talking; aggressive students are generally so emotional at the time, that conversation usually evolves into an argument, which only augments the tension. In analyzing alternative actions to take, the age of the students involved in the aggressive act will help to determine the teacher's approach. For example, if nine-year-old students are having a fight, it would be reasonable for most teachers to stop the fight by restraining the most aggressive student until they have calmed to the point where the anger and frustration can be discussed. It might be very unwise for most secondary teachers to wade into a fight between two sixteen-year-olds. When students this age are fighting and the teacher attempts restraint, the teacher is taking the risk of being hit and seriously hurt. Too, the student who was not held may continue the attack as the teacher restrains the adversary. It is usually advisable for a secondary teacher to send for help and direct bystanders to stay clear of danger while verbally trying to get the two (or more) combatants to desist. The teacher who is dealing with younger students and feels that it is necessary to stop the fight by holding one of them should remember that it is wise to allow the students to stop struggling and arguing completely before attempting to get their cooperation. Since aggressive students can only be dealt with constructively after composure has been regained, it is often best to separate the aggressive student from all sources of tension. It is recommended that during the course of aggressive behavior, the teacher refrain from verbal chastisement and emotional outbursts, which would only further arouse the student's aggression. The teacher should always make it clear to students that physical aggression (e.g. fighting or throwing objects) and verbal aggression (e.g. sassing the teacher or calling names and bullying classmates) are unacceptable behaviors in any social group, especially in the classroom. Students who are chronic problems must be either isolated from the group or punished by having certain privileges taken away. The teacher, however, must go beyond merely dealing with the aggressive outbursts. Attempts should be made to discuss the source of the aggression with the students after they have regained their composure. Often, students exhibit aggressive behavior because something is happening at school that is causing them great frustration. The teacher should listen patiently to the students and attempt to help them relieve these frustrations. If the source of frustration is not removed, the student is likely to become chronically aggressive or develop a dislike for or mistrust of the total school environment. Fundamentally, aggression should be thought of as a symptom of a more complex source of frustration. It is the role of the teacher to help the student deal with the frustration or to locate others who are more qualified to do so.

4.5. Attention-Seeking

For years, teachers and parents alike have discussed the fact that some students seem to break behavior rules simply to get the attention either of their peers or the adults in charge. These students often seek attention by trying to "entertain" the other people in the group. As a result, they are frequently labelled *SHOW-OFFS* or *CLASS CLOWNS*. Some younger students receive the label *TATTLETALE* because they try to get the teacher's attention by *TELLING* when others have broken rules or done something of which the teacher would not approve. Of course, peer pressure abates tattling as the students get older (i.e. upper elementary and secondary levels). It must be remembered that attention-seeking, like most other types of misconduct, is a symptom of some other problem.

Students who are attention-seekers are usually trying to compensate for a real need. These students frequently are not getting the kind of attention in their home life that they need for proper social adjustment at school. Basically, many *SHOW-OFFS* and *CLASS CLOWNS* are insecure individuals searching for feelings of *LOVE* and *BELONGING*. All attention-seekers are not unloved children with tyrannical parents or from broken homes, but many of them are. Finding the exact source of such problems is often difficult, sometimes even impossible, yet teachers can make things somewhat easier for these students.

Since attention-seekers are characterized by insecurity, the teacher must avoid *PUTTING THEM DOWN* by telling them they are *SILLY* or *ACTING LIKE BABIES*. Avoiding this temptation is often difficult because the chronic attention-seeker can try the patience of the most even-tempered of teachers at the end of a tedious day. Ironically, it is usually the most trying students who need the greatest understanding. There are, fortunately, some important things that teachers can do to help change unwanted student behaviors. While the teacher should give these students attention to the degree that it is possible, the teacher should only reinforce them for appropriate behavior (Good and Brophy, 1973). It will often be necessary to delay attention-seekers instead of refusing them. With this in mind, it is important that teachers plan to give such students some daily, individual attention in order that they may learn that they can receive approval without displaying deviant behavior. Although the *CLASS CLOWN* can sometimes be entertaining and can provide a pleasant break even for the teacher, the teacher must avoid reinforcing such behavior if at all possible. In fact, ignoring the attention-seeker is probably a more profitable approach than trying to use a coercive strategy to change unwanted behavior. Attention-seekers, however, should be reassured that they are important, respected members of the group. This, of course, must be done without giving rewards for seeking attention in unacceptable ways.

4.6. Defiance

Students who refuse to do what the teacher asks or boldly talk back to the teacher in a threatening way are categorized as defiant. The behavior of such students must concern teachers very much. The defiant student, probably more than any other, clearly creates situations where the teacher, as leader of the group, could possibly exhibit retreating behavior. If the teacher gives directions to a student and that student refuses to follow the teacher's directives, the deviant behavior must be corrected or the teacher may no longer be seen as the leader of the classroom group. Nothing short of true physical danger should be seen as a greater threat to a group leader. Defiant students are communicating to the teacher that they no longer MUST do what they are told to do.

The causes of defiance are quite often deep-seated. Students usually have a level of anger and frustration that has reached a point that can no longer be contained. For these students, this anger and frustration may have been building up over years of negative school experience. (Additional sources of defiant behavior could be found in the home; students who are having problems relating to authority figures in the home may very well react defiantly toward teachers and administrators in the school.) While this is the case, it is very likely that the teacher can have some control over the development of a deviant attitude on the part of the students. Something in the classroom atmosphere or even the teacher's own behavior could possibly be a cause of the defiance. For example, the teacher could, unknowingly, be doing something which makes students feel unliked (e.g. never calling on them), or the teacher could unintentionally be placing one or more students in a stressful situation (e.g. a poor reader being embarrassed because of oral reading assignments as a classroom activity).

Teachers should be cautious when dealing with a hostile student; such a student is not likely to comply automatically to the verbal commands of the teacher. Interaction with such a student is apt to increase hostility because the student is often aware of the fact that serious, deviant behavior has already been exhibited. Rather than take offense at what has already been said and done, the teacher should stay calm and, if at all possible, direct the hostile student out of the classroom. Removing such a student from the classroom has the advantages of (1) giving the student time to get under control, (2) taking away the peer audience which could reinforce further defience, and (3) removing the need for the deviant student to KEEP FACE in front of the entire class. All defiance is not so hostile as to require the immediate removal of the student involved; however, any act of defiance is reason enough for the teacher to hold a PRIVATE conference with the student. Such a student may have corrected the unwanted behavior, but the source of the anger and frustration causing the defiance might be expected to exist long after the original incident has been forgotten. A teacher-student conference may help the student view the teacher as being fair and concerned about his well-being. Through this building of rapport, the student may be able to see why the teacher could act negatively. Since the teacher interacts with these students on a one-to-one basis, the teacher can feel freer to admit mistakes and talk to the student about what can be done to improve the classroom climate and avoid future defiance. The teacher must deal with deviant behavior in such a way as to avoid the act of RETREATING. That is, defiant behavior should never be ignored, since such student behavior must be viewed as a type of power struggle in the classroom. To lose such a power struggle is to relinquish the role of group leader, which would certainly be disastrous to the teacher.

4.7. Dishonesty

Dishonesty is a trait which, as a rule, has always been viewed as totally unacceptable in the school setting. Probably the most common type of dishonesty is cheating; no doubt, this type of behavior takes place at all levels of schooling. Students in the early elementary grades may not have important exams to worry about, but they might decide to copy each others' quiz papers or get someone else to do their homework assignments. Obviously, the telling of untruths and even stealing takes place in many social settings, not only in the school. Certain amounts of dishonest behavior are, regrettably, expected from school-age youths; although teachers certainly do not want to condone dishonest conduct on the part of their students, it must be remembered that children and adolescents are still in the formative stages of moral development. That which may seem to be very deviant to an adult may not seem to be serious misconduct to students. For example, students may actually steal a copy of an exam before the testing date simply to have an adventure, not to really cheat and steal in the sense that a teacher may view this type behavior. In fact, many children in the early elementary grades do not have clear concepts of *OWNERSHIP* and *TRUTH.* Nonetheless, teachers have the responsibility to help students learn acceptable standards for behavior. Dishonesty should always be cast to be seen in a very unfavorable light. Teachers must remember, however, that students are not born with middle-class, adult standards of behavior common to most teachers. Students must learn acceptable behavior in the home, community, and school.

Just as there are a variety of dishonest behaviors, there are a variety of causes for such behaviors. It is a reality of the times that many students come from home and community environments which do condone and even model dishonest behavior; these students are likely to copy those behaviors. Moreover, students can get in the habit of relying upon dishonesty in order to function in the school environment. Some students habitually copy homework from others and cheat on tests to the point where they do not know how to exist in an academic setting without using such tactics. Cheating of this nature can be a characteristic of students having poor self-concepts. These students have failed so frequently that they feel it impossible to get acceptable grades without cheating. It is also possible that during adolescence, students become involved in some less-than-honest deeds simply to appear courageous, adventurous, or mature in the eyes of their peer group. The problem that teachers and administrators face with this type of *RITE OF PASSAGE* is that if one student is successful in gaining peer approval through dishonest acts, other students will try to get approval through the same behaviors.

Dishonest behavior often does not pressure the teacher into the kind of immediate action that aggression or defiance demand. As long as dishonest behavior does not hurt other group members, many students are unaware of its existence. When stealing or cheating on tests become known by the group, however, the teacher can no longer only analyze behavior. At this time, the teacher must take action to correct the unwanted behavior. It is necessary that the students know the teacher does not condone dishonesty. Repeated cases of dishonest conduct may require such corrective strategies as deprivation of privileges. First and foremost, it is important for the teacher to determine if the student is being assigned work on an appropriate instructional level; a student who cheats may be in a curriculum that is too demanding. Such a student should be placed in a content area where success is possible without having to rely upon dishonest tactics. In dealing with students who have been dishonest (e.g. cheated, stolen, or lied), the teacher must be cautious not to label the student. It must be clear that it is the deed that is dishonest, not the person. If a student is labelled as a *CHEAT* or a *THIEF*, the possible ill effects on the self-concept is an unnecessary consequence that should be avoided. Telling students they are bad or dishonest may cause them to think of themselves negatively and begin more consistently assuming the role of a dishonest person.

Formative Evaluation: Section 4*

1. Define and provide an example of each of the following specific control problems: inattention, disruptive talking, unruliness, aggression, attention seeking, defiance, dishonesty.
2. Suggest possible underlying causes of each of the specific control problems listed in question one.
3. Outline at least two preventive measures that a teacher could take to avoid each of the specific control problems listed in question one.

---

*See the Appendix for suggested answers to these questions.

REFERENCES

Bernstein, B. Language and social class. *British Journal of Sociology,* 1960, 11, 271–276.

Biehler, R., and Snowman, J. *Psychology applied to teaching* (4th ed.). Boston: Houghton Mifflin, 1982.

Charles, C. *Educational psychology: The instructional endeavor* (2nd ed.). Saint Louis: C.V. Mosby, 1976.

Charles, C. *Building classroom discipline.* New York: Longman, 1981.

Dreikurs, R. *Psychology in the classroom* (2nd ed.). New York: Harper and Row, 1968.

Dreikurs, R., and Cassell, P. *Discipline without tears.* New York: Hawthorn Books, 1972.

Glasser, W. *Reality therapy: A new approach to psychiatry.* New York: Harper and Row, 1965.

Glasser, W. *Schools without failure.* New York: Harper and Row, 1969.

Good, T., and Brophy, J. *Looking in classrooms.* New York: Harper and Row, 1973.

Good, T., and Brophy, J. *Educational psychology: A realistic approach.* New York: Holt, Rinehart, and Winston, 1980.

Gordon, T. *T.E.T. teacher effectiveness training.* New York: Wyden, 1974.

Hill, W. *Principles of learning: A handbook of applications.* Sherman Oaks, CA: Alfred Publishing Company, 1981.

Hunt, G., and Bedwell, L. An axiom for classroom management. *The High School Journal,* 1982, 66(1), 10–13.

Kounin, J. *Discipline and group management in classrooms.* New York: Holt, Rinehart, and Winston, 1970.

Schlechty, P. The psychological bias of American educators. *Ball State University Faculty Lecture Series.* Muncie, IN, 1969.

Schlechty, P. *Teaching and social behavior: Toward an organizational theory of instruction.* Boston: Allyn and Bacon, 1976.

Travers, R. *Essentials of learning.* New York: Macmillan Publishing Company, 1977.

Waller, W. *The sociology of teaching.* New York: John Wiley and Sons, 1932.

Walters, G., and Grusec, J. *Punishment.* San Francisco, CA: W. H. Freeman Publishers, 1977.

CHAPTER SIX

THE TEACHER AS AN
EVALUATOR OF PERFORMANCE

A classroom presents an environment that is both intricate and fast-paced. The teacher who becomes effective, who learns the many cause-and-effect relationships between teacher behavior and student behavior, between planning and implementation, between motivation and hard work, between leadership and followership will have gained these insights only through developing proficiency in evaluation. As professionals, teachers must evaluate student behavior and social climate by comparing actual behavior with stated expectations for behavior. Teachers must also evaluate student achievement, taking into consideration specified standards, and, at the same time through self-evaluation, evaluate materials, performance, and overall classroom interaction.

In this chapter, emphasis will be placed on the evaluation of student performance; several techniques will be suggested and described which aid in this process. The following performances should be mastered after careful study of this chapter.

1. Describe three major steps in the evaluation process.
2. List sources of student evaluation information.
3. Describe an approach to the analysis of evaluation information.
4. Describe several test construction concerns.
5. List characteristics of each of five major types of test items.
6. Construct quality test items representing each of the five major types.
7. Outline major approaches to grading.
8. Explain techniques that may be used to enhance communi-

cation with parents and the benefits possible through increased communication.

9. Describe two approaches to record management.

SECTION 1. EVALUATION AS A THREE-STEP PROCESS

Evaluation is essentially a three-step process which begins with (1) the collection of information, continues with (2) the analysis of information, and concludes with (3) the making of decisions. For instance, when asked to choose between two series of textbooks, one begins by examining each textbook in the series (collecting information), comparing the texts to valued criteria for textbooks (analysis), and then deciding on one series because it contains many of the valued criteria, whereas the other series did not.

Obviously, all decisions are not so simple to make; consequently, the teacher, rather than thinking through the situation in a linear, sequential fashion, is often faced with a more complex evaluation situation. Because of this, the process should be thought of as one in which the original three steps are considered and reconsidered in light of continued interaction with students. Besides being a logically oriented process, evaluation is the means by which people make judgments concerning persons, ideas, or things. With this in mind, teaching is seen to be comprised of a series of continual judgments in which the teacher is constantly (1) observing the classroom and related environment for information, (2) processing the information, and (3) making significant decisions for the improvement of instruction and student performance.

1.1. Collecting Evaluation Information

As evaluative decisions are made, it must be remembered that these decisions are only as accurate as the information that has been acquired. If this information is misinterpreted or in any fashion incorrect, the quality of the evaluation will be diminished. Accordingly, a rash judgment or intuition is to be viewed as suspect; at times, however, situations are such that these judgments are the only ones possible. As long as the untenable nature of these decisions is considered, the teacher should not hesitate in making them. Generally, most situations will allow the teacher to collect or, at least, identify the significant places to locate the needed facts in order to weigh them and make a confident evaluative decision. Knowing that it is rare to (1) have *all* the facts on hand, (2) have sufficient time to interrelate *all* the variables, and (3) make a *conclusive* judgment, evaluations should be completed with only a relative degree of confidence. The more facts that are considered, the more confidence should be placed in the evaluative process.

The collection of evaluation information must be based on the goals and objectives of instruction. Thus, in order to obtain quality information to be used in evaluation, the effective teacher must first carefully determine what the students will be expected to do following instruction (see Chap. 1). Given careful planning of goals and objectives, one need only examine the planned objectives, particularly the criterion statement portions, in order to determine what information must be obtained. It may be discovered that (1) a test must be given in order to collect the information, (2) student assignments and other products should be collected, and/or (3) the teacher should use informal observation to collect information concerning student performance.

Formal Testing

Evaluation and testing, both critical to effective teaching, are often described by teachers and students as synonymous terms. Whereas testing refers to the measurement of student abilities through some formal means, evaluation is actually a more inclusive term that encompasses measurement in all its quantitative and qualitative forms. Testing is merely one of the means of collecting information to be used in evaluation.

Tests serve to aid the learning process in several ways. First, well-planned testing at regular intervals communicates to students the significance of the learning process. In this manner, testing can serve to motivate student learning. If tests are written to assess the higher levels of the cognitive domain, this likewise should stimulate greater effort toward learning at the higher levels. Too, since feedback is essential to learning, tests also serve as an aid in the retention and transfer of learning. Additionally, testing helps to increase the amount students learn and the likelihood that what is learned will be of permanent, lasting value. The end result of an emphasis on testing to students is that a greater understanding of themselves will be gained. Periodic testing will assure consistency in feedback of what each student knows and does not know. It will also help each student clarify misconceptions and reinforce what is known. In short, testing is a decisive factor in what a student learns and how significant that learning is.

Realizing the consequences of the testing program for students, though, is only a portion of its significance. Well-conceived and implemented tests are essential elements in producing data for teachers so that they may evaluate instructional effectiveness. Tests, then, serve both students and teachers and can give insight into proper instruction. Tests are one of the most commonly used evaluative devices and, thus, will be stressed in subsequent sections of this chapter.

Student Products and Assignments

There are, in the typical public school setting, a great variety of student abilities and talents. As a teacher, you will want to give all of your students an opportunity for success. Some students find it very difficult to perform well on traditional paper-and-pencil tests; however, many of these same students have the skills necessary to learn and demonstrate their learning in other ways. The student who may not read or write sufficiently to function successfully on a social studies test, for example, may be able to create a replica of the American flag. Or, the student who might not display competence on a test of poetry scanning may be able to create poems on an audiotape. Obviously, such a variety of evaluation procedures will offer a teacher numerous options concerning the procedures they believe assess significant learnings on the part of students. The use of a variety of procedures, then, will allow more students to demonstrate their skills and knowledge. Furthermore, such a program of alternatives will give the teacher the opportunity to measure levels of ability in all students which cannot always be measured easily with traditional paper-and-pencil tests.

Informal Observation

Along with verbal questioning, informal observation is another common form of collecting evaluation information. This is particularly the case at the primary school level. This formal monitoring function, which must be developed, demands that teachers know what student behaviors to look for and then fit this information into a meaningful set of cause-and-effect relationships. At the very least, the insight into those variables that potentially fit that kind of relationship will be acquired. For example, if a teacher desires the students, at the completion of a lesson, to know what to do in sequence and to exhibit comprehension of the chosen material, it is critical that the teacher monitor student reactions from the beginning of the lesson until the students have completed their tasks. In this process, important cause-and-effect relationships concerning student behavior will, no doubt, be identified. All teachers should be skilled enough to pose probing questions to help answer the basic question, "What has been accomplished?"

Informal observation takes place in many ways as a teacher moves through the classroom monitoring students as they work. This type of observation, which is common practice by early childhood teachers, should be relied on heavily at all levels. As students work on their assignments, it is recommended that teachers make extensive observations, taking careful note of such information as who is having problems and who is not being challenged. Such observations should include the extensive use of probing questions to determine progress. Obviously, there is a degree of subjectivity to informal evaluation and teachers frequently do not allow this type of feedback gathering to affect student grades. However, if the teacher feels that such evaluations clearly add to the knowledge of a student's performance, it, at times, may be appropriate to alter a grade based on informal observation.

1.2. Analyzing Evaluation Information

The evaluation process would yield little worthwhile information if the data received was not carefully analyzed. Essentially, teachers must ask themselves questions about evaluation results that will help to determine if the information they have received is indicative of what the students have actually learned.

In examining test data, teachers should first look carefully at the test itself. Are there questions that were missed by all students? Are there questions that were frequently answered with the same incorrect response? If the answer to either of these questions is in the affirmative, it is possible that the items were not lucid. Also, the teacher must determine if some students missed questions because of their inability to read the test item or if it was because they did not know the necessary information, or both.

When analyzing student products and assignments, teachers have to carefully examine the final product. Is the product an example of the student's own work? Often, students receive "outside" assistance on projects and other assignments. How much learning has actually taken place? Some products are both large and attractive while representing very little learning.

When informally observing students, the teacher must be aware of individual performances. Is this student ready for the material to be learned? Is this student having unique problems? Are several individuals having similar problems? Are some students too advanced for the material under study? Often, very important decisions are made based on informal observations of student behavior. After seeing a student perform and after asking a few verbal questions, you will frequently know if the student involved is working under the best possible conditions for learning.

The following questions should be considered when analyzing evaluation information:

1. Are some test questions missed by all students?
2. Are some test questions frequently answered incorrectly with the same response?
3. Do testing items pose a reading difficulty problem?
4. Does a student project or assignment really represent student work?
5. In making informal observations, are any students having a particularly unique problem?
6. In making informal observations, are some students having the same specific problem?

7. In the evaluation procedure, does the evaluation represent an appropriately difficult exercise?

1.3. Making Evaluation Decisions

After analyzing the evaluation data, certain decisions must be made. Should the lesson or even the unit be retaught? If reteaching is necessary, should instructional strategies be altered? Should new grouping formats be employed to address individual as well as group concerns? These and other important questions can be answered only after analyzing evaluation information.

The answers to questions such as these will have a great impact on the direction of learning and the development of the curriculum. You will not always be able to arrive quickly at answers to such questions. Evaluation decisions must be made over time and should never be thought of as final in nature. For example, decisions based on a test given on one day may need to be changed based on further information gained from tests or other measures on subsequent days. A continuous, decision-making process is necessary to accomplish meaningful evaluation.

The following questions should be considered in the decision-making process:

1. Does student performance indicate that part or all of the information should be retaught?
2. If the decision is made to reteach previously taught material, should the same or altered instructional strategies be utilized?
3. Have appropriate grouping approaches been used in the previous instruction?
4. Has ample observation been made of the evaluation performance to allow a valid conclusion to be drawn?
5. Has the evaluation process been a continuous one, over time, to allow student performance to be revealed throughout numerous evaluation settings?

Formative Evaluation: Section 1*

1. Describe each of the three major steps in the evaluation process.
2. What are three possible sources of student evaluation information?
3. What are two of the questions that a teacher must consider when analyzing evaluation information?

SECTION 2. TEST CONSTRUCTION

The ability to construct tests that are suitably based upon the attainment levels of students while, at the same time, adequately sampling the content at a variety of cognitive levels is surely one of the most difficult tasks facing the classroom teacher. It is necessary to be aware of the purposes of the test, the types of questions available, and how to construct effective test items.

2.1. General Considerations in Test Construction

It might be thought that test construction begins with writing test questions; instead, several concerns must be addressed prior to writing items which will help make certain that the test is readable, appropriate, and valid. As the teacher begins to prepare a test, the general purpose that the test is to perform is the real key to its successful development. If a valid test is to be prepared, it must be logically linked with the goals of instruction.

Educators sometimes want to determine how well certain students are progressing when compared to other similar students across different classes, schools, and states. With this purpose in mind, an appropriate standardized test must be used. Since test standardization is a most complex process, such tests are usually purchased from a commercial concern. Most school systems purchase standardized tests from professional testing firms which not

---

*See the Appendix for suggested answers to these questions.

only furnish tests but also score them and report comprehensive descriptive statistics.

A basic purpose for giving a test is to determine if students have learned the content which has recently been taught. This type of test is often referred to as being *summative* in nature. A summative test is one designed to reflect a summation of student learning in a given content area. As you already no doubt know, teachers frequently give this type of test and then record student scores for grading purposes. The test should be designed to measure only those learnings the teacher feels that students need to know or be able to do in order to demonstrate achievement of prestated objectives. Basic guidelines that teachers should follow include:

1. Be certain the test measures the objectives which were stated prior to instruction.
2. Always ask a sufficient number of questions to properly sample the content being tested.
3. Be conscious of the need to sample enough behavior over time to provide students with adequate feedback concerning their performance.

For the specific purpose of improving ongoing instruction, teachers often diagnose their students to determine strengths and weaknesses. The results of these diagnostic efforts are not used for grading purposes as was the case with summative tests discussed earlier. The results of these tests can be used to group students for instruction, make decisions concerning the need to reteach the material, determine the readiness level of individual students as new content areas are approached, and identify the causes of student failure. Since these tests are often thought of as a means to gather information for future structuring of learning experiences, they are typically referred to as being *formative,* as opposed to *summative,* in nature. Formative evaluations are sometimes referred to as "en route" evaluations, as they assess students' progress as they move toward the point where the summative evaluation will be conducted. After teachers have examined the results of their students' diagnostic tests, it becomes much easier to prescribe the best learning experiences for small group as well as individual instruction.

Once the teacher has determined the purpose of a particular test and realizes how it relates with course goals and objectives, the overall plan of the test must be considered. Should the test be a type of written test or would an oral or performance test be more suited to the material covered? There is a definite reason for oral assessment where quick recall is the aim. In a similar vein, it is necessary for some subjects such as typing, woodworking, and gymnastics to have a substantial performance testing component. Regardless of the type of test chosen, the kind of test questions will be determined by such conditions as the level of cognitive functioning desired, class objectives, student maturity level, and student familiarity with the testing format.

Even though the teacher may have a clear conception of the test's purpose and overall make-up, the development of a good test is still not assured. For instance, a general set of directions is, unfortunately, frequently omitted because it is sometimes felt that these specifications are either superfluous or can be given orally by the teacher. In fact, general directions can be very helpful to the student, especially on longer and more advanced tests. General directions should be clear, concise, and on the reading level at which the students are functioning. Students who have had to struggle through difficult content only to be overwhelmed by the reading level of the test are in a situation that is unfair to them. General directions should include all information and guidelines that students need in order to complete each question and to record each answer as expected. Such directions are necessary so that each student knows what is expected, the point value awarded for each question, and what is to be done in response to each item. Additionally, although not part of the written directions, care must be taken to develop optimal testing conditions, both physically and psychologically.

An effective teacher also knows that test item arrangement may influence the students taking the test. It is recommended that the least complex questions be placed at the beginning of the test and the more difficult ones toward the end. The following hierarchical list, taken from Merwin, Schneider, and Stephens (1974, p. 230), serves as a guideline to follow in positioning questions (see Fig. 6–1).

Type of Test Items	Knowledge 1.0	Comprehension 2.0	Application 3.0	Analysis 4.0	Synthesis 5.0	Evaluation 6.0
1. True-False	B	X	–	–	–	–
2. Completion	B	X	–	–	–	–
3. Matching	B	B	X	X	–	X
4. Multiple-choice	X	B	B	B	–	X
5. Essay questions	X	X	B	B	B	B

Least Complex ↑ Most Complex ↓

Key: X = Appropriate to the level indicated
      B = Best level at which to use this item
      - = Not ordinarily used to evaluate this level

Figure 6-1. Relationship of test items to the cognitive domain of the taxonomy.

Therefore, if a test had all five types of questions, true/false and completion should be at the beginning and multiple choice and essay located toward the end, assuming all other concerns are equal. However, the content of the items must also be considered. If several different parts of a subject are tested, each part should be grouped together rather than being placed in different places throughout the exam. The latter type of placement forces the student to consider a mental construct time and time again, rather than answering all questions about a certain topic at one time. For those complex tests with many questions of many types, it is advised that teachers also group (1) question types in ascending order from the beginning, (2) similar content in question clusters, and (3) items of difficulty in ascending order within each content area.

2.2. Item Preparation

The five question types identified in Figure 6-1 can be grouped into two major categories by the type of response they require from students. Students may be asked to either SELECT the correct answer from stated alternatives or to SUPPLY the proper answer in response to a question. Selection items include many of the most commonly used test questions: *true-false, matching,* and *multiple choice.* Supply items are the remaining major types of written test questions: *completion* and *essay.*

Each question type has its own unique characteristics along with specific advantages and disadvantages. Selection questions may demand only an acquaintance with the subject and may seemingly require less in-depth understanding. Nevertheless, sophisticated test construction can elicit rather high levels of thinking on these types of questions. Indeed, if care is not taken, even supply-type questions which are often known for requiring higher level responses can require only low level performance.

Major benefits of selection items are that they (1) can provide great structure, forcing a single, predetermined, easy-to-evaluate response, (2) can be used to measure a variety of learnings from simple to complex, and (3) are suited well to the coverage of a wide range of content on a single test. Requiring students to choose among different alternatives, or whether a statement is true or false, is the intellectual process necessary in answering these items. Thus, selection items can be used at the knowledge level or, through the use of creatively written multiple-choice items, challenge the student at the higher cognitive levels. When this is coupled with ease of scoring that the selection item offers, it is little wonder that much classroom testing is of this nature.

Evaluation that only requires the identification of correct answers and never the written development of solutions to complex problems is an insufficient form of evaluation. Learners must be expected, for example, to exhibit such behaviors as to supply the list of steps necessary to "log on" to the computer, an explanation of their field trip to the power station and how electricity is generated, or to describe the major characters in Hemingway's *A Farewell To Arms*. Such responses will clearly require performances beyond low level cognitive memory.

In order for higher intellectual skills to be fully assessed, the essay-type supply item is often needed. Even though multiple-choice items can be written above the knowledge level, their use beyond comprehension is not extensive because of difficulty in construction. Whereas the selection item often requires only recognition, the supply item generally demands a more creative response on the part of the student. Some professionals would argue that without at least some supply items, it is possible for test takers to have only the most minimal type of acquaintance with a subject. Since there is a decidedly low probability of students guessing or memorizing the correct answer for this type of question, a more rigorous process of education typifies the class in which supply items are used. Of course, the grading of essay questions, in particular, is time consuming and mentally demanding; on the other hand, the phrasing of questions and the test, as a whole, is fairly straightforward.

It is sometimes felt that extensive written work may penalize the less expressive of two students who knows the same amount of material as the more verbal counterpart. This is just one of several ambiguities that beset teachers. Further complicating the grading of supply items is the problem of spelling and grammar. When and how much should spelling and grammar be counted on tests (especially those other than English)? We feel that spelling and grammar should always influence the evaluation of supply items because written expression is such an important aspect of a quality education. It will, of course, be up to each individual teacher to determine how much these factors will influence a student's grade.

The remainder of this section is designed to aid in the development of tests that are both challenging and which produce helpful information about students for evaluation purposes. Each of the five major types of test items previously mentioned will be considered.

True-False Items

Perhaps because it is so simple to employ, the true-false item is one of the most frequently used items. However, the true-false item has the least flexibility and is extremely difficult to employ properly. For this very reason, it is advised by many educators that the use of true-false items be limited (Travers, 1950; Gage and Berliner, 1975). In spite of these cautions, teachers still frequently desire to and do use true-false items. Perhaps this is due to the fact that through their use, much subject matter can be tested in a short period of time and the items are generally quite easy to score. But, true-false items typically measure only low level learning, and this may not be the teacher's goal. Although the following items are acceptable, they measure only the lowest level of cognition.

_____ 1. Dallas is the capital city of Texas.

_____ 2. Alexander Bell invented the telephone.

_____ 3. A spider is an insect.

Care should be given in the construction of true-false items to avoid misinterpretation of what is expected. For example, the following question is ambiguous because one does not know whether land area or population is the feature being referred to in the question.

_____ 1. Alaska is the largest state.

This item can easily be improved with the addition of a short clarifying phrase. For example:

_____ 1. Alaska is the largest state in total land area.

True-false items also increase the probability of students guessing the correct answer. The guessing problem may be lessened somewhat by incorporating large numbers of items into a given test. However, it can be a very difficult task to construct large numbers of meaningful true-false items. To use fewer questions and to improve the item type, the "modified true-false" item is helpful. To prepare the modified true-false item, state in the directions the following:

> If the item is correct, put the letter T for true in the blank provided, but if it is incorrect, change the underlined word(s) to make it correct.

An additional option to modifying true-false items is to omit the underlining and direct the learner to underline the false portion if encountered and to write in the correction.

The following guidelines may be helpful in the construction of effective true-false items.

1. Write short, direct statements in which a main idea is stated with only minimal additions.
2. Put only one idea, fact, or generalization in each statement.
3. Avoid words which are indefinite, i.e. be specific.
4. State items positively rather than negatively in order to exhibit clarity.
5. Avoid clues such as *all, never, usually, every, always,* and *often* which are typically indicative of false statements.
6. Avoid the tendency to create trivial items.
7. Include a minimum of 30 statements to lessen the influence of guessing.

Matching Items

The matching-type test item has great utility in test construction, even though it does have limitations. This item, commonly used at both the elementary and secondary levels, requires students to associate two groups of facts, concepts, or generalizations. It is this relating of two groups of words, phrases, or symbols that gives this type of item its versatility. For example, matching items may be constructed to associate such things as names with significant events in history, great paintings with techniques, or related scientific concepts with their applications. Consider the following example:

Directions: Place the letter of the event in the blank next to the matching name.

Name	Event
_____ 1. G. Washington	a. Served the most years in the Presidency.
_____ 2. A. Lincoln	b. Known as the "Father of Our Country"
_____ 3. F. Roosevelt	c. Was assassinated in Dallas, Texas
_____ 4. R. Nixon	d. President during the Civil War
	e. Resigned from office due to scandal

Although it can be seen that the above example exhibits a tremendous economy of space, can be constructed without great difficulty, can be scored easily, and lowers the possibility of guessing, there are pitfalls which teachers must avoid. In constructing this type of item, two columns—a premise and a response—should be developed in which there is a definitie "similarity" of terms. Notice in the following example that the premises are concerned with both plays and poetry. This provides a mix-match of ideas that should be avoided.

Premise	Response
_____ 1. *Hamlet*	a. The hero searches for great deeds even when there are none.
_____ 2. *Man of La Mancha*	b. A poem about the meaninglessness of our modern world.
_____ 3. "The Hollow Men"	c. The hero meets a tragic end.
_____ 4. *Oedipus Rex*	d. The protagonist kills his father.
	e. The hero returns from the dead.

When producing items to test a topic, refrain from including parts from any other topic; keep all premise words homogeneous.

Mixing classes of premises may allow clues to be given about those things to be matched. Another concern to be noted is the use of synonyms or words of the same or similar derivation in both the premise and response. For instance:

Premises	Response
_____ 1. Great Lake	a. Lake Baikal
_____ 2. Small barren sea	b. Lake Erie
_____ 3. Largest lake in the world	c. Dead Sea
	d. Mediterranean Sea
_____ 4. A sea separating Africa and Europe	e. Chesapeake Bay

Since it is obvious that the lakes and the seas match, there are really two separate question types with only two alternatives; each of which is much too simple.

Four is the minimum number of reasonably similar paired terms to match and approximately ten the maximum. If more than ten items are desired for a matching exercise, it is recommended that the number of desired matching items be separated in groups of from four to ten. As an aid in preparing the matching type test item, consider the following guidelines:

1. Use words or short phrases in both premise and response.
2. Eliminate clue words and mixing of topics.
3. Keep the number of response alternatives between four and ten, if possible.
4. Lower the probability of guessing by adding extra responses.
5. Put all the premises and responses on the same page (to prevent turning back and forth).
6. Arrange the response alternatives in a logical sequence (e.g. alphabetically). This is especially true if there is a long list of alternatives.
7. Indicate the basis for the relationship between the two groups (e.g. if the states are the premises and the capitals are the responses, be sure to label both columns appropriately).

Multiple Choice

Acknowledged as one of the most versatile of all items (second only to the essay), the multiple-choice item is laborious to construct. Whereas other supply items test knowledge and comprehension, multiple-choice items can be used to test at the higher cognitive levels. No other item type, except essay, can be used so broadly; however, though the essay item may be easy to construct, it is also very difficult to score. Multiple-choice items, conversely, are simple to score: just check the proper letter or response made.

In construction, multiple-choice items require a stem and from three to six alternatives offered as correct choices. Of these alternatives, one should be obviously wrong, one correct, one similar to the correct answer, and the others somewhere between obviously incorrect and almost correct. The emphasis during development should be to make the student think and discern gross and slight differences between distractors (i.e. alternative answers).

Even though multiple-choice items can be used to measure simple recall of facts and knowledge, their usefulness is especially noted when they are directed beyond this minimal level. It is advised that true-false and matching items be used to test lower cognitive performance since these items are relatively easy to construct; whereas multiple choice items are not.

Examples of multiple-choice items are as follows:

1. Which of the following is a primary color?
   a. Red
   b. Brown
   c. Black
   d. Orange
2. Where should you ride your bicycle when in traffic?
   a. On the left side
   b. On the right side
   c. In the middle near the dividing lines
   d. It really does not matter if you are careful
3. Which of the following paintings most utilizes the idea of linear perspective?
   a. *Descent from the Cross*
   b. *The School of Athens*
   c. *Guernica*
   d. *Le Moulin de la Galette*

There are definite educationally valid reasons for selecting multiple-choice items when constructing a test. First, they can be graded quickly with immediate feedback provided. Second, they provide helpful practice for students since virtually all standardized tests use the multiple-choice item. Finally, they are valued in that they can be so constructed as to measure high levels of cognition. There are, however, cautions identified in the use of the multiple-choice item. For example, the construction of good multiple-choice items is a difficult procedure; it is easy to make them too difficult or ridiculously easy. Another concern grows out of the desire to have students communicate ideas. The multiple-choice item requires no writing on the part of students. If multiple-choice items are used exclusively, students would never be required to express their ideas in writing on a test.

The following guidelines should prove helpful in constructing multiple-choice items:

1. Avoid having an item with a multiple focus; there should be a central question in each item.
2. Keep all wording concise and clear.
3. Make all alternatives, whether correct answer or distractor, of similar length.
4. Write all distractors, even those that are clearly wrong, so that they are plausible.
5. Be sure that there are no clues in any of the distractors (e.g. all options must be grammatically consistent with the stem).
6. Include some items that require fine distinctions.

Completion Items

One of the most commonly used items at the elementary level is the completion (fill-in-the-blank) item and is both easy to use and easy to misuse. Since textbooks generally represent the primary learning aid, it becomes natural, because of the importance of the text, to take whole sentences from the text with key words omitted. Caution must be exercised when using such a procedure because the overuse of blanks may make even the simple task of recall difficult. For example:

> Weather satellites are beneficial for weather _____ because they take _____ pictures.

The fact that "forecasting" and "cloud" make sense when they are presented does not simplify the task in the completion item above; for example, "watchers" and "accurate" also make sense as well as many other possibilities. Even if the sentence is quoted from a textbook, the item is not appropriate and would be better phrased as a short-answer question.

Completion items that have a specific stem with a sufficient description of the missing word(s) are necessary. For example:

> Granite is a commercial rock which always contains _____ and _____.

"Always contains" is the specific description of "granite" that furnishes the learner with a valid indication of what is being requested in the response. When used in a direct manner, the completion item is most useful. For example:

> A noun names a _____, _____, or _____.
> The name of the capital city of Indiana is _____.
> The molten material that flows from volcanoes is called
> _____.

A variation of the completion item, the short-answer item requires only that students produce a sentence or perhaps a phrase. The teacher need only take a completion item and rephrase it in the form of a question to develop the short-answer item. For example:

> What is a noun?
> What is always found in granite?
> What is one benefit of weather satellites?

A response to the short-answer item allows the student more

freedom in supplying information beyond basic memorization. Such items represent a step toward approximating the complexities in answering essay items. For this reason teachers should particularly refine their skills in constructing this type of item and in teaching students how to phrase their answers. Moreover, middle school and secondary teachers should not relegate this item only for use with lower grades. This type item should be used regularly at all levels where students are capable of taking paper-and-pencil tests.

Consider the guidelines below as an aid in the construction of completion items:

1. Write the item so that only a single word or brief phrase is required.
2. Use direct, clear sentences with the missing word(s) at or near the end of the sentence.
3. The missing word(s) should be the major point of the statement.
4. Determine the amount of clues that are appropriate for the grade level of the student; use sentences directly from the text when you wish to prepare easier items for the early elementary grades, but create completely novel sentences for older children and adolescents.
5. Carefully use the length of the line. Shortly after introducing this question type in early elementary grades, it should be noted that the length of the line should no longer vary as an aid in determining the answer. From that point on, use the same length line for all words.
6. State during instruction that correct spelling is important.
7. Give any specifications that will insure a unitary response such as in mathematics:

   A room that is 9 ft. by 3 ft. is _____ sq. ft.

This specification insures an answer in feet rather than inches or yards.

Essay

The usefulness of the essay item is in the flexibility that it allows the teacher and the freedom of response it allows the student. Additionally, students, through the performance of constructing a written, original response to a given problem or question, demonstrate their ability to conceive a problem, organize the facts and concepts needed to answer, and learn to communicate effectively in writing. Thus, the essay permits the teacher to observe students' thoughts in their essays as well as evaluate their written expression. Effective communication and the development of thinking skills are certainly two of the most important outcomes of schooling. Because of this, the importance of the essay item cannot be overemphasized.

Essay items may ask the student to list, outline, compare and contrast, defend, summarize, or evaluate. Such items are generally used to measure higher level thought processes. For example:

1. Describe how life would be in this country without any cars. Include effects on mobility and the use of leisure time.
2. Analyze the way your life might be if you lived in a communist country. Include reference to freedom of religion, education, and government participation.

There are primarily three major reasons for using essay items. First, they tend to measure higher levels of cognition. Second, they encourage students to communicate their thoughts in writing. Third, the essay item tends to reward creativity (i.e. divergent thinking) on the part of the student.

The disadvantage of using essay items comes in their scoring. The items are subjective; this is to say, it becomes difficult to evaluate each student's response the same way on the same set of criteria. Secondly, a student's verbosity and writing skills may create a *halo effect* in that the teacher gives certain students good grades because their papers look good, not because their answers are complete. The reverse is also a distinct possibility in reference to less-capable students.

Consider the following guidelines:

1. Carefully construct each question so that it gives sufficient direction to the student to complete the item as intended.
2. Outline a model answer to insure greater objectivity and that the question is specifically phrased.
3. Include several shorter essay items rather than few longer ones.
4. Write essay questions so that higher levels of student thought are required.
5. Use questions which the student will find new and challenging yet answerable. The question should indeed require the student to do more than produce a memorized answer.
6. Grade all essays without noting the name of the student.
7. While grading, write comments on all students' papers.

Formative Evaluation: Section 2*

1. Describe four general concerns to be aware of in constructing a test.
2. List two characteristics to be considered in the use of each of the five major types of test items.
3. Select a topic and write at least one item representing each of the five major types of test questions.

SECTION 3. GRADING AND RECORD MANAGEMENT

Grading, once a heated, controversial topic (Glasser, 1969; Ebel, 1974; Holt, 1974), is still not fully resolved in educational circles. Yet, grading is almost universally applied with only slight variation in all schools. The issue may not seem controversial until the effects of grading are assessed. Many educators and parents still decry the deleterious effects of constant failure on the self-concept of children and adolescents. Teachers must be cautious of the manner in which grades are determined and how this information and other evaluative data are communicated to students. Grades, along with other forms of feedback, are part of the information

---

*See the Appendix for suggested answers to these questions.

used to keep students abreast of their progress. The more frequently this is done, the less misunderstandings that will occur.

Because of the variation in student ability, experience, and achievement, teachers are also faced with great difficulty in record management; students complete assignments at different speeds and with different levels of understanding. Properly grouping or working with learners on an individual basis will meet many student needs. Without an orderly management of assignments, however, the teacher can become confused as to which assignments are due at a particular time and what those students who have completed assignments early should do next.

3.1. Grading Procedures

Teachers have traditionally varied in the procedures they use to ascertain grades. Although some procedures are more systematic and effective than others, all teachers must choose a system that coincides with their personal philosophy of student evaluation. However, it is most important that every teacher makes his grading procedures clear to students before summative evaluation takes place.

Some teachers employ what has been commonly referred to as *grading on the curve*. These teachers assume that student abilities are dispersed around a central point in a consistent way. In this system, the middle half of the grades are labelled as being C's. Approximately 20 percent of the grades immediately above C are awarded B's, and approximately 20 percent of the grades immediately below C are awarded D's. There remains two small groups: one, approximately 5 percent extremely above average receiving A's and another approximately 5 percent extremely below average receiving F's. We do not feel that such a system is advisable in the typical classroom situation because it falsely assumes that grades on teacher-made tests are, or even should be, normally distributed in a fashion expected of standardized tests.

Many teachers prefer a procedure commonly called *scaling grades*. In this procedure, the teacher takes the highest score achieved and treats it as if it were 100 percent correct and scales all other grades based upon it. For example, if the highest raw score obtained on a test were 92 percent, eight points would be added to that score to make it total 100 percent, and eight points would then be added to each of the other test scores (e.g. a raw score of 75 percent would then become 83 percent). At this point, teachers either assign grades to scores using the curve or one of the other procedures discussed in this section. Teachers often use this system to hide the fact that some students are not doing as well as should be expected or the fact that the test items being used inadequately sample the students' learning.

The *inspection method* of grading is another procedure sometimes used. This method requires the teacher to record all test scores on a continuum from high to low and then assign a grade to each cluster. The best way to display such scores is a frequency continuum as shown in Figure 6-2. Considering these scores, it can be seen how they "group themselves" in clusters for a class of twenty-five students.

SCORES	FREQUENCY OF SCORE	GRADE ACHIEVED
98	2	
95	3	A
88	2	
86	3	
85	1	
84	4	B
78	2	
77	1	
76	2	C
71	1	
70	1	D
65	1	
61	2	F

Figure 6-2. Worksheet to employ the inspection method of grade assignment.

Obviously, this unscientific procedure has its basic weakness in that most distributions can be broken down in several different ways. Therefore, the system is often unreliable and individual grades are hard to justify.

Another, and probably more common, procedure is the use of the *standardized grading scale*. This procedure is recommended over the rather haphazard inspection approach. Many teachers are required, or simply prefer, to use the grading scale established for the school in which they teach. However, it is not uncommon for teachers to formulate their own scales. A traditional scale would be as follows: A = 93–100%, B = 85–92%, C = 77–84%, D = 70–76%, and F = 69% and below.

A final type of grading, called *criterion-referenced*, is currently being used by many teachers for some, or all, of their grading procedures. Criterion-referenced grading is used to denote mastery of material; specifically, student performance is compared to announced standards (criteria). There are no student-to-student or student-to-class comparisons. Simply stated, it seeks to uncover whether or not students possess minimal competence in the stated objectives of instruction. The only comparison is to the learning of the material. Did the student learn it at the minimal level or not? The teacher's major task in interpreting performance is to initially set the standards for successful completion. Often, minimal competency is set at 70–80 percent mastery of the material. This is typically done in a pass-fail manner. In criterion-referenced grading, the grade report form can vary significantly. Parents usually receive a report card on which all the mastered objectives (criteria) are merely checked as met or not met.

Criterion-referenced grading and reporting has been growing in use with primary grade children. Communicating achievement in this fashion is seen to be less threatening to students while adequately expressing progress to parents.

3.2. Recording Student Performance

Once grades have been determined for a grading period, teachers typically send home some type of report to parents; teachers acting *in loco parentis* have a responsibility to keep parents informed about the students' progress. Since all students do not put into their parents' hands the schoolwork sent home, teachers must not surprise parents at the end of the grading period with a less-than-expected report. To avoid surprises, teachers should communicate through one of the following techniques: (1) telephone or send home a written message to parents concerning student progress, especially for those who are performing below average; (2) send home a weekly or bi-weekly progress report or packet of student work to be signed by the parents; or (3) request a conference with parents. It is suggested that teachers who make the effort to communicate achievement in these ways will be rewarded by having some parents take more interest in their youth's schoolwork, require the student to do better work (e.g. spend more time on homework, study for regular spelling, vocabulary, or mathematics tests), and not become dissatisfied and call or come to the school wanting to know why their offspring is doing less well than expected.

In order to report student achievement to parents, careful record-keeping procedures must be utilized. Recording by objectives is a commonly used record-keeping format when criterion-referenced grading is used. It can be seen in Figure 6-3 that students *four, five,* and *six* all have completed one enrichment assignment, whereas students *two* and *three* have completed none. It is evident in this sample record which students have completed which objectives; this can be verified by a quick inspection. Taking just those students included in Figure 6-3, it can be seen that three student groups can be formed: (1) student *one* working at an accelerated pace, (2) students *four, five* and *six* working together at approximately the same rate, and (3) students *two* and *three* meeting minimal requirements.

Most teachers, however, do not use this involved criterion-referenced recording process. Instead, the more common procedure involves keeping a typical grade book with each student's name and the scores made on each class assignment or test (see Fig. 6-4). In this method, it is assumed that each quiz or test adequately samples the stated learning objectives.

Regardless of the recording system being used, it is strongly suggested that teachers keep complete, updated records of their students' scores along with individual folders containing examples of each student's work. A complete record system and examples of student work will allow teachers to make a more accurate assess-

NAME	Objective 1	Objective 2	Objective 3	Objective 4	Objective 5	Objective 6	Objective 7	Enrichment Objective A	Enrichment Objective B	Enrichment Objective C
1.	X	X	X					X	X	X
2.	X	X	X							
3.	X	X	X							
4.	X	X	X					X		
5.	X	X	X					X		
6.	X	X	X					X		

Subject: SCIENCE — Unit: Weather

Figure 6-3. Record keeping by objectives.

ment of performance over time and prove helpful when communicating progress to the students themselves as well as their parents.

Formative Evaluation: Section 3*

1. Outline the major characteristics of five approaches to grading.

---
*See the Appendix for suggested answers to these questions.

Subject: Math Unit: Geometry	unit 5 exam	quiz	constructions	quiz	test chapter 16	quiz	quiz	assignment	test chapter 17	quiz	quiz	test chapter 18	unit 6 exam	
1.	83	90	87	80										
2.	91	88	94	90										
3.	78	86	80	74										
4.	89	94	90	82										
5.	72	60	81	79										

Figure 6-4. A typical teacher's grade record.

2. List three techniques which may be used to communicate with parents.
3. Describe the major characteristics of two approaches to record management.

REFERENCES

Ebel, R. L. Should we get rid of grades? *Measurement in education.* 1974, 5(4), 1–4.

Gage, N., and Berliner, D. *Educational psychology.* Chicago: Rand McNally, 1975.

Glasser, W. *Schools without failure.* New York: Harper and Row, 1969.

Holt, J. Marking and grading. In M. D. Gall and B. A. Ward (Eds.), *Critical issues in educational psychology.* Boston: Little, Brown and Co., 1974.

Merwin, W., Schneider, D., and Stephens, L. *Developing competency in teaching secondary social studies.* Columbus, OH: Charles E. Merrill, 1974.

Travers, R. *How to make achievement tests.* New York: Odyssey Press, 1950.

APPENDIX

FORMATIVE EVALUATION FEEDBACK

Feedback Box: Chapter 1, Section 1

1. AUTHORITARIAN   Refer to part 1 for feedback
   LAISSEZ–FAIRE   or discuss this with your
   AUTHORITATIVE   instructor and/or study
                    partner.
2. The best answer deals with the manner in which students would respond to the authoritative style. For example: Students are more likely to (1) develop a positive attitude toward learning, (2) develop a sense of autonomy, and (3) become active participants. Thus, they will learn more effectively (Part 1).
3. Your answer should indicate that centered-instruction refers to: Who is the main focus of instruction, the teacher or students? In this section an argument was presented favoring student-centered instruction (Part 2).
4. These two inventories are examples of the kind of instrumentation which could be utilized to obtain more knowledge concerning your total class group in order to more effectively structure student-centered instruction (Part 2).

Feedback Box: Chapter 1, Section 2

1. To obtain feedback concerning your answer, refer to Figures 1-1 and 1-2.
2. Among your suggestions should be these:
   - High ability students work in individualized, self-paced groups
   - Average students work in medium-size subgroups
   - Low ability students receive much direct instruction

251

- Challenge high ability students and provide enrichment curriculum
- Provide much immediate reinforcement for low ability learners (Parts 1 and 2)

3. Among your suggestions should be these:
    - Have enrichment work planned for those who finish early
    - Allow students to work in subgroups
    - Provide differing levels of instructional materials for students of differing ability
    - Make use of special techniques such as learning centers and individual student projects (Parts 1, 2, and 3)

4. Learning style refers to the manner in which individual students are able to respond to differing instructional methods; they do not all achieve at their optimal level through the use of the same instructional methods and settings. Several suggestions for accommodating differences in learning styles are presented in Part 3 under the headings: Environmental Elements, Emotional Elements, Sociological Elements, Physical Elements, and Sense Modalities. Your suggestions should be similar.

Feedback Box: Chapter 1, Section 3

		Conditions Statement	Performance Statement	Criterion Statement
1.	a.	given regulation track shoes and the use of an outdoor cinder track	run one mile	in seven minutes or less
	b.	given a current map of Africa	list the countries that lie in the Sahara Desert area	all of
	c.	without the use of aids	write definitions of spelling words	all in unit one

2.–7. It is necessary that you consult with your instructor and/or study partner for feedback on these items.

Feedback Box: Chapter 1, Section 4

1. Pre-Instructional Development Stage: . . .
   Instructional Planning and Implementation Stage: . . .
   Post-Instructional Stage: . . .
   Compare your description with your study partner's and refer to the text.
2. Possible unit topics for the goal "Learn how to be a good manager of money, property, and resources" for the subject matter area of mathematics/social studies are (1) Developing a Weekly Financial Budget, (2) Using the Bank, and (3) Becoming a Wise Consumer. For additional feedback, discuss your unit titles with your instructor.
3. Your components should include as a minimum: goals, objectives (Section 3, Part 1–5), experience with the subject matter, evaluation, and materials (Section 4, Parts 1 and 2).
4. Check your plan using the lesson plan checklist (See Fig. 1-12) and discuss it with your study partner and/or instructor.
5. Your description should stress the importance of this stage for the overall evaluation of the planning process. Refer to Part 3 for details and discuss your work with your instructor and/or study partner.

Feedback Box: Chapter 2, Section 1

1. Your answer should include reference to the communication process as an interaction among senders, receivers, and messages.
2. Nonverbal communication includes all human responses which are not overtly spoken or written words. Verbal communication includes speaking, writing, reading, and listening.
3. Speaking, writing, reading, and listening.
4. Refer to the end of Part 2 for a listing of suggestions.
5. The six nonverbal language symbols are: Kinesics, Proxemics, Haptics, Oculesics, Vocalics, and Environmental Factors. See Part 3 for descriptions of effects.

Feedback Box: Chapter 2, Section 2

1. Generalizations explain a total situation or summarize a large body of data; value statements function either as justification for a course of action or as a basis of rating objects, events, persons, or situations. Facts are verifiable or something thought to be verifiable. Concepts serve to define and are, essentially, mental images of an object or event. Consult your instructor and/or study partner for feedback concerning your examples.
2. Your answer should indicate that a concept represents a mental image of an object or event and serves to define it.
3. Refer to Part 3 for a brief summary of the three types.
4. Successful demonstration of a skill is dependent on some form of conceptual understanding.

Feedback Box: Chapter 2, Section 3

1. Refer to Part 1 in relation to the processes induction and deduction in building the concept.
2. Your description should include (1) the analysis of the concept, (2) lesson procedures and materials, and (3) an evaluation related to the lesson presented.
3. Your concept analysis should include reference to (1) the concept rule, (2) critical and non-critical attributes, (3) examples and non-examples, and (4) questions and cues.
4. Compare your plan with the sample plan provided in Figure 2-6. Also, check with your instructor.

Feedback Box: Chapter 3, Section 1

1. (1) Appropriate Developmental Level, (2) Address Stated Objectives, (3) The Motivational Aspect, (4) A Variety of Grouping Structures, (5) Active Involvement of Learners, (6) Working at the Application Level, (7) Determination of Student Learning, (8) Students Receive Feedback.
2.-3. Refer to Parts 1–8 in this section and consult with your instructor.

Feedback Box: Chapter 3, Section 2

1. (1) C, (2) CM, (3) CM, (4) CM, (5) E, (6) E, (7) C, (8) CM, (9) D, (10) CM
2. Some possible questions are listed below. Discuss these with your study partner and/or instructor.

Cognitive Memory

1. In what city was the Declaration of Independence signed?
2. Which colony was the largest in population of the original thirteen?

Convergent

1. What was the significance of the Boston Tea Party?
2. What was the purpose in writing the Bill of Rights?

Divergent

1. How might our nation be different if we had never had the Declaration of Independence?
2. What could life be like today if the colonists kept doing only what the British wanted them to do?

Evaluative

1. If you had the opportunity, what would you propose as a new amendment? Why?
2. Was England right in waging war against us for declaring our independence? Why?

3. Refer to Part 4 to evaluate your answer.

Feedback Box: Chapter 4, Section 1

1. Your procedures should address the ROPES format; also, give special attention to Figure 4-4, items 1, 2, 3, and 9.
2. Your procedures should address the ROPES format; also, give special attention to the appropriate "teacher should" figure.
3. Make sure that your objective includes condition, performance, and criterion statements. You may wish to refer to Chapter 1, Section 3. Your procedures should address the ROPES format; also, give special attention to the appropriate "teacher should" figure.

Feedback Box: Chapter 4, Section 2

1. Compare your contract with the example provided in Part 1.

2. You should refer to Figure 4-13 for an explanation of each of the major components of a LAP. Next, refer to Figure 4-14 which can be used for a checklist to evaluate your development of this LAP.

3. Depending upon which strategy you chose, you should refer to either Figure 4-15 (Learning Centers) or Figure 4-16 (Independent Study Projects) in order to determine if your description is appropriate.

Feedback Box: Chapter 5, Section 1

1. Your answer should note that, although the psychological approach considers the individual and the sociological approach concentrates on group behavior, each orientation has made significant contributions to good classroom management practices (e.g. Psychological: information concerning motivation, reinforcement, and needs of the individual. Sociological: interaction effects, social order, and influence of peers). You should also mention that the two orientations complement each other.

2. Some possible answers might include:
   a. Driekurs' Model: *defines degrees of misbehavior, emphasizes one-to-one conference*
   b. Glasser Model: *involves Reality Therapy, emphasis on classroom meeting*
   c. Skinnerian Model: *emphasizes reinforcement, precludes punishment*
   d. Kounin's Model: *emphasizes Ripple Effect, focuses on teacher leadership*
   e. Gordon's Model: *emphasizes caring attitudes of teacher, "I" messages*

3. Your answer might include: In each model, students are responsible for their own behavior and must accept any negative consequences that might result. Each model emphasizes the importance of students helping to establish

rules for proper conduct. Too, each has elements of both the psychological and sociological approaches.

4. Review the appropriate models to verify your answer and consult with your instructor and/or study partner.

Feedback Box: Chapter 5, Section 2

1. The seven behaviors in order of presentation are: Thorough Preparation, Development of Routines, Calm and Confident Behavior, Professional Demeanor, Recognizing Inappropriate Behavior, Avoidance of Retreating, and Preventing Problems. Refer to the text description of each to verify your description.
2. Your answer should be similar to this: Teacher issues a directive, student(s) ignore or indicate unwillingness to comply, teacher ignores fact that students continue unwanted behavior after being directed to stop.
3. Possible actions include:
   a. Adjust the curriculum difficulty to more nearly match student ability.
   b. Enter the classroom with the attitude that you are in charge.
   c. Develop the support system of parents and administrators.
   d. Pre-plan with the class for dealing with unexpected events.
   e. Develop classroom routines.
4. Discuss your checklist with a study partner and your instructor.
5. See the last paragraphs of Part 6 to verify your answer.

Feedback Box: Chapter 5, Section 3

1. Refer to the appropriate strategy to verify your descriptions. Your answer should be similar to the following:

   Normative: An ideal type of control in which students conform to the directives of the classroom leader (typically the teacher) because the group acknowledges the leader's right to direct. This conformity is usually the result of the leader's actions as a competent individual who should be respected.

Coercive: Requires leaders to demonstrate their power. This type of control may be exhibited directly in the form of force or indirectly in the form of threats to use power.

Remunerative: In this type of control, leaders take on a very different role in which they gain their power by administering a series of rewards. Force is not used.

2. You could mention that neither deals with solving the cause of the behavior, remunerative strategies could have a negative effect on those not receiving rewards, and punishment and other coercive strategies can have a negative psychological effect if the student's self-esteem is attacked. Re-read the paragraphs concerning the two strategies for other ideas and discuss this question with your instructor.

3. Discuss your answer with your instructor and refer to Part 4.

Feedback Box: Chapter 5, Section 4

1. a. Lack of on-task behavior — Reading the assigned science text during an explanation of multiplication of fractions.

   b. Talking that interferes with the designated class goals — Whispering during the Uninterrupted Sustained Silent Reading (USSR) period.

   c. Broadly defined as lack of control; acting in an undesirable fashion — Running in the cafeteria.

   d. Emotional behavior that is directed toward someone with the potential for physical harm — A loud argument in which the ownership of a cosmetic case is in dispute. Threats and pushing accompany the disagreement.

   e. Behavior exhibited to entertain or impress someone — Repeatedly making "wise cracks" during class discussions.

   f. Openly refusing to follow the teacher's directives — Telling the teacher that you will not do your assignment and that you will go out to recess with the others in spite of orders to the contrary.

g. Telling untruths, cheating or the like—Handing in your older friend's report on *Hamlet* rather than doing one yourself.

2. a. Monotonous, uninspired, unorganized teaching where students have few, if any, opportunities for active participation in the lesson and are just inattentive. Besides these teacher weaknesses, students may become inattentive because of personal concerns that occupy their minds.

 b. Students who do not understand or cannot complete an assignment will be more likely to talk than those who understand an assignment.

 c. During exciting school events students can become unruly if they have not been taught acceptable behavior. For example, during an assembly, students who have been taught to applaud at appropriate times and that whistling, hooting, etc. are inappropriate will be less likely to become unruly.

 d. Frustrating experiences at school or at home are frequent causes of aggressive behavior.

 e. A student who rarely receives praise might "clown around" or make a scene.

 f. A teacher who constantly belittles students runs the risk of inducing defiance.

 g. Parents who overtly or covertly approve of dishonest behavior may instill this trait in their children.

3. a. Plan for students to actively participate in every lesson by talking, writing, or moving (e.g. in a laboratory experiment, skill practice, skit). Get to know your students so that you know their needs and can address them yourself or see that this is done by a support staff member.

 b. Practice giving simple directions with the demonstration of the required work as an example. Additionally, you can prevent disruptive talk for those who finish early by having enrichment or further assignments ready to be completed.

 c. Occasionally, some students become unruly because

they sit next to another person who incites their emotions. Separating such students prevents unruly outbursts. An even better measure is to go over rules of proper behavior whenever you think students need to be reminded of their conduct.

d. The only ways to prevent aggression are to teach students alternative strategies to vent their emotions, or to anticipate the aggressive tendencies and intervene before they overflow to full-blown aggression.

e. Give attention-seekers responsibilities like: checking roll, taking messages to other teachers, and cleaning erasers. Another way to prevent disruption from attention-seekers is being sure that they are given work for which they may receive praise.

f. The best way to prevent defiant behavior is to develop a relationship with students in which you are seen as the leader. Therefore, making assignments that students must complete and rules that must be obeyed will develop in students the habit of following directives. Students who have become accustomed to obeying the teacher's dictates will, in all likelihood, not defy authority. Another strategy to prevent defiance would be to meet with a student in a private conference before unruliness actually reaches a point of defying authority.

g. Stating rules of behavior that stress honesty and integrity will foster positive attitudes towards being honest. The teacher should insure that all students are working on appropriate material; overly difficult work could stimulate cheating and negative emotional outbursts.

Feedback Box: Chapter 6, Section 1

1. Your description should include: (1) *Collecting evaluation information*—use a variety of sources such as tests, projects, and informal observations and base the collection of information on the goals and objectives of instruction. (2) *Analyze the evaluation information*—carefully examine all information to determine its validity and evidence of stu-

dent progress. (3) *Make evaluation decisions*—the decision should be based on collected and analyzed information. This process must be continuous if it is to be effective.

2. Formal testing, student products and assignments, and informal observation.
3. Any two of the seven questions listed in Part 2 would be acceptable.

Feedback Box: Chapter 6, Section 2

1. (1) Purpose(s) of the test, (2) quality of the directions, (3) sequence of the questions, (4) relationship of questions to instructional objectives.
2. Your answer may include such characteristics as those listed below:

True-False	1. requires a large number of items
	2. measures low level learning
Completion	1. use equal size blanks
	2. avoid too many blanks per item
Matching	1. requires that premise and response lists be homogeneous
	2. allows for versatility in content covered
Multiple Choice	1. requires considerable effort to construct
	2. can measure high levels of cognition
Essay	1. allows for the measurement of student communication skills
	2. are quite difficult to score

3. For feedback on this question, refer to the examples in this section and confer with your study partner or instructor.

Feedback Box: Chapter 6, Section 3

1. The major procedures are (1) grading on the curve, (2) scaling grades, (3) the inspection method, (4) the standardized grading scale, and (5) criterion-referenced grading; refer to Part 1 for detailed characteristics of each.

2. Written or telephoned messages, weekly or bi-weekly progress reports to be signed, and parent/teacher conferences.
3. Your answer might include such characteristics as those listed below:

    Recording by Objectives: 1. used primarily with criterion-referenced grading
                                2. displays individual progress by objectives
    Traditional Grade Book   1. records grades on individual assignments and tests
                                2. is the least complex method of recording progress

INDEX

Grading (*Continued*)
    scaling, 245
    standardized grading scale, 247
Group strategies, 117–145 (*see also* Individual
        strategies)
    defined, 117
    lecture contrasted with inquiry, 117
    major considerations summarized,
        144–145
    types of, 117–145
        demonstration, 125–127
        discussion, 127–130
        drill, 141–142
        field trip, 134–138
        game, 138–141
        guided inquiry, 118–123
        laboratory, 133–134
        lecture, 123–125
        panel, 130–133

H

Homework (*see* Assignments)

I

Illustrations (*see* Clarity; Demonstration)
Inattention, 204–206
Independent study, 160–162
Individual differences, (*see* Ability grouping)
Individual strategies, 145–165 (*see also* Group
        strategies)
    defined, 146
    major considerations summarized, 164
    types of, 147–163
        contracts, 147–152
        independent study, 160–163
        LAPs, 152–157
        learning centers, 157–160
Instruction, 18–20, 33–54, 79–80, 89–102,
        115–165 (*see also* Active student
        involvement)
    address stated objectives, 93–95
    adjustment to learning styles, 15–20
    appropriate level, 89–93
    developing high levels of
        thinking, 100–101
    developing strategies, 115–165
    direct, 13

dyadic, 14
effects of community on, 51–52
feedback and monitoring, 101–103
grouping of students, 97–99
instructional stage, 38–46
motivational aspects, 95–97 (*see also*
        Motivation)
objectives for, 21–33
of concepts, 79–80
planning, 33–45
postinstructional stage, 46–53
preinstructional stage, 34–37
revision, 31, 46–53
tutor, 14
types of strategies, 116
variety
    importance of, 116–117
Instructional (curriculum) materials
    media (*see* Media)
    use of, 14
Intellectual skills (*see* Cognitive learnings)
Interest of students, 43, 158
Introductions, 42–43, 81, 96–97

K

Kounin model, 175–176

L

Language, 92
    non-verbal, 57–61, 64–69
    verbal, 57–64
LAP (*see* Individual strategies, types of)
Leadership, 4–10, 179–192
    characteristics of good managers, 179–192
    LEI, SSI, 9–10
    planning (thorough preparation), 179–181
Leadership styles, 4–8
    authoritarian, 4–6
    authoritative, 4, 7–8
    laissez-faire, 4, 6–7
    research on, 8
Learning
    active involvement in, 4, 9 (*see also* Active
        student involvement)
    determining student, 101
    enhancement, 43
    perception of, 9–10